Creature and Creator

Myth-making and English Romanticism

CREATURE AND CREATOR

Myth-making and English Romanticism

PAUL A. CANTOR

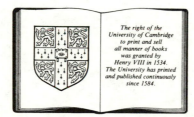

The right of the
University of Cambridge
to print and sell
all manner of books
was granted by
Henry VIII in 1534.
The University has printed
and published continuously
since 1584.

CAMBRIDGE UNIVERSITY PRESS

Cambridge
London   New York   New Rochelle
Melbourne   Sydney

Published by the Press Syndicate of the University of Cambridge
The Pitt Building, Trumpington Street, Cambridge CB2 1RP
32 East 57th Street, New York, NY 10022, USA
296 Beaconsfield Parade, Middle Park, Melbourne 3206, Australia

First published 1984

Printed in Great Britain at the Pitman Press, Bath

Library of Congress catalogue card number: 83-14255

British Library Cataloguing in Publication Data
Cantor, Paul
Creature and creator: myth-making and English Romanticism.
1. English literature – History and criticism
2. Romanticism   3. Myth in literature
4. Creation in literature
I. Title
820.9′145   PR146

ISBN 0 521 25831 6

Surely your turning of things upside down shall be esteemed as the potter's clay: for shall the work say of him that made it, He made me not? or shall the thing framed say of him that framed it, He had no understanding?

— Isaiah, 29:16

In man *creature* and *creator* are united: in man there is material, fragment, excess, clay, dirt, nonsense, chaos; but in man there is also creator, form-giver, hammer hardness, spectator divinity, and seventh day: do you understand this contrast?

— Friedrich Nietzsche

Contents

Preface

In the 1790's a new genre appeared in English literature, or rather an ancient genre reappeared: the creation myth. The first clear-cut example of this new form is Blake's *The Book of Urizen* (1794), and at least through *The Four Zoas*, Blake devoted his artistic career to shaping a poetic account of the creation. Blake often seems to be the odd man out among the Romantic poets, but he was not alone in his interest in creation myths. The second generation of Romantics, presumably without knowledge of Blake's work, also were drawn to primitive mythic material, stories of divine conflict and the origins of man. In *Prometheus Unbound* and *Frankenstein*, Percy and Mary Shelley both turn to the myth of the Greek Titan, first presented in Hesiod, as a means of exploring contrasting visions of human destiny. Byron returns in *Cain* to the Bible's account of man's genesis. And finally, in his *Hyperion* poems, Keats attempts to chronicle the triumph of the Olympian generation of gods over their predecessors.

As diverse as these works are, there are enough parallels among them to suggest some kind of common enterprise. The most striking common denominator is what one might call their sympathy for the devil. They tend to raise doubts about the established order of gods, questioning their motives for creation, while giving justifications for rebellion against the reigning divine power, indeed finding nobility in revolutionary figures. The unorthodox bias of these Romantic creation myths is most clearly evident in Blake and Shelley. In his earlier formulations of his myth, Blake portrays the traditional God of orthodox Christianity in the repellent form of the tyrant Urizen, and at the same time treats sympathetically the figure who revolts against Urizen, the fiery Orc, who clearly embodies elements from the traditional image of Satan. In Shelley's mythic formulation, he clearly sides, not with the reigning god of the Greek pantheon, Jupiter, but with the rebel against Heaven, Prometheus. At least in Blake and Shelley, the break with traditional religion seems complete. What was once viewed as divine is now seen as demonic, while the traditional devil figure is recreated as the savior of mankind.

To be sure, once one studies these writers carefully, one finds that their sympathies are not as one-sided as they might at first appear. As we shall see, as Blake worked on reformulating his myth, he began to efface the sharp opposition between Urizen and Orc. In *Frankenstein* and *Cain* the issue of rebel vs. tyrant is complicated by the discovery that in the process of revolution, the rebel threatens to turn into a tyrant himself. And Keats is distinguished precisely by the even division of his sympathies between the winners and the losers in the divine struggle he portrays. But bearing all these important qualifications in mind, one can still discern a change of direction in Romantic creation myths. None of these writers – not even the most conservative of them, Mary Shelley – simply returns to the traditional conception of the divine and the demonic. And all the works at least begin by exploring the possibility that overturning the established divine order might be a form of liberation or progress for mankind.

The distinctive orientation of Romantic creation myths, particularly the tendency to invert gods and devils, is known in the history of religion as gnosticism.[1] In the original Gnostic versions of the Garden of Eden story, for example, Jehovah appears as an arrogant or deluded deity, usurping dominion over Adam and Eve, striving to keep them ignorant and hence under his control by denying them the Tree of Knowledge. The villain in the orthodox version of Genesis, the serpent, becomes the hero in Gnostic versions, teaching Adam and Eve the true path to divine illumination.[2] In Gnosticism, what was traditionally viewed as the fall of man is reinterpreted as the first step toward his salvation, while the traditional act of creation is reinterpreted as the work of a fallen being. In Gnostic myth, the creation and the fall are in effect conflated into a single event. The parallels between authentic Gnostic and Romantic myths are often so striking that one is tempted to assume direct influence. In the case of Blake, there can be no doubt of his familiarity with Gnostic literature, even if he could not have read the wealth of Gnostic documents that have surfaced only in this century.[3] Shelley's interest in heretical ideas probably led him to at least some first-hand acquaintance with Gnostic texts as well.[4] But from the point of view of literary criticism, it is unnecessary to document a direct line of influence from the original Gnostics down to Romantic myth-makers. Whether the writers we will be studying worked from models or shaped their creation myths independently, the fact is that their myths take a gnostic turn. Even in the case of Keats, who as we shall see does not present any of his mythic figures as devils, his poetry can best be understood as the result of his working through the gnostic myths of his predecessors. Only by being aware of the initial sharpness of the battle lines drawn in the myths of Blake and Shelley can we fully appreciate the significance of their blurring in Keats.

II

The sudden and widespread interest among Romantic writers in the creation myth as a literary form may at first seem puzzling. The creation myth is one of the most primitive forms of literature.[5] In most languages, some of the oldest surviving texts deal with the generations of the gods and the creation of the world. Why should sophisticated modern authors deliberately seek out an ancient and seemingly antiquated form? Only by bearing in mind the gnostic twist in Romantic creation myths can we understand the appeal of a primitive genre to a group of avant-garde writers. Some of the most interesting recent criticism of Romanticism, notably the work of Harold Bloom and his students, has already shown the value of analyzing Romantic myth in terms of gnosticism.[6] For Bloom, gnosticism is an appropriate response to the problem posed for modern poets by the phenomenon he has called the anxiety of influence. Gnosticism is a particularly ingenious way of overcoming the block to creativity that results once any sort of canon has been formed and rigidified.[7] This is exactly the situation the original Gnostics faced, as most of the books which comprise what we know as the Old Testament had acquired, or were just in the process of acquiring, canonical status by the time of Christ. The Gnostics learned that the only way to add to a supposedly complete revealed text is, not as one might suppose at the end, but rather at the beginning. Gnostic myths developed by writing the pre-history of creation, hypothesizing more and more stages in the fall that led to the creation as we know it, and hence pushing back the material that appears in the first chapters of Genesis to a later and later point in Gnostic accounts. One of the initial surprises in reading Gnostic myths is to see how long they sometimes take to get to the Garden of Eden.[8] But it is characteristically in the blank pages before the opening of Genesis that the Gnostics found the clean slate they needed for creating their new myths.

The Romantics faced a similarly frustrating situation as artists, a seeming impasse in mythic creativity. By the end of the eighteenth century, traditional sources of mythic inspiration seemed exhausted. Classical mythology had clearly lost its vitality, serving at most a purely decorative function in literature.[9] As for Christian mythology, Milton was seen as having already done whatever could be done with the Bible in literature. In this historical context, the appeal of gnosticism as a mythic technique is understandable. It offered a way of finding new meaning in the old myths, of turning well-worn paths into new avenues of creativity, simply by travelling them, as it were, in the opposite direction. As we shall see, Romantic myth-makers follow the gnostic pattern of pushing their narratives further and further back in time, in a quest for the absolute origin which would make all other creation accounts seem displaced and derivative. In shaping an alternative to Milton's account of man's genesis, the Romantic myth-makers aspired to supplant Milton in his enviable position as *the* poet of origins. To establish an account of the first things is in a sense to establish oneself as the first of poets. In general, the Romantic fascination with creation myths can be viewed as an attempt to find radically fresh themes by learning to deal with cosmic beginnings. If one can present for the first time a true account of man's origins, one can legitimately claim to have found a way of writing about what no man has ever written about before. The Romantic quest for origins is profoundly connected with the Romantic quest for originality.[10]

The one limitation of Bloom's otherwise extremely fruitful approach is that it sometimes gives the impression that the Romantics were interested in inverting the hierarchy of traditional myth merely for the sake of novelty. Romantic myth-makers were indeed obsessed with surpassing Milton's achievement as a poet, and, following the lead of Bloom and others, I will be devoting much of this book to tracing the Romantic battle with *Paradise Lost*. But this must not be viewed as a narrowly literary battle. Romantic myth-makers did not start a quarrel with Milton just for the sake of making themselves heard in a distinct voice. They had a genuine disagreement with Milton concerning the nature of man, and in order to express their new vision found it necessary to recreate Milton's myth in gnostic fashion. One must always remember that authentic Gnosticism was not an aesthetic but a religious movement. The original Gnostics were not interested in creating myths for myth's sake. As Jonas and others have demonstrated, the twists and turns of Gnostic myth reflect a fundamentally new conception of man's place in the cosmos.[11] The Romantic creation myths we will be studying similarly reflect a revolution in philosophy. By calling attention to the ideas behind these myths, I hope to restore a sense of balance that I fear is being lost in the study of Romanticism. I genuinely admire Bloom's work, and, as will be obvious in the course of this book, have learned a great deal from it. Nevertheless, it seems to me that readers of his recent work could be losing sight of the fact that the Romantics were interested, not just in revolutionizing poetry, but in revolutionizing the world.[12] I realize that this book will seem old-fashioned to some in its naive effort to comprehend the meaning of Romantic creation myths, to uncover what these Romantic authors were trying to say about human nature. But I believe that they themselves would have been appalled to hear that their poems are merely about other poems, and not about anything in the real world. I take very seriously, as Bloom once did,[13] the identification both Blake and Shelley make between the poet and the prophet, and hence assume that their poetry contains a message, a very complicated one perhaps, but one that can be communicated to a reader.

III

In studying the creation myth as a genre, and emphasizing its intellectual content, I hope, then, to return to a sense of Romantic authors as presenting, not just a distinctive voice in literature, but a distinctive set of ideas as well, above all a new conception of human nature. Romantic myth-makers realized that a myth of creation occupies a privileged position in any system of beliefs. In particular, they realized that the creation account accepted in the Christian tradition was not simply a quaint old tale for children. Nor was it of merely theoretical interest, a way of satisfying man's abstract curiosity about his origins. As Blake and Shelley understood, the Biblical account of creation as conventionally interpreted was intimately bound up with the efforts of the old regime to preserve the *status quo* in Europe. The Garden of Eden story embodies a conservative moral. God created a perfect world for man, a world in which he had the opportunity to be completely happy. Only man's error in breaking God's commandment ruined his paradise. The lesson to be learned is that man should never again try to improve upon God's handiwork, but instead obey Him without question, which in practice means to obey His constituted authorities in church and state on earth. Man cannot hope to recapture paradise by his own efforts. He can only hope that out of His grace God will somehow return man to his original happy state. As long as one believes that man was created by a benevolent deity, one must learn to accept the human condition as one finds it, and endure its pains with patience and humility.

The peculiarly gnostic form of creation myth provides the revolutionary reply to this religious conservatism.[14] To portray a demonic creation is to throw off the restraints on man's efforts to improve himself and his condition. Whether one pictures the creator-god as malevolent, or as simply mistaken as to how to make man happy, or perhaps just incompetent in carrying out basically good intentions, the liberating effect of these gnostic visions of the creator is the same. Man need no longer be in awe of his creator; he need no longer even feel grateful for being created. He can turn his back on God with a good conscience and set about charting his own course, seeking out ways to remake an imperfectly created world, and even to change his own nature for the better. The denigration of God as a creator in Romantic myth is for the sake of exalting man's own creative potential.

Behind the reappearance of the creation myth as a genre in Romantic literature thus lies a new fascination with the idea of remaking man. I will argue that this idea has its roots in the thought of Rousseau. Thus a subsidiary aim of this book is to re-open the question of Rousseau and Romanticism. Certainly the claim that Rousseau is important for understanding Romanticism will strike no one as a revelation. But since the pioneering work of Irving Babbitt, most studies of Rousseau and Romanticism have been distorted by the effort to see Rousseau himself as a Romantic, or at least as a proto-Romantic.[15] Critics have concentrated, often with valid results, on Rousseau as a precursor of Romantic modes of feeling or perception, or they have viewed Rousseau's way of life as a prototype of Romantic existence. They have therefore tended to focus on Rousseau as a literary figure, and neglected his status as a philosopher. Babbitt's bias is clear in the fact that he derives his image of Rousseau almost exclusively from his most "Romantic" works, the *Nouvelle Héloïse*, the *Confessions* and the *Reveries*. By neglecting one whole side of Rousseau's writings, represented by such works as the *Social Contract* and the *Emile*, critics like Babbitt miss the genuine complexity of his philosophy.[16]

I believe that a new picture of the relation of Rousseau and Romanticism will emerge if we take into account his more clearly philosophical writings, above all his *Second Discourse*, a work which he called "of greatest importance," the one in which he claimed to have developed his principles "completely."[17] By not regarding Rousseau merely as the source of vague Romantic attitudes, but by treating his thought as a coherent whole, I hope to show that he was in fact not simply a Romantic, but rather in certain respects the antithesis of Romanticism. Rousseau in effect set the agenda for many Romantic writers, providing the challenge they rose to meet. If I wanted to be fashionable, I would say that Romantic creation myths arose from a powerful misreading of Rousseau's concept of the state of nature. I prefer to state my thesis this way: the way Rousseau rethought the question of human nature, and in particular of man's original state, gave rise to hopes of man's recapturing paradise. But contrary to the popular understanding of Rousseau, he himself saw no clear path back to the state of nature. The strength and originality of his thought lies in the clarity with which he perceived fundamental contradictions in man's condition: the tension between nature and civilization, the tension between reason and passion, the tension between the extraordinary man and the ordinary community. The Romantic writers who refused to accept Rousseau's statement of the human problem as final tried to go beyond him by seeking out a higher synthesis wherever Rousseau had seen irreconcilable antinomies. Above all, they turned to art itself as the great mediating force, a way of reconciling nature with civilization, reason with passion, and the avant-garde artist with the common run of men. The Romantic myths we will be studying originate in an effort to shape a happy ending to the seemingly tragic history of the human race Rousseau propounded. To see the roots of Romantic myth in Rousseau is one way of realizing the problematic character of the Romantic dream of synthesizing a whole out of all the warring opposites in life, and hence of understanding why such strains developed among the Romantics, particularly in the second generation, as they tried to remain faithful to their original hopes.

One can see the effect of neglecting Rousseau's central importance for the Romantics in M. H. Abrams's *Natural Supernaturalism*. Though clearly one of the most comprehensive surveys of the intellectual backgrounds of Romanticism, Abrams's book tends to minimize the role of Rousseau, while emphasizing the significance of German idealist philosophy for understanding Romanticism. But German idealists like Kant, Schiller, Fichte, and Hegel were themselves reacting to Rousseau, and in fact trying to bring about much the same synthesis out of Rousseauian antinomies that Romantic artists pursued. Thus to look at Romanticism through the lens of German idealism inevitably has the effect of highlighting its positive side and presenting its efforts at synthesis as unproblematic, as Abrams certainly does. Abrams tends to exclude the negative side of Romanticism; for example, he omits Byron completely "because in his greatest work he speaks with an ironic counter-voice and deliberately opens a satirical perspective on the vatic stance of his Romantic contemporaries."[18] Abrams's exclusion of Byron seems related to his comparative neglect of Rousseau in *Natural Supernaturalism*. By returning to Rousseau as the source of Romantic creation myths, we will be aware of the precariousness of Romantic syntheses and hence in a position to hear more clearly that "ironic counter-voice" among the Romantics which Abrams excludes from his survey.

IV

Ultimately, then, I regard this book as a case study in the complex interrelation of philosophy and literature, showing how a new understanding of man in Rousseau inspired Romantic creation myths, and yet came to be distorted in the process, with the result that Rousseau in many ways remains the best critic of the works he influenced. I should make it clear therefore that in concentrating on Romantic creation myths, I am analyzing one aspect or phase of Romanticism, and not offering a theory of Romanticism as a whole. It would indeed be reckless to try to construct sweeping generalizations about Romanticism on the basis of the few works I discuss, even though they are among the more significant achievements of the English Romantics. Romanticism is a notoriously complex phenomenon, and it looks different when approached from different angles, whether, for example, one is looking at Romanticism in different nations (England, Germany, or France) or looking at Romanticism in different arts (literature, painting, or music). Recognizing that no single approach can do justice to the richness and diversity of Romanticism, I hope that focusing on one Romantic genre will at least offer a fresh and illuminating perspective on Romantic literature, one which may help to place it in the larger context of intellectual history and also to reveal some of the links between Romantic and modern literature.

The most difficult decision in shaping any book such as this is which works to include. I obviously could have covered more examples of the Romantic creation myth, a work like Peacock's *Ahrimanes*, for example. I at one time planned chapters on Wordsworth and Coleridge, and I think that my thesis could be adapted to works such as "The Rime of the Ancient Mariner" and *The Prelude*. But I did not want to weaken my argument by stretching it to embrace too many examples. What I might gain in comprehensiveness, I might lose in logical coherence. However much Wordsworth and Coleridge may be related to the developments I am discussing, I do not think that either wrote poems that could strictly speaking be called creation myths. I have tried to confine myself to major Romantic works which are clearly transformations of traditional creation myths, specifically works which attempt to recreate *Paradise Lost*. On the basis of this definition, *Frankenstein* may strike some readers as out of place in this book. *Frankenstein* is the one prose work I discuss, and in some respects it seems more properly classified as science fiction than as myth. But, as we shall see, *Frankenstein* does draw upon the Prometheus myth, and combines Milton and Rousseau in just the way the other works we will be studying do. In any case, *Frankenstein* seems to me to deal so directly with the central issues of this book that I could not bring myself to exclude it.

In the end, I make no claim that the texts I have chosen are the only legitimate examples of Romantic creation myths, and all other possibilities are unworthy of consideration. I have necessarily selected the works which I find most interesting and which seem to me to reveal the most about the creation myth as a form in

Romantic literature. And I have tried to take up the works in an order which will at first suggest some inner unity to Romantic creation myths, but which will in the end reveal the diversity even within this one genre of Romantic literature. I have arranged my chapters so that they get a kind of dialogue going within Romanticism. In the first part, I treat Blake's later works as an answer to, and correction of, his earlier versions. In the second part, I treat *Frankenstein* as a kind of proleptic critique of Shelley's vision in *Prometheus Unbound*.[19] In the third part, I view Byron and Keats as questioning the value of the original Romantic quest for paradise. And of course throughout this book, I am dealing with the ongoing dialogue between the Romantics and Rousseau, a debate in which curiously Rousseau gets in a last word when Shelley resurrects him in *The Triumph of Life*.

In short, in order to understand Romantic creation myths, one cannot expect to find all the writers speaking with one voice and shaping the same myth. What in fact makes the Romantic period so fascinating for a study of literary myth-making is that in their search for the one authentic mythic archetype, the Romantics kept broadening the range of possibilities for myth in literature. What ultimately unites the different writers we will be studying is a set of common problems, centering around the question of whether one can recapture paradise and how best to go about it. Each of these writers responds to this basic question in a different way, and therefore shapes a different myth. Studying the Romantic creation myth as a genre provides a model of how I believe the phenomenon of Romanticism has to be understood. Whatever unity Romanticism possesses as a literary movement is a dialectical, not a simple, unity.

Acknowledgements

I first formulated the basic ideas of this book in the course of teaching Humanities 118, "Myths of Creation," at Harvard University from 1972 to 1976. I would therefore like first and foremost to thank the extraordinary run of students who took this course over a five-year span. It was, and I suspect will remain, the most challenging and rewarding teaching experience of my life, and my many conversations with students in the course helped me to shape and refine the ideas of this book. I would also like to thank several friends who read various drafts of the book and made suggestions for improvement, in particular, Allan Bloom, Douglas Hoffman, and Ronald Sharp. I would especially like to thank David Perkins, who helped me in my original planning of what to include in the book and gave the first draft an unusually careful reading, helping me to see where it needed revisions.

Chapter 5 appeared in slightly different form in *The Kenyon Review* (Vol. II, Summer, 1980), under the title "Byron's *Cain*: A Romantic Version of the Fall."

A note on texts

I cite Blake from the newly revised edition of David Erdman's *The Complete Poetry and Prose of William Blake* (Berkeley: University of California Press, 1982), abbreviated as E where necessary. For the works in Illuminated Printing, I cite by plate and line numbers; for all other works, I cite by Blake's page numbers. I cite Byron's *Cain* from the edition of Truman Guy Steffan, *Lord Byron's Cain* (Austin: University of Texas, 1968). All other quotations from Byron's poetry are taken from Robert Gleckner, ed., *The Poetical Works of Byron* (Boston: Houghton Mifflin, 1975). I cite Keats's poetry from Miriam Allott, ed., *The Poems of John Keats* (London: Longman, 1970). My text for *Paradise Lost* is the edition of Merritt Y. Hughes (New York: Odyssey, 1935). For Rousseau's *Second Discourse* (abbreviated as SD), I cite by page numbers the translation of Roger D. and Judith R. Masters, *The First and Second Discourses* (New York: St. Martin's, 1964). For Rousseau's *Reveries* (abbreviated as R), I cite by page number the translation of Charles Butterworth, *The Reveries of the Solitary Walker* (New York: New York University Press, 1979). For Percy Shelley, wherever possible I cite Donald H. Reiman and Sharon B. Powers, eds., *Shelley's Poetry and Prose* (New York: Norton, 1977), abbreviated as R & P. For *Frankenstein*, I cite by page number the edition of Harold Bloom (New York: New American Library, 1965), the 1831 version.

A Discourse on Eden

Thus nature's gentle voice is no longer an infallible guide for us, nor is the independence we have received from her a desirable state. We lost peace and innocence forever before we had appreciated their delights. Unfelt by the stupid men of earliest times, lost to the enlightened men of later times, the happy life of the golden age was always a state foreign to the human race, either because it went unrecognized when humans could have enjoyed it or because it had been lost when humans could have known it.

– Jean-Jacques Rousseau[1]

I

Paradise Lost was the primary form in which Romantic myth-makers confronted the orthodox account of creation. By giving a definitive poetic shape to the traditional understanding of the fall, Milton made possible the distinctive Romantic transformation of the myth. Milton's myth involves three stages, which in altered form provide the framework for Romantic creation myths: paradise, paradise lost, and paradise regained.[2] An initial stage of unity is shattered by a fall, a painful stage of disunity results, with the promise of a third and final stage, in which the divisions of the fallen world will be overcome and the original unity restored, on a higher level. The original stage in Milton is of course the Garden of Eden, portrayed as a state of perfect harmony for man, both internally and externally. Man is at peace with himself, his various faculties functioning together harmoniously. In particular, his reason and his passions do not act at cross purposes, but point to the same ends in life. Correspondingly, in the small community of Eden, social harmony prevails, as Adam and Eve divide up their tasks and work together for the common good. Finally, man is in harmony with the world around him, as shown most clearly by the way he gets along with the whole animal kingdom. With God having ordered all of nature with man's benefit in mind, he lives in an environment perfectly suited to his needs. At one with himself, his society, and his world, man should enjoy complete happiness.

But this paradise is destroyed by the fall. As a result of man's willful disobedience of the divine prohibition, he undergoes a painful self-division. His passions for the first time get out of control and contradict the dictates of his reason (IX.1121–31). Simultaneously his peaceful society falls apart: Adam and Eve almost immediately begin quarreling over who is responsible for the fall (IX.1131–89). Similarly, man's unity with his environment breaks down. Nature turns hostile, as animals run wild and become dangerous to man (X.710–14), while divine adjustments of the heavens produce the alternation of the seasons and hence extremes of cold and heat (X.651–707). The effect of these changes is to introduce suffering into human existence, compounded by the fact that man for the first time has to worry about his mortality.

At first the fall seems to be a total and unmitigated disaster. But in one respect, it marks a step forward for man. The price man paid for his happiness in Eden was his complete dependence on God. Something seems lacking in Eden. Man's original state is primitive, his faculties not fully developed. Eden may be paradise, but it is a narrow one. Eve's susceptibility to Satan's temptation results from her chafing under the restraints of her supposedly perfect state (IX.322–41, 1153–54). Thus the fall, though it introduces misery into human life, also introduces an element of human independence. With nature turned hostile, man is thrown back on his own resources and is forced to become self-reliant. As Michael's prophecy to Adam shows, in response to his new-found misery, man will develop all the arts and sciences lacking in Eden (X.1053–85, XI.556–73). Moreover, as its origin in eating the fruit of the Tree of Knowledge of Good and Evil shows, the fall does involve a gain in awareness for man. Man's new self-consciousness takes the initial form of painful embarrassment at his nakedness. But in a sense, human progress depends on this shame man develops about his bodily nature, and his consequent resolve to rise above it.

We are here confronted with the central paradox which made Milton's task so difficult in *Paradise Lost*, the paradox of the fortunate fall. Milton could not admit to any defects in the original paradise, for that would be to impugn divine providence. Paradise must have been a perfect state, in the sense that man never had to leave it to enjoy a full existence. Nevertheless, like Eve, we may feel dissatisfied with Eden, and Milton himself seems uncomfortable with the idea that man was to live in such a dependent condition forever. Hence, although Milton cannot openly approve of the disobedience which led to the fall, he does view the event as part of a larger providential scheme for the development of the human spirit. Presumably, Milton shares Adam's ultimately ambivalent reaction to the fall:

> O goodness infinite, goodness immense!
> That all this good of evil shall produce,
> And evil turn to good; more wonderful
> Than that which by creation first brought forth
> Light out of darkness! full of doubt I stand,
> Whether I should repent me now of sin
> By mee done and occasion'd, or rejoice
> Much more, that much more good thereof shall spring,
> To God more glory, more good will to Men
> From God, and over wrath grace shall abound.   (XII.469–78)

Paradise Lost portrays a potentially tragic disjunction of human possibilities. In Eden, man is morally innocent and happy, but comparatively ignorant and undeveloped in his faculties. In the fallen world, man gains in wisdom and becomes civilized, but he breaks with the way of God, becoming miserable and morally corrupt in the process. Milton's faith in divine providence requires a third stage in human history, when God will restore man to paradise, but allow him to keep all the benefits he has derived from his long sojourn in the fallen world. Man will be able to cancel out the negative aspects of both the original paradise and the fallen world, while preserving what was positive, and thus achieve a perfect synthesis. Eliminating his initial ignorance and his acquired corruption, man will become both happy and wise at once, a truly higher innocence (XI.26–30, XII.463–65). As Michael promises Adam: "then wilt thou not be loath / To leave this Paradise, but shalt possess / A paradise within thee, happier far" (XII.585–87). With God's help, the potential tragedy of human history will be given a happy ending to match its happy beginning. Man will in fact be better able to appreciate his happiness at the end of history than he was at the beginning, because the fall will have given him a basis for comparison.

From the standpoint of Romantic myth-makers, the most interesting aspect of this third stage in Milton is the internalization of paradise.[3] In general, Milton moves in *Paradise Lost* from portraying Heaven and Hell as physical locations to conceiving of them as mental states. This explains why Satan cannot escape his fate:

> horror and doubt distract
> His troubl'd thoughts, and from the bottom stir
> The Hell within him, for within him Hell
> He brings, and round about him, nor from Hell
> One step no more than from himself can fly
> By change of place.   (IV.18–23)

After the fall, Michael even begins to speak disdainfully of the "narrow bounds" of Eden (XI.341) in an effort to break Adam's attachment to paradise as a physical locale, and tells him that during the Flood the Mount of Paradise will be washed away, "To teach thee that God attributes to place / No sanctity, if none be thither brought / By Men" (XI.836–37). Once one begins to think of paradise, not as a sacred precinct established by God, but as a psychological state, paradise begins to be within the grasp of man. To be sure, Milton does not believe that paradise can be regained by man's own efforts. Divine grace is still needed to restore man's happiness (III.181–82). But Milton's development of the myth of the fall, particularly the notion of a "paradise within," pointed the way to a fully humanized version of the pattern. For a Romantic, what was wrong with Milton's myth is that it makes man's salvation dependent on external forces. Though responsible for his fall, man in *Paradise Lost* is heavily influenced by the machinations of Satan, and he needs the help of Christ to undo the damage. Only by coming up with a purely human version of the fall could Romantic myth-makers put man's fate entirely within his own hands. Paradoxically, they had to increase man's culpability for his fall in order to give him the ability to save himself.

II

The philosophical breakthrough that provided the basis for Romantic creation myths came in the work of Rousseau, specifically his *Second Discourse, On the Origin and Foundations of Inequality Among Men* (1755). The influence of this work was so pervasive in the late eighteenth century that one need not show that

4

individual Romantics had read it in order to claim that it shaped their thinking about human nature.[4] Actually, a great deal of evidence could be cited to show that the Romantics did read Rousseau, although the question of what they made of their reading is complicated. In the case of Blake, for example, virtually all his references to Rousseau are negative in tone and often cast him in a sinister role.[5] But Blake's antipathy to Rousseau seems to be based on a misconception of what he stood for. As shown by the fact that Blake repeatedly pairs Rousseau with Voltaire, Blake evidently thought of him as one of the *philosophes*, which is absurd, since Rousseau devoted most of his career to combatting the *philosophes*.[6] Perhaps, then, Blake may not have had much of a first-hand acquaintance with Rousseau's writings. One way for him to have gained acquaintance second-hand was through his friend Henry Fuseli, who wrote one of the first books on Rousseau in English.[7] Fuseli's brief survey of Rousseau's writings is a basically sympathetic treatment, trying to defend his reputation in light of the negative impact Rousseau's much publicized quarrel with Hume had in England. Given Fuseli's thorough knowledge of all Rousseau's work, he may well have passed the philosopher's fundamental ideas on to Blake, without making him aware of their precise source.

Shelley provides the best case for documenting a direct link between Rousseau and an English Romantic.[8] Thanks to his wife's journal, we have a partial record of Shelley's reading of Rousseau, proving that he was familiar with the *Emile*, the *Nouvelle Héloïse*, and the *Reveries*.[9] Though Mary does not list the *Second Discourse*, we know from Shelley's notes to *Queen Mab* that he had read it carefully.[10] Besides the fact that Shelley actually cites the *Second Discourse* in one of the notes, he makes extensive use of Rousseau's arguments, particularly the idea that man may be by nature a vegetarian. In addition to his first-hand knowledge of Rousseau, Shelley had many opportunities to come under his influence indirectly, especially through his contact with Godwin.[11] Another possible intermediary between Rousseau and Shelley (as well as other Romantics) is Lord Monboddo.[12] Monboddo's monumental work, *Of the Origin and Progress of Language*, follows the *Second Discourse* closely, particularly the idea that language is not natural to man and had to be invented at some point in human history.[13] Monboddo aroused considerable controversy in England in the late eighteenth and early nineteenth centuries, focusing attention on precisely the issues Rousseau raised, such as the question of the difference between man and animal. Monboddo's writings show how quickly Rousseau's ideas became common intellectual property by the turn of the nineteenth century.

Thus to focus attention on Rousseau is not to claim that every single idea of every single Romantic creation myth has to be traced back to the *Second Discourse*. Other eighteenth-century philosophers made major contributions to the rethinking of the question of man's origins, often with profound implications for the intimately related question of how to read the Bible. In the most notable case, Vico, his thought can even claim historical priority over Rousseau's. Nevertheless, the *Second Discourse* is fundamental to understanding the revolution in thinking about man's nature that occurred in the eighteenth century. As the most incisive and daring thinker on the subject, as well as the best known, most widely read, and most influential, Rousseau serves to define the intellectual climate in which Romantic myth-makers approached the problem of the creation of man.

In tracing the genesis of man, Rousseau broke decisively with the traditional concept of human nature. He rejected the long accepted definition of man as the rational animal, and turned attention instead to man's free will as his distinguishing characteristic (SD, 113–14).[14] Concluding that even free will is too determinate a characteristic to be made the basis for defining man, Rousseau finally settled on man's perfectibility to separate him from all other animals (SD, 114–15).[15] The concept of perfectibility comes as close as possible to supplying a purely formal – one might even say empty – definition of man. Rousseau defines man not by saying what he is or what he can become, but by pointing only to the fact that he can become something other than what he originally was.[16]

One cannot fully appreciate the originality of Rousseau's thought if one sees him as simply substituting one definition of human nature for another. What Rousseau questioned was the very idea that one can speak of any kind of fixed human nature, that is, an eternal essence of man, independent of what he happens to become in history.[17] For Rousseau, what man is can only be determined retrospectively, by looking at what he has developed into, in a process which involves many historical accidents and which therefore has an element of arbitrariness in it. As things turned out, man became a rational animal, but under different circumstances, he might have developed differently or failed to develop at all (SD, 112, 140). In Rousseau's view, man's nature is almost infinitely malleable, and one must beware of mistaking any particular stage of his development for the limits of his growth (SD, 178).[18] Our greatest error in thinking about man is to assume that he has always been more or less the way we see him today, and always will remain so (SD, 102). Rousseau's notion of human nature as something which changes and develops over time required a complete rethinking of the question of man's genesis. Man need no longer be viewed as coming into being in a single stroke and as a finished product, as the Bible and Milton portray the creation. In the *Second Discourse*, man only gradually acquires his characteristic traits, his formation requiring millennia and occurring in incremental stages (SD, 178).

Rousseau's new way of defining man gave a great impetus to the ideal of self-development, and specifically freed the imaginative hopes of Romantic myth-makers for making human nature better. In the traditional understanding, either God or nature or both define man's essence and thereby set limits to what he can become. But if man's nature is the product of an accidental historical process, one no longer has reason to believe that he cannot develop further, indeed one cannot be sure that he has hitherto pursued the right path. It sounds highly flattering to human nature to speak of man's perfectibility. But mere perfectibility does not imply that man has reached perfection at any given moment, and he must always be alert to chances for improving himself.[19] The bungling creators of Romantic myth are a way of symbolizing Rousseau's insight that man has to question his origins and decide if he is satisfied with what he has become in history.

The specific course of man's development outlined in the *Second Discourse* bears a curious resemblance to the pattern we saw in *Paradise Lost*. In fact, Rousseau's hypothetical history of mankind reads like a secularized version of the fall of man, and thus supplied what Romantic myth-makers needed to recreate Milton's myth. The first stage of Rousseau's argument, the state of nature, corresponds to the Garden of Eden in Milton. The second stage, the state of civil society, corresponds to the fallen world.[20] Rousseau does not present a third stage in the *Second Discourse*, and indeed the great question in his philosophy as a whole is whether man can ever return to the state of nature. The problem Rousseau bequeathed to his successors is how man can combine the advantages of nature and civilization and thereby transcend the seemingly tragic disjunctions of his history. Rousseau's own solution to the human dilemma was, as we shall see, unacceptable to many Romantics, but he nevertheless defined the terms in which they thought about the problem.

The state of nature Rousseau hypothesizes at the beginning of man's history has much in common with the traditional notion of Eden. Rousseau's natural man leads a largely untroubled existence, unified within himself and with his world. His desires are simple and easily satisfied and hence do not come into conflict with one another. His environment, though not strictly speaking Edenic, provides him with all he needs, and he fits in comfortably to the world of nature, living in harmony with its rhythms (SD, 105–6).[21]

The most important difference between Rousseau's account of man's beginnings and Milton's is that Rousseau has a more radically primitive notion of the original human condition. Rousseau's natural man lacks speech and reason (SD, 116–26). For all Rousseau's praise of the state of nature, we must recognize that he is talking about what we would conventionally regard as man in a subhuman condition. Relatively concealed in one of the footnotes, Rousseau even speculates that some of the great apes may in fact be human beings in the natural state, and delicately proposes a shocking experiment for settling the question (SD, 203–9).[22] We tend to think of Darwin as having first raised the issue of the relation of men and monkeys. But Darwin actually came toward the end of a long controversy, and his notion of the descent of man from some kind of primate species was tame by comparison with Rousseau's suggestion that men and apes may simply be the same species at different stages of their history. Throughout the eighteenth century, Europeans were fascinated by the reports travellers, merchants, missionaries, and explorers brought back from Africa and Asia about primate behaviour. Whether authentic or fabricated, these reports of apes using tools, communicating, and forming societies suggested that the line between the animal kingdom and man is harder to draw than had been traditionally supposed. The orangoutan, whose name means "inhabitant of the woods" (SD, 206), became a particular focus of controversy.

8

Rousseau gave wide currency to the philosophical question of the status of the orangoutan, and the issue was popularized in England by the writings of Monboddo. As late as 1815, we find Coleridge writing to Wordsworth wishing that he had used his *Recluse* poem to explode "the absurd notion of . . . Man's having progressed from an Ouran Outang state."[23]

The importance of Rousseau's insistence that natural man is indistinguishable from an animal is that it sharpens the antinomy he creates between nature and civilization. Rousseau would have said in criticism of Milton that he blurs the issue by giving man in his original state many of the traits he develops only in civilization (SD, 102), thus concealing the radical character of the choice man has to make. Far from idealizing natural man, as is commonly supposed, Rousseau had no illusions about the limitations of the state of nature, especially the intellectual limitations. The virtues Rousseau attributes to natural man are the corollaries of what from another perspective might be regarded as his defects. For example, if natural man is spared the anxieties and alienation of social man, it is only because he leads a solitary existence, and thus is denied the benefits of society as well. Rousseau admires the independence, autonomy, and self-possession of natural man. But these qualities are achieved only at the expense of any lasting bonds to other members of his species (SD, 120–21).

Rousseau is famous for the claim that man is naturally good. But in the context of the *Second Discourse* all this means is that the state of nature exists prior to any moral distinctions between good and evil: "Thus one could say that savages are not evil precisely because they do not know what it is to be good" (SD, 130). In order to understand the *Second Discourse* fully, one must penetrate its rhetorical surface. Mainly concerned with using the idea of the state of nature to criticize civil society, Rousseau does everything he can to exaggerate its virtues and minimize its defects (SD, 104). But a careful reading of the *Second Discourse* reveals that Rousseau actually has a balanced view of the state of nature, and does not simply prefer it to civilization. Rousseau's primitive man is at one with the natural world only because he is completely absorbed in it. His harmony with the animals is not the result of some divinely imposed peace but simply the result of the fact that man is originally no more than an animal himself (SD, 115).

Creature and Creator

III

The *Second Discourse* thus tells its own version of a fortunate fall. If man had remained in the simple happiness of the state of nature, he would have stayed ignorant and left his faculties undeveloped. But one must not underestimate the price Rousseau sees man paying for his progress into the state of civil society. Man makes himself thoroughly miserable, losing the certainty of following his impulses and the independence of acting on his own, destroying even his physical health by all the artificial needs and desires he generates in society (SD, 109–10, 185–200). The fundamental institution of society for Rousseau is private property. The attempt to delimit one man's possessions from another's leads to all the apparatus of society, above all, the system of laws which circumscribe man's freedom to act as he chooses. Left to accumulate as much property as possible, men begin to compete with each other for increasingly scarce resources, and lose the state of equality they enjoyed naturally. Wealth and social position become the only measure of human worth, and men are no longer free to generate their own self-esteem as they were in the state of nature (SD, 149, 175). What is most soul-destroying for Rousseau about the state of civil society is that men learn to live in the opinion of others, forced to value themselves by social standards (SD, 179–80). For the harmony of the state of nature, society substitutes a system of conflicting economic interests and the struggle for recognition and mastery among men (SD, 155–56, 193–95).

These social divisions are matched by divisions within man's soul. Once he abandons the sure guide of his natural impulses, he no longer acts singlemindedly. Man experiences doubt and indecision, as for the first time competing desires struggle for ascendancy within him. The main psychological result Rousseau sees from the development of civil society is a split between reason and the passions. One of the most revolutionary aspects of the *Second Discourse* is Rousseau's rethinking of the relation between reason and passion, and hence his reformulation of the fundamental problem of ethics. Traditionally, finding a way of restraining the passions had been regarded as *the* task of ethics. Without some form of restraint, the passions were thought likely to run wild, and hence reason had to step in to devise ways of ordering man's soul. Rousseau set out to clear the passions of what he saw as centuries of false charges, and to show that reason is in fact the cause of man's ills.[24] Rousseau argues that when left to themselves in the state of nature, the passions are quite orderly, because they are easily satisfied: "Everyone peaceably waits for the impulsion of nature, yields to it without choice with more pleasure than frenzy; and the need satisfied, all desire is extinguished" (SD, 135). According to Rousseau, it is the attempt to restrain the passions in the state of civil society which inflames them. By creating artificial scarcities, society makes the passions a source of conflict among men, as Rousseau tries to show in the specific case of sexual desire: "the obligation to eternal fidelity serves only to create adulterers" (SD, 137). Hence, when reason claims the right to restrain the passions, with moral laws, it is presenting itself as the solution to a problem it created in the first place.

Rousseau's ethical revaluation of reason and passion is the most clearly Romantic element in his thought, though it must be remembered that he is remote from any sort of Romantic titanism.[25] He defends the passions by arguing for their inherent moderation, and hence cannot be calling for their unrestrained liberation. In fact Rousseau sees infinite desire as one of the prime defects of civil society. When man's desires become learned rather than spontaneous, they lose their natural finitude, as men seek to acquire more and more in a social spirit of competition and rivalry. The second part of the *Second Discourse* shows how reason creates infinite desire in civilization. Reasoning is a process of comparing, and hence involves men in a ceaseless and frustrating struggle to surpass their neighbors:

Each one began to look at the others and to want to be looked at himself, and public esteem had a value. The one who sang or danced the best, the handsomest, the strongest, the most adroit, or the most eloquent became the most highly considered; and that was the first step toward inequality and, at the same time, toward vice (SD, 149).

Thus Rousseau would have rejected Blake's characterization of human nature in *There is No Natural Religion* (b-VII): "The desire of Man being Infinite the possession is Infinite & himself Infinite." For Rousseau, infinite desire characterizes man only in civil society, not in the state of nature. This suggests that had Rousseau lived to witness the rise of Romanticism, he might have regarded it as a kind of hypertrophy of civilization, rather than a genuine return to man's natural origins. But still, in one decisive respect, Rousseau did prepare the way for a more positive evaluation of the passions among Romantic writers. By blaming reason for the inflaming of man's passions, Rousseau undermines its traditional status as the arbiter of ethics, and indeed suggests that far from being the cure for man's unhappiness, reason is its principal cause. The traditional definition of man as rational animal puts a premium on rationality in his behavior. If man is distinguished from animals by his reason, then he ought to work to suppress his passions as part of his lower, animal nature. Rousseau's new understanding of man sees his passions as more basic to his character than his reason: "we seek to know only because we desire to have pleasure; and it is impossible to conceive why one who had neither desires nor fears would go to the trouble of reasoning" (SD, 116). In Rousseau's view, then, the full realization of man's potential requires allowing room for his passions to develop as an integral part of his character. Rousseau raised the question of whether man is most fully man in his ability to restrain his impulses or to express them.[26] Clearly Romantics like Blake identified with the second position.

This new conception of the relative merits of reason and passion underlies Romantic reinterpretations of traditional creation myths. According to Blake, for example, the conventional accounts have all been written from the point of view of reason against the passions. A common image in orthodox creation myths is a god in the sky, suppressing the rebellion of monstrous forces from below in the earth. For Blake, this way of portraying the superiority of the head to the heart lies behind all the world's legends of titanic wars in heaven and defeated giants, whether in Hesiod, the Bible, or Norse mythology. It reflects a false understanding of the proper ordering of the human whole:

The Giants who formed this world into its sensual existence and now seem to live in it in chains; are in truth. the causes of its life & the sources of all activity, but the chains are, the cunning of weak and tame minds. which have power to resist energy according to the proverb, the weak in courage is strong in cunning (*Marriage*, Pl. 16).

Accordingly, Blake seeks to redress the balance, and write creation myths from the standpoint of the passions against reason. That is why he gnostically reverses the evaluation of heights and depths in his mythic system. Blake portrays the sky-gods as sinister figures, and sympathetically treats the demons chained down below, welcoming their breaking loose from their imprisonment.[27] He thus turns *Paradise Lost* on its head: "It indeed appear'd to Reason as if Desire was cast out but the Devils account is, that the Messiah fell. & formed a heaven of what he stole from the Abyss" (*Marriage*, Pl. 5).

We can now begin to see how the essentially secular and scientific account of human development in the *Second Discourse* could serve the purposes of Romantic myth-makers. Rousseau's reformulation of the problem of ethics, his asking of the supposed chaos of the passions "whether these disorders did not arise with the laws themselves" (SD, 134), suggests that the ethical orientation of traditional creation myths has to be inverted. More generally, as far removed from myth as the *Second Discourse* is, it ends up posing the same dilemma for man that *Paradise Lost* does: whether to remain happy but ignorant, or to become wise but unhappy. But the fact that Rousseau poses this dilemma in purely natural terms means that he fundamentally transforms the problem. In Rousseau's version, no supernatural forces are needed to account for the "fall." Purely natural catastrophes, like earthquakes, floods, or volcanic eruptions, destroy the original abundance of the state of nature, and force man to develop the arts and sciences in response to the newly imposed conditions of scarcity (SD, 143, 148).[28] Nature's lack of providence is what spurs human progress, which takes the form of making up for the defects of nature.[29]

Hence there is nothing sacred about the history Rousseau narrates in the *Second Discourse*, no reason to suppose that the course man's development has taken is sanctioned or directed by any higher power. Recognizing that he has been impelled along in his development by the essentially blind forces of nature, man can pause and reflect on where they have taken him and ask with an open mind: "Where do I want to go from here?" Rousseau in effect redefined the traditional problem of evil.[30] For centuries men had wondered why the human race suffers when an omnipotent and benevolent God created it. But for Rousseau, natural forces and human effort combine to make man what he is, and therefore man himself must take the blame for his current condition. The question which Rousseau posed and which Romantic creation myths attempt to answer is: Why, when man has it within his own power to change himself, does he continue to endure a miserable condition?

13

IV

The influence of Rousseau's new science of man on Romantic creation myths may at first seem paradoxical. We generally think of Romantic writers viewing man as potentially godlike. But Rousseau argues that man in his original state is indistinguishable from a beast. How could this lowering of man's self-image lead to the heights of Romantic expectations? Rousseau's analysis strips man of everything on which he prides himself in his civilized state. In the beginning, nature gives man virtually nothing: no reason, no language, no sociability. But if nature gives man nothing, then it does not set limits on him either, for man owes nature nothing in return. By tearing man down in theory, Rousseau leaves open the practical possibility of building him up again into something more glorious. In a nearly contemporary reaction to Rousseau's theories, we can hear the bewilderment of an orthodox thinker at the peculiar blend of bestial origins and godlike possibilities in the *Second Discourse*:

We have . . . been amused with strange, and monstrous tales of that mute, as well as ill-conceived quadruped, *Man*, – a being, who, for a series of ages, crawled upon the earth, before he began, occasionally, to assume an erect posture, and walk upon his hinder feet; who afterwards made slow progress through the monkey, and the savage, *accidentally* acquired *speech* and reason; till at length, forming himself into a kind of terrestrial God, he established a dominion over his brethren of the forest.[31]

As Edward Davies suspects, a man who thinks of himself as "ill-conceived" to begin with will eventually get the idea of trying to form himself into a god.

Rousseau's reconstruction of human history thus requires men to think carefully about their future, and chart the new directions, if any, in which they ought to develop. In Rousseau's view, man is poised between the bestial happiness of the state of nature and the civilized misery of society, unable to be satisfied with either. Criticizing civil society in the name of the state of nature is the main thrust of the *Second Discourse*, and Rousseau thereby undermines traditional supports for man continuing to lead the life he does. But contrary to the popular view of Rousseau, he does not advocate simply rejecting civilization and returning to the state of nature.[32] He makes this point explicitly: "What! must we destroy societies, annihilate thine and mine, and go back to live in forests with bears?

A conclusion in the manner of my adversaries, which I prefer to anticipate rather than leave them the shame of drawing it" (SD, 201). Rousseau realizes that turning our back on civilization would involve as many losses as gains, since we would have to renounce "its enlightenment, in order to renounce its vices" (SD, 202). Leaving the state of nature changes man in ways which prevent him from ever simply returning. Rousseau counts himself among the men "whose passions have forever destroyed their original simplicity, who can no longer nourish themselves on grass and nuts, nor do without laws and chiefs" (SD, 202).

As we have seen, Rousseau does not present any third stage in the *Second Discourse* which would allow man to synthesize the best of nature and civilization, as Milton's "paradise within" promises to undo the bad effects of the fall. But this does not mean that Rousseau resigned himself to a choice between unpalatable alternatives. Throughout his writings, Rousseau grappled with the question of how man can recapture something of the state of nature within the context of civilized life.[33] To explore the complexity of Rousseau's thought on this subject would require a whole book in itself. For the purposes of understanding Rousseau's influence on Romantic creation myths, a sketch of his solution to the human dilemma will have to suffice. Rousseau actually projected two solutions: one (the social contract) is the better known and is often thought to be the only solution in Rousseau;[34] the other (the solitary walker) is in fact more relevant to Romantic literature. Rousseau ends up recreating the antinomy between civilization and nature in the new form of a bifurcation of humanity into the common men who must learn to live in society and the uncommon men who must learn to go beyond it.[35]

For the majority of men, Rousseau believed that the most that could be regained from the state of nature is the freedom and independence, and hence the sense of dignity and self-worth. This goal can be accomplished by constituting a democratic republic. Men will still be subject to the constraint of laws, but at least they will participate in the creation of the laws. Hence all legislation will become self-legislation and thus a form of autonomy. Rousseau's basic political insight is that restraint becomes less of a burden if it can be interpreted as self-restraint.[36] Rousseau's political writings are largely devoted to showing how a democratic republic can be made to work. These are the writings which are generally neglected by critics like Babbitt, because they reveal the un-Romantic side to Rousseau. Rousseau repeatedly argues, especially in the *Emile*, that an education in moral virtue is the precondition of political freedom. Anyone who insists on regarding Rousseau simply as a proto-Romantic should read his *Letter to M. d'Alembert on the Theatre*, in which he gives the most eloquent defense since Plato's *Republic* of the need for censoring the arts to prevent corruption of a healthy political community (like Geneva).[37] Compared, for example, to Shelley's *Defence of Poetry*, the *Letter to d'Alembert* seems to reveal a Rousseau who is the complete antithesis of Romanticism.

The specific rhetorical intent of Rousseau's political writings is what makes them sound so different from his more theoretical and personal works. Knowing that the majority of men must live under some form of government, Rousseau could not leave them thinking that the state of nature is simply preferable to civil society. As the opening of the *Social Contract* indicates, Rousseau as political writer set out to find some way of presenting social order as legitimate. Taking into account his different practical purpose, Rousseau reverses the rhetorical strategy of the *Second Discourse* in the *Social Contract*. He now does everything he can to exaggerate the virtues of civil society and minimize its defects. Consider the following quotation:

This passage from the state of nature to the civil state produces a remarkable change in man, by substituting justice for instinct in his behavior and giving his actions the morality they previously lacked ... Although in this state he deprives himself of several advantages given by nature, he gains such great ones, his faculties are exercised and developed, his ideas broadened, his feelings ennobled, and his whole soul elevated to such a point that if the abuses of the new condition did not often degrade him beneath the condition he left, he ought ceaselessly to bless the happy moment that tore him away from it forever, and that changed him from a stupid, limited animal into an intelligent being and a man.[38]

The subhuman character of the state of nature, suggested in the text of the *Second Discourse*, but discussed in detail only in the footnotes, is here loudly and clearly proclaimed, while the tendency to corruption in society, the main theme of the *Second Discourse*, is buried in a subordinate clause ("if the abuses of the new condition ..."). In contrast to the *Second Discourse*, the most theoretical of Rousseau's works, the *Social Contract* is addressed to a non-theoretical audience, as Rousseau subtly hints when he says right after this passage: "the philosophic meaning of the word *freedom* is not my subject here."[39] When speaking to the common man and his legislators about the fundamental needs of society, Rousseau takes pains to obscure and conceal his "Romantic" praise for the state of nature, and indeed presents himself as a kind of latter-day Lycurgus, legislating men into moral virtue.

But we must not go to the opposite extreme from Babbitt and let the "anti-Romantic" side of Rousseau now stand for the whole of his thought. Just as a careful reading of the *Second Discourse* reveals the limitations of the state of nature, even the *Social Contract* hints at the limitations of civil society. Rousseau may have found a way to make man's chains appear legitimate, but he never denies that they are still chains. One can see the problem for Rousseau with the democratic republic as a solution to the human dilemma in the fact that it would have to exclude him from its ranks, much as his own Geneva once shut its gates on the young Rousseau for being a wayward citizen. Rousseau's theories would undermine the practical premises of the community, especially its religious beliefs, and his behavior would not be compatible with the strict moral virtue Rousseau himself required of democratic man.[40] Rousseau could not abide any form of restraint in his own life, and thus his course led him away from conventional society:

I have never been truly suited for civil society where everything is annoyance, obligation, and duty and my independent natural temperament always made me incapable of the subjection necessary to anyone who wants to live among men. As long as I act freely, I am good and do only good. But as soon as I feel the yoke either of necessity or of men, I become rebellious, or rather, recalcitrant; then I am ineffectual (R, 83).[41]

In his later works, particularly in his last and in many respects his most peculiar book, *The Reveries of the Solitary Walker*, Rousseau explored a new remedy to man's painful separation from the state of nature. Since it requires dropping out of society and living on its fringes, this solution is not available to all men, but only to a few sensitive individuals, like Rousseau, who cannot find fulfillment in ordinary pursuits and are willing to strike out on their own. Though Rousseau is unable to break with civilization entirely, he does all he can to leave the city behind him and re-establish an immediate relationship with nature by living in the country. His aim is to achieve a state of reverie, in which his conscious mind is suppressed and he is able to experience nature directly, feeling once again the sense of unity with the whole world which natural man enjoyed. Rousseau realizes that the most problematic aspect of civilized life is man's painful sense of self-consciousness, and he seeks to overcome the division man has created between his mind and the world. In reading Rousseau's *Reveries*, we encounter for the first time what was to emerge as the distinctive Romantic sensibility, the feeling of consciousness dissolving back into nature, the merging of subject and object.[42] At times, Rousseau's reveries read like Romantic lyrics in prose.[43]

The first example Rousseau cites is particularly strange. As the result of a near-fatal collision with a Great Dane, Rousseau is knocked unconscious and awakens in a daze. The result of this literal fall, which turns Rousseau upside-down, is to undo the effects of the metaphoric fall into civilized self-consciousness:

I was born into life at that instant, and it seemed to me that I filled all the objects I perceived with my frail existence. Entirely absorbed in the present moment, I remembered nothing; I had no distinct notion of my person nor the least idea of what had just happened to me; I knew neither who I was nor where I was; I felt neither injury, fear, nor worry. I watched my blood flow as I would have watched a brook flow, without even suspecting that this blood belonged to me in any way. I felt a rapturous calm in my whole being; and each time I remember it, I find nothing comparable to it in all the activity of human pleasures (R, 16).

As odd as it may seem to treasure such a moment, Rousseau has come as close as possible to feeling the way natural man did, as the line between his own consciousness and his surroundings blurs in his mind.[44] Rousseau is totally absorbed in the present, just as he described natural man's condition: "His soul, agitated by nothing, is given over to the sole sentiment of its present existence without any idea of the future" (SD, 117). Untroubled by any thoughts of the past or the future, Rousseau is able to enjoy perfect peace. His normally painful sense of separate identity is submerged in a pleasurable sense of belonging to a larger whole.

This feeling is what Rousseau keeps trying to achieve. He has his greatest success during the period of his retreat to Lake Bienne in Switzerland. In the most Romantic passage in the book, Rousseau allows the waters to lull him into unity with nature:

There, the noise of the waves and the tossing of the water, captivating my senses and chasing all other disturbance from my soul, plunged it into a delightful reverie in which night would often surprise me without my having noticed it. The ebb and flow of this water and its noise, continual but magnified at intervals, striking my ears and eyes without respite, took the place of the internal movements which reverie extinguished within me and was enough to make me feel my existence with pleasure and without taking trouble to think (R, 67).

Rousseau has found the only true form of absolute happiness:

But if there is a state in which the soul finds a solid enough base to rest itself on entirely and to gather its whole being into, without needing to recall the past or encroach upon the future; in which time is nothing for it; in which the present lasts forever without, however, making its duration noticed and without any trace of time's passage; without any other sentiment of deprivation or of enjoyment, pleasure or pain, desire or fear, except that of our existence and having this sentiment alone fill it completely; as long as this state lasts, he who finds himself in it can call himself happy . . . What do we enjoy in such a situation? Nothing external to ourselves, nothing if not ourselves and our own existence. As long as this state lasts, we are sufficient unto ourselves, like God (R, 69).

Rousseau suggests how some men can transcend the self-division and alienation of civil society and achieve a divine state. At the same time, the experience can be viewed as a return to the self-sufficiency and self-possession of the state of nature, although presumably the solitary walker, with his experience of civilization behind him, is better able than natural man to understand and appreciate, and hence to savor, this form of happiness.[45]

V

In describing a way to ease the burden of self-consciousness through absorption in nature, the *Reveries* obviously points ahead to Romantic poetry. Rousseau's solitary walker, leaving the ordinary paths of men to seek out the lakes and forests and commune with nature, might be regarded as a prototype of the Romantic artist.[46] But there are ominous implications in the way Rousseau portrays his life in the *Reveries*. He remains isolated from the rest of the human race, and if they ever realize what he is doing, they treat him with contempt or horror. Moreover, in the first reverie Rousseau describes, the desired extinction of consciousness is closely associated with death, and one gets the impression that Rousseau's way back to nature leads to the grave. Clearly the solitary walker is at best a problematic solution to the human dilemma. One reason for studying Rousseau as the background to

Romantic creation myths is to be alert to the potential for tragedy that lurks beneath Romantic visionary ideals.

But we must first look at the original Romantic attempts to avoid the tragic implications of Rousseau's thought. Many Romantics hoped not to have to make the difficult choices Rousseau poses between nature and civilization, between the social contract and the solitary walker. Hence they sought to find the third stage of history Rousseau deliberately omitted (the same goal pursued simultaneously in the philosophical systems of German idealism). In particular, the Romantics did not want to have to abandon the faculties man has developed in civilization in order to recapture a natural quality, for among these faculties is the imagination, and all the arts in which the Romantics hoped to distinguish themselves. The defect of Rousseau's solitary walker is that he seems to jettison too much of the positive achievement of civilization in his eagerness to get back to nature. Though in many respects the solitary walker has the sensibility of a Romantic artist, he does not exhibit the full creative power. The solitary walker is too passive in his relation to nature to be a creative artist. He allows nature to overwhelm him and is so absorbed in the present moment that he cannot shape anything out of it: "A sweet and deep reverie takes possession of his senses then, and through a delicious intoxication he loses himself in the immensity of this beautiful system with which he feels himself one" (R, 92). Rousseau admits that when he is in the state of reverie, he cannot write about it: "In wanting to recall so many sweet reveries, instead of describing them, I fell back into them" (R, 13). Rousseau senses that to think about translating his reveries into artistic form would be to lose the very immediacy of experience which attracted him to the state of reverie in the first place. This may explain why Rousseau calls the *Reveries* a "shapeless diary," stressing the spontaneity and lack of art in the book's organization (R, 6–7). He renounces the ordinary ambitions of an artist, writing the *Reveries* only for himself and caring nothing for the reception of the book: "now that the desire to be better understood by men has been extinguished in my heart, only profound indifference remains about the fate of my true writings" (R, 7).

From the point of view of a creative artist, the most negative aspect of the solitary walker's return to the condition of natural man is the return to his indolence. As Rousseau describes his experience at Lake Bienne: "The precious *far niente* was the first and principal enjoyment I wanted to savor in all its sweetness, and all I did during my sojourn was in effect only the delicious and necessary pursuit of a man who has devoted himself to idleness" (R, 64). In particular, Rousseau takes joy in leaving behind all the symbols of cultural mediation and artistic achievement: "one of my greatest delights was to leave my books well packed up and to have no writing table" (R, 64). At times one gets the sense in the *Reveries* that the solitary walker dissolves so fully back into nature that he might well leave no record of his existence. Of course the *Reveries* is a record of Rousseau's reveries, indeed a beautifully written, at times even poetic record. But the fiction of the *Reveries* is that it is not a finished work of art, but a kind of unpolished self-communion.[47] In leaving behind the constraints of civilization, the solitary walker seems to leave behind its forms as well, and even its form-giving impulse. The solitary walker's world changes from moment to moment: "Everything is in continual flux on earth" (R, 68). Thus although Romantic authors could admire the *Reveries* and learn from it, the kind of literature Rousseau writes could never fully satisfy Romantic ambitions for lasting artistic achievement. If the solitary walker could shape the content of his experience into some kind of permanent artistic form, he would be combining the immediacy and spontaneity of nature with the mediacy and self-reflexive character of civil society. This is the way Romantic authors hoped to reunite nature and civilization in art.

Some Romantics also hoped to overcome the division Rousseau posited between the extraordinary individual and the ordinary community. The idea of the solitary walker was unacceptable to many Romantics because it excludes the majority of men from the highest form of human existence, and thus is profoundly undemocratic. At times Rousseau seems to be condemning most men to the drudgery of bourgeois existence, which supplies the necessities of life, so that a few men like Rousseau can enjoy the luxury of living a life of reverie:

Most men, agitated by continual passions, are little acquainted with this state . . . It would not even be good in the present structure of things that, avid for these sweet ecstasies, they should become disgusted with the active life their ever recurring needs prescribe to them as a duty (R, 69).

But Rousseau's democratic ideal of the social contract was in its own way equally unacceptable to many Romantics, because it excludes the creative individual, who might threaten the community's beliefs. One Romantic response to the split between the social contract and the solitary walker in Rousseau was to attempt to combine his two solutions in one grand synthesis: a universal and democratic community of free and creative individuals.[48] This ideal, which remains powerful to this day, provides the third stage Romantic myth-makers envisage completing history. Unlike Rousseau, many Romantics foresaw a radical transformation of the world which would fundamentally alter human relations and make it possible for everyone to participate actively and harmoniously in the creative life. This is the stage portrayed in the apocalyptic phase of Romantic myth, symbolizing some form of revolution, originally conceived as coming about through political means, but later thought of as a more purely spiritual liberation, accomplished through art itself.

The antinomy of nature and civilization in Rousseau thus gave birth to the dialectical patterns of Romantic myth. Blake's notions of Innocence and Experience, for example, correspond in many respects to Rousseau's state of nature and state of civil society, and Blake's search for a higher form of innocence is an effort to synthesize what Rousseau believed must forever remain sundered. Rousseau posed a challenge to man's longing for perfection, and many Romantics took it up. In one of his earliest works, Shelley states the task he saw before him in terms which are clearly derived from Rousseau:

The supereminence of man is like Satan's a supereminence of pain; and the majority of his species, doomed to penury, disease, and crime, have reason to curse the untoward event that, by enabling him to communicate his sensations, raised him above the level of his fellow animals. But the steps that have been taken are irrevocable. The whole of human science is comprised in one question: How can the advantages of intellect and civilization be reconciled with the liberty and pure pleasures of natural life? How can we take the benefits and reject the evils of the system which is now interwoven with all the fibres of our being?[49]

By providing a secular equivalent of the paradise–fall pattern in Milton, Rousseau pointed the way for man to seek to recapture paradise without divine aid. But to show how man can get from his current state to a restored paradise taxed the powers of Romantic myth-makers, and provided the real test of profundity in their creation myths. The initial euphoria created by the American and French Revolutions made it at first look easy for modern man to bring on the apocalypse. But as the hoped-for paradise failed to materialize, Romantic myth-makers had to rethink the question of how man had fallen prey to tyranny in order to find a way of escaping it. In the logic of myth, Genesis necessarily precedes Exodus.

The complexities of Romantic creation myths result from this rethinking, the effort to understand the psychological process of man's self-division and self-enslavement. The more complicated the account of the fall grew, the more difficult it became to see a way to overcome it. As a result, even some of the most poetically successful of Romantic creation myths remained incomplete and fragment-ary.[50] But in uncovering the mental forces that block a genuine liberation of man's potential, Blake and Shelley explore new psychological depths in poetry, even if they cannot always shape solutions to the problems they uncover. By virtue of their effort to go beyond Rousseau, they were drawn in to his attempt to broaden the conception of man by means of a new investigation of his distant past and origins. It is fitting that in Shelley's *The Triumph of Life*, his final – and fragmentary – attempt to understand man's fallen condition, he summons up Rousseau himself to serve as his guide in his search for man's beginnings. Though Rousseau helped to inspire the Romantic imagination, with his refusal to conceive of man ever fully regaining paradise, he shadowed its dreams. Rous-seau's appearance in Shelley's last poem may signal that toward the end of his life, the poet began to despair of overcoming the antinomies of history and to accept the tragic implications of the philosopher's thought. As we shall see, in Mary Shelley, Byron, and Keats, the tragic undercurrent in Romanticism, at first suppressed by its apocalyptic expectations, begins to come to the surface.

VI

To sum up the importance of Rousseau for Romantic myth-makers: by portraying man's development as the result of an accidental concatenation of blind natural forces and his own actions, Rousseau removed the aura of sanctity surrounding human nature and made it possible for man to think of improving upon what had traditionally been thought of as God's immutable handi-work. Rousseau thus prepared the way for a new conception of the creature and the creator in the human condition. Traditionally, man had been regarded as pure creature, the perfectly designed and executed product of a divine creator, whose intentions must not be questioned and whose work must not be tampered with. But in Rousseau, man becomes both creature and creator. Though in his idea of the subhuman natural man, Rousseau in many ways heightened man's sense of his creatureliness, in his idea that we are what we make of ourselves, Rousseau pointed to man assuming the traditional prerogatives of God. Romantic myth-makers dreamed of the creator in man remaking the creature into something divine.

The title of Byron's strangest work might well serve to sum up this Romantic goal: *The Deformed Transformed*. As long as man thinks of himself as deformed in his origins, he will seek to transform himself into something more closely approaching perfection. In some ways, Byron's portrait of a lonely, outcast hunchback seeking the devil's aid to become a handsome hero reveals the deepest stratum of Romantic yearning: "You both see what is not, / But dream it is what must be" (I.i.289–90). In one of the weirdest scenes in all Romantic literature, Byron allows his hero, Arnold, to shop for a new body among the great figures of antiquity, rejecting Caesar, Alcibiades, Socrates, Mark Antony, and Demetrius the Macedonian to settle finally on the heroic figure of Achilles. But as fantastic as Byron's opening scene may be, its action goes to the heart of the Romantic ideal of autonomy. Total self-determination ultimately requires total self-creation. If all value is a human product and everything is to be the result of man's own will, then even his body ought to become a matter of free choice. The grotesque image of the human body Blake's Los shapes in *The Book of Urizen* reflects the depth of the Romantic protest against man's inherited condition. But at the same time it paradoxically embodies the poet's hope that man can use the future to correct the past errors of God.

But in reading the hopeful visions of Blake and Shelley, we must bear in mind the possibility of a dark side to Romantic literature. Many Romantics sought to liberate the creative energies of man. But they could not always be sure what forces they were unleashing on the world, or whether they themselves could live with their new freedom. Mary Shelley's *Frankenstein* provides a nightmare vision of what it is for man to try to replace God's creativity with his own.[51] The human creator turns out to be as isolated and power-mad as the demonic creator of Romantic myth. Byron's *Cain* and Keats's *The Fall of Hyperion* both develop this theme of the loneliness and tragic suffering of the solitary creative ego. The gnostic form of creation myth originally served as a means for Romantic authors to distance themselves from the traditional image of God. But as we shall see, Keats, in rejecting gnostic myth, identifies with the gods he portrays, precisely in their frustrations as creators. In Keats's myth, the fallen god in fact becomes an image of the Romantic artist himself.

PART ONE

Paradise Lost and Paradise Regained

CHAPTER I

The Demonic Creator

I

Although some of Blake's earliest works, *The Book of Thel* and the *Songs of Innocence*, show affinity with the Bible's portrait of Eden, his first sustained effort at retelling Genesis was *The Book of Urizen*. Almost immediately after writing *The Book of Urizen*, Blake went on to write *The Book of Los* (1795), covering much the same narrative ground from a slightly different perspective, as if he were already having second thoughts about the details of his creation account. At that point, Blake abandoned his original plan for a Bible of Hell and spent approximately the next ten years recasting his mythic material into the fullest and most complex of his creation accounts, *The Four Zoas*. The fact that Blake left this poem in manuscript in an unperfected state suggests that he was never fully satisfied with this version of his creation story. Blake's last two major poems, *Milton* and *Jerusalem*, which he did engrave, are not, strictly speaking, creation myths at all, though they do contain a great deal of cosmological material, take up the issue of the fall of man, and articulate much that is new in Blake's understanding of creativity. But in breaking with conventional linear narrative, both these poems move away from the traditional form of the creation myth, and in particular depart from the idea that the cosmos had a definite beginning.[1]

For the purposes of studying Romantic creation myths as a genre, *The Book of Urizen* seems to be the best choice for careful analysis.[2] Blake's first attempt shows in sharp relief the direction in which Romantic myth-makers developed the form, portraying the establishment of man's current condition as the work of a demonic and incompetent demiurge in order to free man to improve upon his lot. To be sure, by comparison with *The Four Zoas, The Book of Urizen* offers an overly simplified view of the creation and the fall. But the price Blake pays in his later work for developing a more complex understanding of the role of the various elements of the psyche in its disintegration is that he obscures the clear outlines of his myth, leaving the reader unsure what caused the fall or even when exactly it took place.[3] *The Book of Urizen* may give a one-sided account of reason's responsibility for the fall, but at least it gives an initially clear view of what the sides in Blake's cosmic drama are. After analyzing *The Book of Urizen* thoroughly, one should go on to study Blake's major prophecies to see how he refined and elaborated his myth of creation. But it is questionable whether he ever expressed his basic ideas with greater power or intensity than he did in 1794, when Urizen's "shadow of horror" first arose in Blake's Eternity.

The Preludium to *The Book of Urizen* calls to mind the opening of *Paradise Lost*, as Blake announces his subject and briefly summarizes the story he is about to tell. Blake invokes his own mythic creations, the Eternals, as his muse, and presents himself in the Miltonic role of a cosmic recording secretary, taking dictation from a higher power (2:5–6). But in the first chapter of *The Book of Urizen*, we find ourselves plunged into a world very different from that of *Paradise Lost*, or rather Blake seems to have conflated Milton's Book VII with his Book I. Blake's Urizen is a demonic and frightening power, who reminds us of Milton's Satan, especially in his arduous journey through Chaos. But Urizen is doing the work of Milton's God, dividing things into categories, establishing time and space, and thus creating the world as we know it. Blake has evidently run together the fallen angel and the creator god of Milton's story, thereby achieving the characteristic gnostic inversion of mythic values.[4]

Blake's illustrations make the identification of Urizen with the Old Testament God more convincingly than any literary allusion in the text can. Blake's old man with a white beard clearly is the being men worship under the name of Jehovah, but Blake wants us to take a fresh look at this being and to re-evaluate the morality he supports. In traditional accounts, the creation reflects God's omnipotence and benevolence.[5] But in Blake's version, the creation takes on a sinister cast, appearing as the work of a self-interested and self-glorifying being, who cannot even successfully carry out his own plans. The Biblical creator operates out in the open: he can be proud of what he accomplishes and has nothing to hide. Urizen works in secret, unseen by his fellow Eternals, trying to conceal his activity from their curious eyes (3:2, 6–7, 10, 24–25). Whereas the

Biblical creator encounters no opposition in his plans and simply wills whatever he wants into existence, Urizen has to struggle to accomplish his purposes, meeting up with fierce opposition from forces resisting his creation and even having to fight his own passions to continue with the task:

> For he strove in battles dire
> In unseen conflictions with shapes . . .
> Dark revolving in silent activity:
> Unseen in tormenting passions;
> An activity unknown and horrible.
>
> (3:13–14, 18–20)

In Genesis, the creation seems to be a testimony to the overflowing goodness of God, an expansive movement, as the divine power flows into the world and brings it to life. God is continually making full what had been empty: bringing order out of chaos, light out of darkness, and abundance out of nothing. Urizen, by contrast, is paradoxically "unprolific" (3:2) as a creator. Taking a hint from certain Kabbalistic doctrines, as well as one enigmatic passage in *Paradise Lost*, Blake portrays Urizen's creation as a process of contraction.[6] Moving in a direction opposite to that of Jehovah's creation, Urizen's results in a "void" and a "chaos," a "soul-shudd'ring vacuum" (3:4–5, 26). Urizen brings his world into being, not by creating something out of nothing, but by staking out boundaries in what had been an undifferentiated unity, by in effect fencing in a fraction of the world and treating it as the whole.

If the Biblical creation is a model of selflessness, with God voluntarily using his power to bring something new into being, Urizen's creativity is rooted in selfishness. He is merely seeking to heighten his sense of power by harnessing a part of an already existing world as his private domain. Blake stresses Urizen's solipsistic character: he is "self-closed, all-repelling . . . a self-contemplating shadow" (3:3, 21). Far from standing above his creation in sublime repose like the Biblical God, Urizen seems to have willfully isolated himself from the world around him, partly out of arrogance, partly out of fear. In creating, Urizen is learning to say *I* with a vengeance, to establish his separate identity over against a world beneath him which he rules: "self balanc'd stretch'd o'er the void / I alone, even I!" (4:18–19). On one level of interpretation, the rising up of Urizen over the waters symbolizes the ego emerging from the whole of man's psyche, more particularly, the attempt by reason to assume dominion over the passions.[7] To vary an old phrase, in Blake cosmogony recapitulates ontogeny. In narrating what appears to be the genesis of the universe, Blake is really portraying the genesis of human consciousness. The only way to make sense out of the often puzzling events in *The Book of Urizen* is to look for the psychological reality they mirror.[8]

As if he were following in the footsteps of Kant's "Copernican Revolution," Blake understands that the question of how man's world comes into being is really a question of how man comes to perceive the world as he does. *The Book of Urizen* portrays, not the creation of the objective world, but the process of objectification itself, the way man comes to posit the distinction between the objective and the subjective in the first place. Fundamentally, Urizen is battling to take the emotions out of his world, that is, to achieve a form of dispassionate perception, in which things will appear as they "objectively" are, uncolored by the force of man's fears or desires. Only in this sense can Urizen's creation be regarded as any kind of fortunate fall. His actions do bring about an advance, or at least an articulation, of consciousness. Still, in Blake's view, Urizen's creation involves a process of abstraction (3:6), and hence an impoverishment of man's view of reality. Though Urizen's suppression of the passions allows for a greater control of the environment, enabling the newly created realm of objectified things to be manipulated at will, he is closing his eyes to a whole side of existence, the world which has emotional meaning, the world which Blake hoped modern man could still recapture, despite the apparent triumph of a mechanistic world-view in the eighteenth century.[9]

II

To understand Urizen's motives as a creator more fully, we must examine the world he rejects. Unfortunately, *The Book of Urizen* is sketchy about the original state which prompts Urizen's withdrawal into a private universe:

> Earth was not: nor globes of attraction
> The will of the Immortal expanded
> Or contracted his all flexible senses.
> Death was not, but eternal life sprung (3:36–39)

The only information one can gather with certainty from this description is that the original state was not as yet articulated into separate entities (the "globes of attraction"). The "Immortal" is probably a prototype of the primeval cosmic giant Blake was later to call Albion, and in any case represents the unity of Urizen and the other Eternals, at one with each other and with their world. Fortunately, we can fill in our picture of Blake's view of the original state by turning to *The Book of Los*. The aged Mother, Eno, recounts a vision of man's original state, the "Times remote," when "none impure were deem'd" (3:7–9), that is, before Urizen, as part of his struggle with the passions, created the concept of sin:

> Covet was poured full:
> Envy fed with fat of lambs:
> Wrath with lions gore:
> Wantonness lulld to sleep
> With the virgins lute,
> Or sated with her love.
>
> Till Covet broke his locks & bars,
> And slept with open doors:
> Envy sung at the rich mans feast:
> Wrath was follow'd up and down
> By a little ewe lamb
> And Wantonness on his own true love
> Begot a giant race. (3:14–26)

This passage sounds strange only because, as so often happens, Blake is forced to use the vocabulary of a fallen world to describe an unfallen state. Blake is not praising the passions we know as covetousness, envy, wrath, and wantonness, but suggesting that before these passions were distorted by the artificial scarcities and restraints of civilization, that is, when they were fully satisfied rather than dammed up, they were a source of unity among men, rather than the divisions they now cause in their fallen forms.[10] Eno's vision reflects Blake's basic conviction that until reason turned against the passions and tried to dominate them, the passions were inherently rational. Blake believed that, left to themselves, the passions would not get out of control. Animals, after all, lack reason, and yet they are not torn apart and destroyed by conflicting passions. As paradoxical as it sounds, animal passions are in fact more "reasonable" than human passions. Animals live in harmony with their world, their passions suited to their environment, kept in check by natural limits. Only man, with his reason and civilization, can develop "unnatural" desires. For example, only man has learned to kill his fellow creatures, not to satisfy his legitimate needs, but to feed his pride.

Blake thus carries on Rousseau's revolutionary rethinking of ethics:[11] man's difficulty lies not in the way his passions interfere with the rule of his reason but in the way his reason has interfered with the free play of his passions. In Blake's view, as in Rousseau's, it is only civilization's attempt to restrain the passions which inflames them, and leads to conflict among men. Allowed to satisfy themselves freely ("Covet was poured full"), the passions would stay within reasonable limits, and remain harmless ("Wantonness lulld to sleep"). That is the meaning of Blake's famous statement in *The Marriage of Heaven and Hell*: "Reason is the bound or outward circumference of Energy" (Pl. 4). Reason should not be pictured as a separate, independent force, necessary to stand above the passions and keep them in line. On the contrary, the passions will on their own and of themselves fall into ordered and harmonious patterns, and this form is what we – after the fact – call reason. What Blake rejects is any attempt to impose prior restraints on the passions according to abstract rational dictates, rather than allowing them to take their own course. This ideal Blake found expressed in the Gospels: "Jesus was all virtue, and acted from impulse: not from rules" (*Marriage*, Pl. 23–24).

For Blake, then, man's fundamental mistake is to think of reason and passion as originally at odds in his nature. In Blake's view, man's energies are not a source of chaos but express themselves precisely by taking shape, or as he put it in one of his earliest works, *The French Revolution*, "fire delights in its form" (l. 189). Fire would seem to be an excellent symbol for the supposedly uncontainable and uncontrollable force of the passions. Yet flames do assume a definite outline on their own: it is just that the particular shape of a given fire is everchanging according to the law of its inner nature, and certainly cannot be predicted or circumscribed in advance. Taking shape without the imposition of an external pattern, fire becomes for Blake a symbol of the potential harmony of reason and passion: "living flames / Intelligent, organiz'd" (*The Book of Los*, 3:28–29).

It is this original unity of reason and passion which Urizen chooses to shatter, thus precipitating what Blake regarded as the

34

true fall of man, the self-division of his faculties. The central question Blake grappled with in his creation myths is: Why, when man originally enjoyed harmony within himself and with his world, did he ever provoke an internal crisis, setting his reason at war with his passions? What Urizen evidently objected to in the original state was its fluidity. With man's energies freely flowing in any direction and expressing themselves as they pleased, taking any form and changing it from moment to moment, Urizen could find no stable point of reference in his world, nothing solid to grab hold of, nothing clearly outlined he could call his own, in short, nothing with his name stamped on it:

> Hidden set apart in my stern counsels
> Reserv'd for the days of futurity,
> I have sought for a joy without pain,
> For a solid without fluctuation
> Why will you die O Eternals?
> Why live in unquenchable burnings? (4:8–13)

While Urizen represents the faculty of reason in particular, more generally he embodies man's boundary-making impulse, his urge to create horizons for himself.[12] Urizen wants certainty in his world, and that means the certainty of possession, above all, self-possession.[13] He does not want to lose himself in a larger whole, to have his sense of separate identity dissolved in an all-embracing feeling of community. To Urizen the free interchange and transformation of energies in man's original state seems like death, for he cannot conceive of himself as existing except apart, in a single, definite form:

> Let each chuse one habitation:
> His ancient infinite mansion:
> One command, one joy, one desire,
> One curse, one weight, one measure
> One King, one God, one Law. (4:36–40)

Urizen's obsession with stability of identity explains his peculiar attitude toward time. Unable to appreciate anything he cannot hold on to forever, his thoughts are always running off into the future, trying to guarantee the permanence of his possessions, with the ironic result that he cannot take pleasure in the present, and hence cannot take pleasure in anything.[14] As Blake wrote in a brief lyric entitled "Eternity":

35

He who binds to himself a joy
Does the winged life destroy
But he who kisses the joy as it flies
Lives in eternity's sun rise.

Holding himself "reserv'd for the days of futurity," Urizen tries to arrest the joy of the moment, but drains the present of all vitality in the process.

Urizen's concern with setting boundaries also has a political dimension. On one level of interpretation, Urizen is the creator of private property. The moment when he proclaims his separate realm mythically dramatizes the already semi-mythic moment in the *Second Discourse* when property first appears:

The first person who, having fenced off a plot of ground, took it into his head to say *this is mine* and found people simple enough to believe him, was the true founder of civil society. What crimes, wars, murders, what miseries and horrors would the human race have been spared by someone who, uprooting the stakes or filling in the ditch, had shouted to his fellow men: Beware of listening to this impostor; you are lost if you forget that the fruits belong to all and the earth to no one! (SD, 141–42)[15]

Under the guise of cosmogony, *The Book of Urizen* portrays the genesis of society as well as the genesis of consciousness. In Blake's view, these two developments are inextricably intertwined. The growth of consciousness is a social process, involving encounters with other men, and, in particular, struggles for mastery among them. At the same time as he creates his world, Urizen founds with one stroke the realms of politics, religion, and morality: "One King, one God, one Law."

For Blake, morality is a special case of Urizen's impulse to categorize. Refusing to embrace life in its wholeness, Urizen substitutes a rigid compartmentalization of man's impulses for the fluid interplay which according to Blake characterized the original harmony in man. Morality tries to elevate one side of man at the expense of the other, to break apart the dialectical unity of reason and passion and turn them into warring opposites:

Without Contraries is no progression. Attraction and Repulsion, Reason and Energy, Love and Hate, are necessary to Human existence.

From these contraries spring what the religious call Good & Evil. Good is the passive that obeys Reason. Evil is the active springing from Energy. Good is Heaven. Evil is Hell. (*Marriage*, Pl. 3)

Urizen's actions as a creator dramatize this process through which morality emerges. He will not accept the unity of contraries in life: "I have sought for a joy without pain" (4:10). Urizen struggles to force down his passions, and eliminate them entirely, in order to become pure reason:

> First I fought with the fire; consum'd
> Inwards, into a deep world within:
> A void immense, wild dark & deep,
> Where nothing was. Natures wide womb
>
> And self balanc'd stretch'd o'er the void
> I alone, even I! the winds merciless
> Bound; but condensing, in torrents
> They fall & fall; strong I repell'd
> The vast waves, & arose on the waters
> A wide world of solid obstruction (4:14–23)

This passage clearly echoes the opening chapter of Genesis and *Paradise Lost*. But though the imagery is cosmological, Blake is portraying something happening within man's psyche. Urizen is fighting to establish modern man's self-image: a rational head above controlling a passionate heart below. He sunders man's original unity and spontaneity of impulse by inventing the concept of sin, stamping the body's natural urges as evil and attempting to cast them out:

> Here alone I in books formd of metals
> Have written the secrets of wisdom
> The secrets of dark contemplation
> By fightings and conflicts dire,
> With terrible monsters Sin-bred:
> Which the bosoms of all inhabit;
> Seven deadly Sins of the soul. (4:24–30)

The core of Urizen's creation is his invention of the concept of holiness (4:7), the idea that only part of man (his reason) is sacred, and all the rest is profane. Against this assault on the diversity and complexity of human nature, Blake championed the right of individuality: "One Law for the Lion & Ox is Oppression . . . For every thing that lives is Holy" (*Marriage*, Pl. 24–25).

III

When one looks at Urizen's moral tyranny, the results of his creation seem uniformly negative. But a full understanding of

37

Urizen's role in Blake's thought requires appreciating the positive effects of his activity. Along with creating the concepts of sin and holiness, Urizen has, after all, taken the first steps on the road to civilization. The positive side of Urizen's rejection of the passions is his attempt to rise above the animal nature of man and develop the distinctively human faculties. For example, Urizen's attitude toward time may well drain life of joy, but one must nevertheless recognize in this attitude the beginning of the capacity for delayed gratification which in some sense makes man superior to the animal kingdom. Though Urizen has gone too far in losing touch with the present, he has at least introduced the notion of planning for the future, and thereby given man a new freedom, liberating him from his total absorption in the moment to pursue long-term goals and projects.[16]

The best way of grasping the ambiguity of Urizen's achievement is to realize that he is the creator of language. It is no accident that Urizen's principal action is a speech from his "dark solitude" (4:6). In the deepest sense, this speech *is* Urizen's act of creation. Blake understood the force of the Bible's "In the beginning was the Word." Urizen's activities as a creator truly begin when he first "utter'd / Words articulate" (4:3–4). His function is in fact to articulate consciousness into words. The one common element in all of Urizen's activities is the act of naming.[17] He names the holy, and separates the sacred from the profane. He names sin, and separates good from evil. He learns to say *I*, and separates himself from his fellow Eternals. One might even say that his decisive action as a creator is to forge himself a name. The name of Urizen appears to be the first word spoken in Blake's cosmos (3:6).

The Book of Urizen embodies a profound understanding of how the emergence of language is bound up with the emergence of humanity as we know it. As we have seen, Urizen's act of creation can be interpreted in many ways: as the development of self-consciousness, as the objectification of the world, as the elevation of reason over the passions, as the beginning of man's orientation by the future, as the invention of property, and as the foundation of politics, religion, and morality. Blake's fundamental insight is that all these processes are ultimately one and the same, and are identical with the creation of language. Man becomes man as we know him in civil society by interposing a set of symbols between himself and reality, thus breaking the immediacy of the hold his environment has on him, giving him a sense of himself as a separate being, and freeing him to gain control over his environment and his animal impulses.[18] All of human culture and civilization, all of man's higher achievements, are the result of this one decisive step. The reason Blake portrays this process of creation as a fall is that, like Rousseau, he realizes that man pays a great price for his attempt to rise above his animal nature. Urizen originates every form of progress – cultural, scientific, technological – modern man takes pride in. But at the same time he is responsible for leading man away from the primitive happiness of his original state.

The reason why one may at first overlook the positive side of Urizen's achievement is that Blake has deliberately obscured it, following the same strategy as Rousseau in using the notion of a primeval state as a means of criticizing modern man's existence in civil society. As we have seen, in order to heighten the power of the state of nature as a critical standard, Rousseau does everything he can to highlight the ways in which it is superior to civil society, and consistently plays down the ways in which it might strike a modern man as distinctly inferior. Rousseau further manipulates his reader by invoking the myth of the golden age, describing a half-way point between the state of nature and the modern world, when man had acquired some of the benefits of civilization without all the complexities and problems (SD, 150–51). Many readers of the *Second Discourse* come away with the impression that this happy medium between nature and civilization is in fact Rousseau's idea of the state of nature itself.[19] This is a false impression, but one which Rousseau may have encouraged, since it suits his intention in the *Second Discourse* of raising doubts about the value of modern civilization.[20]

Similar considerations may account for Blake's virtual silence about the original state in *The Book of Urizen*.[21] Blake confines himself to indicating that it was a state of unity, presumably of the harmonious functioning of man's instincts and hence of happiness. But one must pay careful attention to what Urizen brings into the world to understand what was lacking in Blake's Eternity. The absence of fully developed human faculties is easier to detect in Blake's earlier portrait of the unfallen state, the state of Innocence, shown in *The Book of Thel* and the *Songs of Innocence*. Thel herself feels unfulfilled in the Vale of Har, and unless she forces herself to leave, we assume she will be trapped on the level of animal existence, locked into the cycles of nature and denied all human progress.[22] Blake's children in the *Songs of Innocence* lead happy lives, at peace with their world, but we sense that they are still children, and have a limited understanding of the world.

In Blake's earlier poems, he makes it clear that man's original state was somehow primitive and undeveloped, and that a fall from this state was necessary for the sake of human growth, even though it involved exchanging happiness for misery. Blake's recasting of his myth of the fall in *The Book of Urizen*, the replacement of Innocence by Eternity, may reflect a rhetorical decision that to portray man's original state as primitive makes it too easy for sophisticated modern man to reject his beginnings as beneath his contempt and remain satisfied with the "progress" he has made. Blake believed that not enough had been said in favor of the goodness and harmony of man's original instincts, and too much had been said in favor of reason and civilization. To redress this wrong, he cast his myth in *The Book of Urizen* in such terms that none of the defects of man's original state are clearly visible, while Urizen, representing reason, appears as the pure villain of the piece. Living in the Age of Reason, Blake felt compelled to give a one-sided defense of the passions. Reason would not be the devil of Blake's poem if he had not seen it as the god of his age.

The Book of Urizen reveals the fundamental tactic of Romantic creation myths, a tactic exactly parallel to Rousseau's in the *Second Discourse*. Rousseau showed how to progress beyond one's predecessors by seeming to go back in history. The *Second Discourse* develops a revolutionary understanding of human nature. Yet Rousseau presents himself as an archaeologist, as a man who is simply delving deeper and deeper into man's past than any previous thinker: "The philosophers who have examined the foundations of society have all felt the necessity of going back to the state of nature, but none of them has reached it" (SD, 102). Rousseau presents a new understanding of man's nature under the guise of recovering man's archaic state.[23] Just like Rousseau, Romantic myth-makers took the revolutionary ideal of a harmony between reason and passion, which man is to quest for in the future, and projected it back in time, into a primeval past. In order to understand what man can become, one must look at what he once was, for whatever man once was, he can become again. The Romantic attraction to the idea of the fall must be explained by the

Romantic interest in the idea of an apocalypse, a revolutionary transformation of the human condition. Romantic creation myths are fundamentally an attempt to gain the prestige of origins for Romantic revolutionary ideals. One way of avoiding the charge of being a mere utopian dreamer is to claim that one is only trying to recapture a state which has already existed, indeed the oldest state of all.

But this mythic approach runs into a theoretical difficulty: If man's original state was so perfect, why did he ever leave it? More specifically in *The Book of Urizen*, if man's reason and passions were originally in perfect harmony, how did they come into conflict? Must there not have been something lacking in the original state for Urizen to reject it? We seem to be back to Milton's original difficulties in portraying Eden. Given the theoretical function the notion of man's original state was called upon to serve in Romantic myth, a writer like Blake was forced to strike a delicate balance in his portrayal of man's beginnings. The original state must be attractive enough to serve as an indictment of man's current condition. But it cannot be so perfect that one can no longer conceive of how man fell out of it in the first place. Given these conflicting demands upon the conception of the original state, it is not surprising that Blake was somewhat sketchy in picturing it in *The Book of Urizen*, and only succeeded in clouding the issue further when he tried to elaborate on his portrayal of man's beginning in later works, such as *The Four Zoas*.

It has been necessary to dwell on the opening of *The Book of Urizen* in order to show that, however grim a portrait of his demiurge Blake draws, the fall Urizen precipitates must still be regarded as a fortunate fall. For all his dubious motives, Urizen has the courage and daring to do what no other being will do: to seize upon the undeveloped potentialities of nature and make them serve the will of man. Urizen sets in motion a sequence of events which eventually might allow the highest impulses of man's nature to develop. Urizen's selfishness, for example, is paradoxically what makes possible the development of true selflessness in man. In Blake's original state, selflessness is no achievement, since to the extent that separate beings exist, they do not have a distinct sense of self, and thus have nothing to struggle with and overcome. By developing a strong sense of personal identity, Urizen creates the challenge of triumphing over that pride and willfulness for the sake of others. In short, without a sense of self, one cannot experience genuine self-sacrifice. Only by introducing division into the original unity does Urizen make the re-establishment of that unity possible on a higher level and as a meaningful human creation. Romantic myth-makers sought a form of unity that does not require simple homogeneity. The defect of man's beginning is that things harmonize only because they have not yet been differentiated into conflicting opposites. Discord is necessary to permit the articulation of the world into the diversity which is precisely what makes it interesting to a Romantic. The higher form of Romantic unity must be compatible with the heterogeneity of human development.

IV

We have seen how Urizen begins the divison in Eternity; the rest of Blake's poem portrays the deepening, widening, and hardening of this initial rift. Perhaps the best way of describing what happens in *The Book of Urizen* is to use T. S. Eliot's phrase, "dissociation of sensibility."[24] Once Urizen shatters the original unity of thought and feeling, thought becomes increasingly abstract and sterile, while feeling becomes increasingly chaotic and uncontrolled. The reaction of the other Eternals to Urizen's abrupt withdrawal is immediate and decisive: "Rage siez'd the strong" (4:44). The remaining Eternals, who presumably represent the passions, run wild in their fury and begin blazing flames of "intense indignation" at Urizen (4:45–47, 5:11–16). Urizen must build defenses against the Eternals, first piling up "mountains & hills" to protect himself from their fires, and finally framing a "roof, vast petrific around" (5:22, 28). Forced to entrench his position, Urizen ends up making his separation from Eternity more and more permanent by giving it a definite form. In psychological terms, Urizen's fortifications represent the defense mechanisms the ego develops to deal with the subconscious impulses it refuses to recognize. Blake shows how difficult it is to bring reason and passion back into harmony once they turn against each other. Even after Urizen's decision to withdraw from Eternity, all might have been well if the other Eternals had sought to make peace with him, and bring him back into the fold. But the Eternals choose the opposite course of action, and alienate Urizen even further. The fall Blake depicts gathers momentum as it proceeds. Tragically, all efforts to respond to the fall only succeed in prolonging it and making it more difficult to reverse its effects.[25]

The irrationality of the Eternals' reaction to Urizen is in a sense dictated by the logic of the situation. They cannot be expected to act reasonably when Reason has just removed itself from their ranks.[26] Thus Urizen's obsession with order is actually what introduces chaos into the world (5:3–11). Like a self-fulfilling prophecy, his invention of the concept of sin calls sin into being:

> All the seven deadly sins of the soul
> In living creations appear'd
> In the flames of eternal fury. (4:49–5:2)

Blake is mythically portraying how the attempt to dam up the passions ironically results in increasing their force and diverting them into harmful channels. Blake believed that the only healthy way of dealing with the passions is to allow them free expression: "Sooner murder an infant in its cradle than nurse unacted desires" (*Marriage*, Pl. 10). By refusing to recognize the legitimacy of his natural impulses, man ends up forcing them underground, where they fester and grow poisonous, until they find subterranean means of expression, beyond the conscious control of the ego.

Into this impasse, Blake introduces a new character, Los. He is quite literally the central character in Blake's poem, poised between Urizen and the other Eternals, and as such he offers some hope of bridging the gap that has opened up, of providing the third term that could restore the harmony between reason and passion. But stationed as a guard over Urizen's newly created world (5:38–40), Los cannot keep his distance and becomes deeply implicated in the fall, helping to give shape to Urizen's separation. As becomes clearer in Blake's major prophecies, Los represents the power of imagination in man.[27] In the unfallen state, Los stood at the center of man's wholeness, for the imagination, when it is functioning properly, unites reason and passion in the living symbols it produces.[28] An artistic image cannot be classified as either simply rational or simply passionate. The work of art has intellectual content, and yet it speaks to the emotions. The centrality of art in Blake's view of life is rooted in the way it mirrors the original wholeness of man, and thus points toward a restoration of psychic harmony.

The fact that Los gets drawn into Urizen's fall is thus a turning point in Blake's myth, and an example of how the crisis Urizen initiates gradually spreads throughout the mental universe. The imbalance between reason and passion Urizen has caused evidently disturbs the harmonious functioning of the imagination.[29] In its fallen form, the imagination ceases to be the unitary expression of all psychic powers operating together, and becomes a mere image-making faculty, capable of serving either reason or passion separately. Both reason and passion must work through images, for without images they have no access to their separate realities. No matter how irrational the desires become, they still need images of what they long for, and no matter how abstract reason becomes, it can never completely divorce itself from the realm of images, since an abstraction is itself an image. Reason may reject the concrete images of desire as imprecise, shadowy, and overcharged with emotion, but the clarity of its geometric designs or numerical symbols still depends on a productive imagination. The fact that all reality takes shape in images ensures that the imagination retains its central role even in a fallen world. But it also subjects the fallen imagination to great pressures. The psychic forces now at odds make contradictory demands upon the imagination. Reason seeks to purge the imagination of all emotions; passion urges the imagination to run wild.

This is the situation in which Los finds himself, caught in the middle of a dividing psyche:

> Los wept howling around the dark Demon:
> And cursing his lot; for in anguish,
> Urizen was rent from his side;
> And a fathomless void for his feet;
> And intense fires for his dwelling. (6:2–6)

The "fathomless void" represents the realms of abstraction into which reason would lead the imagination, and the "intense fires" are the fierce desires passion would like to see given imaginative embodiment.[30] One way of understanding Los's situation at this point is to see Blake as mythically recreating his own position as a poet in the late eighteenth century.[31] Blake is torn between the path of Dryden and Pope, on the one hand, and that of Cowper and Smart, on the other. The Age of Reason in poetry paradoxically turned out to be the Age of Madness as well. In the seeming absence of more imaginative possibilities, a poet could accept the mechanistic world-view of Newton and seek to give it form in verse, along with the rationalistic ethics it grounded. But in creating a work like

Pope's *An Essay on Man*, a poet was, in Blake's view, significantly lowering his aspirations, surrendering his imaginative freedom, and settling for a prosaic reality in his verse. Unfortunately, when reason became such a narrow ideal in poetry, the alternative seemed to be to reject rational restraint entirely, and flirt with madness. Blake would have seen the abandoning of any pretense to ordinary comprehensibility in the poetry of someone like Smart as simply the other side of the coin of Pope's conventional desire to stay within the bounds of received opinion and be comprehensible to everyone. As a late eighteenth-century poet, Blake knew what it means to see the void of Reason on one side and the intense fires of Madness on the other.

Unable to endure being pulled in two directions at once, Los throws in his lot with Urizen. Los is the best example in the poem of a character whose well-meaning but misguided efforts worsen a situation they were intended to improve. Trying to reduce the suffering Urizen has brought about, Los prolongs man's fallen condition by making it tolerable. As long as the wounds Urizen caused remain open, their painfulness serves as a reminder that the beings in the fallen world are somehow incomplete and should seek reunification. By building a body for Urizen, Los heals the gaping wounds, but in the process finally establishes the fallen state as permanent. Mistakenly trying to save the situation, Los ends up trapping Urizen, and himself, in the fallen world.

But Los evidently cannot help himself. As the formative power in man, he cannot stand back and look passively at the formlessness Urizen has brought into being (6:8, 7:8–9). For Los, any shape is better than none, and so he sets to work on Urizen, who has become a "clod of clay" in his hands (6:10). Perhaps on one level Blake is suggesting that a poet can find a concrete way of expressing even the most abstract and unpoetic of ideas, as witness Pope's efforts at transforming Newton's *Principia* and Bolingbroke's Deism into *An Essay on Man*.[32] The partnership of Los and Urizen may reflect Blake's belief that poetry in his age had formed an unholy alliance with the Newtonian world-view, lending the prestige of the imagination to the most anti-imaginative of forces and thereby obscuring the sharpness of the conflict between the alternatives man faced. In mythic terms, if Los had not ended Urizen's agony by giving him a body, Urizen might have been forced to find a way back to Eternity.

The scene of Los forging Urizen's body is probably the most extraordinary in Blake's myth, both for the daring of its conception and the vividness of its realization. The profound irony of this scene only becomes evident when one recalls the myth Blake is rewriting. In the Bible, Jehovah triumphantly creates man in his own image. In *The Book of Urizen*, the fallen imagination struggles to create its image of divinity on the model of a grotesquely distorted human body. Blake anticipates Nietzsche's biting epigram: "What? Is man merely a mistake of God's? Or God merely a mistake of man's?"[33]

On one level of interpretation, Los is creating the way man perceives the divine. On another level, he is continuing the process of the fall, furthering the contraction of the human spirit into fixed form. Blake comes closest to the mode of gnostic myth in this section, showing the spirit of man imprisoned in the material world, cut off from its eternal home by the weight of an ugly body.[34] One would have to search far and wide for a more frightening depiction of the human form. Blake takes ordinary anatomical details, such as the appearance of the skeleton and the nervous system, and turns them into sinister emblems of man's entrapment in this world:

> From the caverns of his jointed Spine,
> Down sunk with fright a red
> Round globe hot burning deep
> Deep down into the Abyss:
> Panting: Conglobing, Trembling
> Shooting out ten thousand branches
> Around his solid bones. (11:1–7)

But Blake was no Gnostic reviler of the flesh, and one should not interpret *The Book of Urizen* as expressing his disgust for the human form. One must not forget that Blake's poem effectively takes place, not in the objective world, but in the world of consciousness. Los is creating, not man's body, but the way man perceives his body. Once man's faculties fall out of harmony, his image of his body suffers a collapse as well. The hideous form Los brings into being is the visual reflection of Urizen's damning of the body's natural impulses as sinful. If man thinks of his body as monstrous, it will assume a monstrous form in his eyes.

In accord with Blake's focus on perception, Los's creation of Urizen's body centers on the creation of the senses. In Los's mistaken handiwork, the senses become a way of shutting out the world, of hiding from the vibrancy of experience man originally enjoyed when

his "all flexible senses ... expanded or contracted" at will
(3:37–38). Rather than opening up as full a perspective on the
world as possible, the senses as Los creates them contract man's
horizons, letting only a narrow range of experience into consciousness:

> In harrowing fear rolling round;
> His nervous brain shot branches
> Round the branches of his heart.
> On high into two little orbs
> And fixed in two little caves
> Hiding carefully from the wind,
> His eyes beheld the deep. (11:10–16)

Los's ordering of sensory perception is an integral part of
Urizen's program of objectifying the world. Los is filtering out all
the expressive aspects of experience, eliminating everything that
keeps man's senses alive. The result of his labors will be the
objective world of fact, drained of all emotion and hence dead:

> The pangs of hope began,
> In heavy pain striving, struggling.
> Two Ears in close volutions.
> From beneath his orbs of vision
> Shot spiring out and petrified
> As they grew. (11:19–24)

For the ego to maintain control, it must shut out much of the
information impinging on it from its environment, or risk being
overwhelmed by the vividness of its sensations. If man allows his
perceptions to be colored by his emotions, he may be swept away,
against his better judgment, by the current of a momentary mood
or whim. But in Blake's view, for man to break the power of his
emotions by creating an objective world is to achieve a hollow
victory. It leaves man with a perceived reality which is only a
shadow of the world his heightened senses could reveal to him:

If the doors of perception were cleansed every thing would appear to
man as it is: infinite.
For man has closed himself up, till he sees all things thro' narrow chinks
of his cavern. (*Marriage*, Pl. 14)

By the time Los has finished creating senses for Urizen, he may have
reduced the pain he suffers, but he has eliminated much of his
capacity for joy as well.

Once Los has completed his creation, he can step back and contemplate what he has accomplished. But unlike the Biblical God, Los cannot look upon his handiwork and see that it is good. Los is more like Victor Frankenstein, horrified at the monstrous results of his botched creation:

> In terrors Los shrunk from his task:
> His great hammer fell from his hand:
> His fires beheld, and sickening,
> Hid their strong limbs in smoke. (13:20–23)

Los has significantly reduced the possibility of ever overcoming the fall. Though it was bad enough for Urizen to remove himself from Eternity, at least as long as he stayed aware that Eternity exists some hope remained of his returning to his original state. But as a result of Los's labors, Urizen cannot even see Eternity anymore:

> All the myriads of Eternity:
> All the wisdom & joy of life:
> Roll like a sea around him,
> Except what his little orbs
> Of sight by degree unfold.
> And now his eternal life
> Like a dream was obliterated. (13:28–34)

Los deepens Urizen's fall, and, what is worse, he expends so much energy in the process that he weakens himself and begins to lose sight of Eternity as well:

> Los suffer'd his fires to decay
> Then he look'd back with anxious desire
> But the space undivided by existence
> Struck horror into his soul. (13:44–47)

With his fires decaying, Los is losing touch with the element of passion which is an integral part of human wholeness. Fallen into the void of Urizen's abstract concept of space, Los can no longer see or feel a vital link to Eternity. At this point in the story, just when Los needs all the energy he can summon to attempt to recapture Eternity and the wholeness of man, he himself undergoes a further division, thus weakening further his power to undo the fall.

V

Contemplating the disastrous results of his creation, Los literally begins to fall apart. He is wracked by pity for Urizen's miserable condition, though he may be really pitying himself. In any case, "pity divides the soul" (13:53), and the pitying element in Los begins to flow out and form a new being. Perhaps Los is trying to expel whatever pity he feels, in the belief that his misguided sympathy for Urizen is what landed him in his present plight. Los may feel that his situation demands sternness and thus requires rejecting any soft and gentle inclinations in his nature. His casting out of pity leads to the appearance of "the first female form now separate" (18:15), as Los divides into Los and Enitharmon.

In portraying this scene, Blake had in mind several myths which suggest that man's nature originally combined male and female. The story of Eve being created from Adam's rib is obviously one of Blake's sources for the Los–Enitharmon episode. Blake might have derived further Biblical support for the notion of an originally androgynous human nature from the line in Genesis: "male and female created He them" (1:27). Some rabbinic commentators interpreted this line as meaning that "man was created with two faces, that is, a hermaphrodite."[35] Blake was probably also influenced by certain Greek myths: the story of Athena springing full-grown from Zeus's head and Aristophanes' comic account in Plato's *Symposium* of man's original condition, when all human beings were double what they are now, forming three categories (male–male, female–female, and male–female).[36] The Los–Enitharmon episode is a good example of how Blake worked as a myth-maker. Ranging through widely-scattered myths with very different meanings, Blake evolved a single archetype which he no doubt believed embodied the real and original truth behind the distorted versions which have been accepted in the Western tradition.

And once again the truth behind Blake's myth turns out to be psychological. As weird as the creation of Enitharmon may seem when one visualizes it as an event in the material world, the episode reflects a sound insight into the human mind, that it encompasses both masculine and feminine elements (or rather what are defined as masculine and feminine elements in the fallen world, but were characteristic of humans in general in the unfallen state). In his original psychic wholeness, man in Blake's view was capable of feeling both harsh and tender emotions. He could be aggressive and self-possessed, but also compassionate and yielding. The division of mankind into masculine and feminine categories thus represents for

Blake another case of breaking up a harmonious totality into warring elements. Men reject what comes to be known as the feminine side of their nature, trying to repress all their fellow-feeling and emotional warmth, in order to become sternly rational and fiercely independent beings.

This repression is accomplished by means of a process of psychic projection. Men create the concept of the feminine, stamping all their tender emotions as somehow unmasculine, and projecting them onto the females of the species. By appropriating all sternness and rationality to themselves, men create what would today be called the sexual stereotype of the flighty female. Enitharmon is the male dream of feminine weakness brought to life. She evolves out of "fibres of blood, milk and tears" and appears "trembling and pale" before Los (18:4–8). In masculine eyes, women are supposed to embody the soft side of human nature, characterized by fear rather than bravery, intuition rather than reason. Though men claim to despise these feminine qualities, they are secretly in love with them because they are part of their own nature as human beings. For Blake, the great irony of life among the divided sexes is that men, having rejected their own tenderness and warmth as unmasculine, become entranced by these qualities when they find them embodied in female form. The force of passion in sexual love is to be traced to the fact that when a man seeks out a woman, he is seeking to recover his psychic wholeness, to recapture and reintegrate the feminine side into his psyche.[37]

To understand the full significance of the masculine–feminine division in *The Book of Urizen*, one must consider its impact upon Los's prophetic function, his capacity for leading man back to paradise. Once Los splits into Los and Enitharmon, his prophetic qualities cease to function together and instead begin to work at cross purposes. Los as a prophet originally possessed a creative unity of wrath and pity. But in his fallen form, his wrath gravitates toward his masculine side and his pity toward his feminine. This development proves disastrous for Los's mission, because to accomplish his task, a prophet must be simultaneously stern and sympathetic with his fellow human beings. He must express indignation at their lapses, and remind them of their need to rise above their fallen state. But he cannot be so harsh with them that they despair of amending their condition or reject his teaching as inhuman. The prophet must temper his indignation with compassion, showing sympathy for the fact that men are after all only human and have their failings. But the prophet cannot allow his compassion to go too far. Out of pity for mankind, he might concentrate all his efforts on ameliorating their current condition, and lose sight of the higher goal of restoring man to his original wholeness. For Blake, pity goes wrong when it helps to perpetuate man's fallen condition by making it more tolerable. The compassion of the prophet must be held in check by his indignation at how low the human spirit has fallen. His anger prevents him from resting content with half-way measures, and enables him to rouse mankind to true spiritual exertions. When indignation and compassion are combined in the prophet's soul, they work to moderate each other and see that neither gets out of hand. But in the fallen world, the prophet becomes self-divided, and wavers between excessive wrath and excessive pity. Los's division into masculine and feminine is in its own way as damaging a dissociation of sensibility as the original split between reason and passion. It leaves man with a wrath that fails to allow for human shortcomings and a pity that fails to preserve human dignity.[38]

VI

The next chapter of *The Book of Urizen* finally introduces us to a recognizably human situation, the family. We see the immediate result of the appearance of Enitharmon, as the Battle of the Sexes begins in earnest:

> But Los saw the Female & pitied
> He embrac'd her, she wept, she refus'd
> In perverse and cruel delight
> She fled from his arms, yet he followd   (19:10–13)

Los tried to externalize his pity in the form of Enitharmon, but ironically he ends up pitying her anyway. In fact, he becomes obsessed with what he had tried to reject just moments before.

The perverse struggles for domination which characterize fallen sexuality divert man from his real task. Los tries to recapture his wholeness, not by seeking to regain Eternity, but by seeking to regain Enitharmon.[39] The result of Los's persistence is the first sexual union:

> Eternity shudder'd when they saw,
> Man begetting his likeness,
> On his own divided image.   (19:14–16)

The mating of Los and Enitharmon ought to signal a major reversal in *The Book of Urizen*. Up to this point, all we have seen is one thing dividing from another. The sexual attraction of Los and Enitharmon provides the first movement toward unity in the poem. But in the fallen world, the sexual act does not restore human wholeness. It merely involves, in Blake's remarkably apt character-ization, "man begetting his likeness, on his own divided image." The sexual union of male and female produces just another male or female, and not the original male–female being the logic of myth would seem to dictate.

But all is not lost: even when Los and Enitharmon seem to be perpetuating humanity in its divided state, the first hopeful sign in *The Book of Urizen* appears. In the upside-down world of the fall, however, this sign is misinterpreted by all concerned as a bad omen. The mating of Los and Enitharmon results in the first human child, Orc. To the Eternals, and no doubt to Enitharmon herself, the child seems monstrous, associated throughout his gestation and at the time of his birth with animal forms and forces, especially the hissing, poisonous serpent (19:16–46). But from the "fierce flames" (19:45) accompanying Orc, we recognize that he somehow embodies the power of passion, and thus may provide the energy needed to restore man to Eternity. For the moment, though, the birth of Orc seems like an unmitigated disaster, since it provokes the Eternals into completing the Tent of Science and thus closing off man's view of his original state: "No more Los beheld Eternity" (20:2). Perhaps Los's recognition of what his child has cost him explains why he evidently rejects Orc and hands him over to his mother (20:3–5).

Blake's poem now moves into another archetypal mythic situa-tion, the conflict of father and son, best known in two versions: the Biblical tale of Abraham and Isaac and the Greek legend of Oedipus.[40] In portraying the conflict as arising from the father's side, Blake stays closer to the Biblical version. Or rather Blake in effect calls our attention to the fact that Oedipus did not begin the tragic sequence in which he became involved. It was Oedipus's father, Laius, who set events in motion, by his decision to expose his child, rather than allow the fulfillment of the oracle which said that the son would kill his father. With his revolutionary impulses and sympathy for the young, Blake viewed what one might call the Laius complex as prior to what we have come to call the Oedipus complex. Freud, who was fundamentally conservative in his outlook, saw the origin of familial strife in the jealousy the son develops over his father's possession of his mother.[41] Blake might have pointed out that with the father's superior ability to understand the situation, he is likely to initiate the jealousy, in his case jealousy over the way his infant is taking away his wife's affection. Blake makes it explicit that Los turns against Orc out of jealousy (20:24), but leaves the motive of his jealousy unclear. Perhaps Los resents the greater energy of Orc. Los has expended much of his own energy in the actions which have led up to the birth of Orc, and it would be frustrating for him to see himself displaced by the very being he created.[42]

Throughout his writings, Blake focuses on the hostility of the old and the young. In *The Book of Urizen*, he suggests that it is the old who begin the hostility, largely out of jealousy and fear that the young, with their superior vitality, will replace them.[43] The scene of Los chaining Orc to the mountain symbolizes the way the older generation attempts to repress the energy of the young. Blake may be depicting the process of psychological sublimation. Chapter VII comes the closest of any part of *The Book of Urizen* to suggesting how reason gets the energy to fight the power of the desires. One passion, jealousy, combines with reason to keep the other passions under control. Los's efforts seem to succeed in diverting Orc's newly created energy into Urizen. Urizen, who for some time has been lying in a deathly torpor, begins "to awake to life" (20:29) when he hears the cries of Orc, almost as if, like a vampire, he wants to drink the blood from the sacrifice of Orc to restore his own vitality (20:30–31). Blake's philosophical monism would seem to depend on some such process of reason tapping the energy of the passions in order to combat them, or, as Blake mythically pictured it in *The Marriage of Heaven and Hell*: "the Messiah fell. & formed a heaven of what he stole from the Abyss" (Pl. 5–6).

Brought back to life, Urizen attempts to order the fallen world and restore his dominion over it. Still obsessed with the regularity of mathematical form, he tries to impose it on reality (20:33–40). But Urizen's rage for order still only results in chaos, and characteristically his world consists of fragments (23:2–7). Faced with incontrovertible evidence, Urizen must finally recognize that his efforts to establish the unitary rule of reason have failed. The

vitality of the world resists confinement in his rigid categories
(23:22–26).

In the last chapter of *The Book of Urizen*, we finally reach the
bottom of the fall, which is to say, the world of man as we know it.
The human spirit continues to contract:

> . Till the shrunken eyes clouded over
> Discernd not the woven hypocrisy
> But the streaky slime in their heavens
> Brought together by narrowing perceptions
> Appeard transparent air; for their eyes
> Grew small like the eyes of a man
> And in reptile forms shrinking together
> Of seven feet statute they remain.   (25:31–38)

Blake audaciously tries to break us out of our fallen habits of
perception. When we look at a clear blue sky and think that we can
see to infinity, we are really seeing "streaky slime," the orthodox
idea of heaven, which views the vault of the sky as a cap to human
aspiration. Blake uses an even more daring image: "their eyes /
Grew small like the eyes of a man." We had been assuming that the
shrivelled creatures before us were already men, but suddenly we
realize that, with all the contraction we have witnessed, we have
not quite reached the depressed level of current humanity, and the
name of man can still serve as a standard of smallness. After
shrinking through many stages, Blake's fallen beings are still seven
feet tall, and hence would seem like giants to modern men.

After a blasphemous parody of the sabbath (25:39–42), Blake
finally shows man in a moment from recorded history. And that
state turns out to be Egypt (28:10), the Biblical archetype of
tyranny.[44] In attempting to recreate Genesis, perhaps Blake was
struck by the book's pattern: man begins in paradise, but ends in
Egypt, enslaved by cruel taskmasters. One might sum up the
gnostic twist of Blake's creation account by saying: Blake did not
see Egypt as the unintentional result of Jehovah's original planting
of his "garden of fruits" (*Urizen*, 20:41). On the contrary, for
Blake, one and the same spirit moved over the waters and moved
over the pyramids, and its name was Urizen, the spirit of moral
tyranny.

CHAPTER 2

The Myth Unbound

I

The Book of Urizen seems to give the most pessimistic picture possible of the human condition. Man ends up enslaved, his senses contracted, his vision of all his higher potential blocked off, his inner strength exhausted. The image Blake creates of the human form in Chapter IV is among the most repellent in all literature. Coming to the end of *The Book of Urizen*, one might conclude that Blake had given up all hope for mankind in disgust. But Blake originally designated the poem *The First Book of Urizen*, and indeed it provides only the beginning of man's story. Blake hoped to take the story from the depths of man's enslavement to the heights of an apocalyptic moment of liberation. *The Book of Urizen* reveals the magic act of Romantic creation myths: the most optimistic view of man's future is grounded in the most pessimistic view of his present. Precisely because man's situation has gotten so bad, a complete turnaround in his prospects is viewed as inevitable.

Thus to examine only the moment of creation in Blake's myth would give a one-sided view of his system. And without surveying Blake's attempts to show the end of history, one cannot understand why he kept altering his view of the beginning. Blake's earliest prophetic poems tended to concentrate on the apocalyptic phase of history. *The French Revolution*, *The Marriage of Heaven and Hell*, *America*, and *Europe* all reflect the millennial hopes raised by political events in the late eighteenth century. Like many of his contemporaries, Blake saw the revolutionary political movements in America, France, and even England as heralding the dawn of a new era of complete liberation for mankind. In these early poems, Blake shows the forces of liberty rising up vigorously to challenge the forces of oppression, whom he portrays in disarray and paralyzed with fear, evidently ready to be overthrown. In *America*, Blake pictures revolution as a direct confrontation between Orc and Urizen, a struggle in which Urizen is barely able to hold on to his power, and then only by delaying tactics which will not prevent Orc's triumph for long. One might speculate that if all had gone well with the French Revolution, and its spirit had spread success-fully to England, Blake might never have felt compelled to write a creation myth at all.

But of course all did not go well with the French Revolution, as even Blake eventually had to realize, and events in France only provoked a period of reaction in England. We can never know Blake's intentions in choosing his mythic subjects with certainty. But it does seem as if the frustration of his immediate apocalyptic hopes led him from celebrating the end of history to investigating its beginning. If one looks for a pattern in the order of composition of Blake's minor prophecies, one sees how the apocalypse was the guiding idea in Romantic myth and shaped the understanding of the creation and the fall. The earliest poems Blake wrote deal with the latest events, and vice versa. Blake's choosing of *The Book of Urizen* as a subject reflects a desire to understand why the apocalyptic liberation of Europe had been delayed. By tracing the roots of man's current enslavement, Blake hoped to discover the forces inhibiting the release of his energies.

But in a sense Blake may have done his job in *The Book of Urizen* too well. By giving a psychological account of the fall, he threatens to take its undoing out of the ordinary realm of political action. If man's enslavement is a form of self-enslavement, then his liberation must proceed from within as well. Blake's earliest prophetic poems portray man's problem as basically external, and hence solvable by conventional political means. The forces of rebellion are arrayed against the forces of reaction, and Blake can side unequivocally with the former against the latter. But *The Book of Urizen* shows that the force of reaction is a component of every human psyche, and thus cannot be isolated in one political party and purged. If Urizen is a part of every man, ending his dominion may be more difficult than Blake originally believed.

One can see how Blake's portrait of man's beginnings in *The Book of Urizen* complicated his thinking about the apocalypse by turning to the sequel he wrote immediately, *The Book of Ahania*. In Blake's "Bible of Hell," *The Book of Ahania* ought to play Exodus to *The Book of Urizen*'s Genesis. In leading a rebellion against his father Urizen, Fuzon seems to be headed in the right direction. Associated with the element of fire, Fuzon has the passionate energy of Orc, and ought to be able to free desire from the tyranny of reason. But from the beginning, Fuzon's revolt takes an ominous turn. When we first see Fuzon, he is imitating Urizen even in the act of rebelling against him:

> On clouds of smoke rages his chariot
> And his right hand burns red in its cloud
> Moulding into a vast globe, his wrath
> As the thunder-stone is moulded.
> Son of Urizens silent burnings   (2:5–9)

The way Fuzon instinctively resorts to Urizen's characteristic activity of englobing suggests that far from liberating himself from his father's influence, Fuzon is merely following in his footsteps. Fuzon's mistake is to attempt to use his father's weapons against him, to fight globes with globes, violence with violence.[1]

Fuzon is not a true fighter for freedom because he does not object to domination as such. What he evidently resents is the fact that he is not the one doing the dominating. He is more interested in overthrowing Urizen than in replacing tyranny with freedom. Hence it is not surprising that when he believes his rebellion has succeeded, his first thought is to step into his father's shoes. Originally the champion of youth against age, Fuzon immediately tries to reverse roles with his father and establish his own venerability. Like many a tyrant, Fuzon tries to rewrite history:

> While Fuzon his tygers unloosing
> Thought Urizen slain by his wrath.
> I am God. said he, eldest of things!   (3:36–38)

In the course of his rebellion, Fuzon in effect turns into Urizen.[2] The way Blake's rebel becomes a tyrant may specifically reflect the poet's disillusionment with the course the French Revolution took in the Reign of Terror.[3]

Blake recognized that many attempts to lead man out of slavery have only resulted in the imposition of new forms of tyranny. In Blake's interpretation, the original Exodus merely resulted in the exchange of Egyptian bondage for the equally restrictive moral law of the decalogue, which probably explains the enigmatic reference to Mount Sinai in *The Book of Ahania* (3:45). The perversion of Fuzon's rebellion makes the apocalypse seem more remote than ever in Blake. By itself, the force of passion cannot undo reason's tyranny, especially when the guiding passion of rebellion is hate.

Blake seems to have reached an impasse in his minor prophecies. He portrayed the end of history and then its beginning, but when he tried to get from the beginning to the end, his myth became locked into a cycle of rebellion and tyranny, the so-called Orc cycle. The "Africa" section of *The Song of Los* reads like a frantic attempt to build a bridge between the Genesis material of *The Book of Urizen* and the beginning of the apocalyptic phase of Blake's myth in *America*. But Blake's effort to tie his minor prophecies together is unconvincing and he himself evidently became dissatisfied with trying to organize his shorter poems into a comprehensive myth. He attempted to recast his material into a single large myth in *The Four Zoas*, and in the process rethought the question of how to get from the creation and the fall to the apocalypse.

II

The apocalypse in Night IX of *The Four Zoas* is the most firmly and confidently realized part of Blake's vision. He knows where he wants history to end, and from the way he rewrites *The Book of Urizen* in the center of his new poem (Nights IV–VI), it appears that he has not substantially changed his idea of where man starts from in his struggle for liberation. But even in his new version of his myth, Blake could not settle upon a clear path from man's present to his future.[4] The evidence of the manuscript shows that one of the points at which Blake had the most trouble arriving at a definitive formulation of his myth is precisely the transition from the fallen world to the apocalypse. Blake did much of his tinkering with the poem in the area between Night VI and Night IX. He evidently could not decide what to do about Night VII, which portrays the crucial sequence of events leading up to the apocalypse. Blake seems to have produced two versions of Night VII, referred to by Erdman as VIIa and VIIb. Editors of *The Four Zoas* are never sure how to arrange these two versions. Erdman, for example, originally printed VIIa as part of *The Four Zoas*, while placing VIIb at the end of the poem as a kind of appendix. In his newly revised edition, he places the whole of VIIb in the middle of VIIa, attempting to form a continuous narrative.[5] We may never know what the proper relation of the two versions should be. But the textual evidence does at least seem to suggest that VIIb is the version Blake wrote first.[6] By regarding VIIa as embodying Blake's later thoughts about the true path to apocalypse, we may get a clue as to how *The Four Zoas* as a whole attempts to correct Blake's myth in his minor prophecies.

Blake's uncertainty about this stage of his myth in *The Four Zoas* is actually greater than at first appears, because the earlier version of Night VII exists in two forms itself. In Blake's first arrangement of the pages of VIIb, he was basically following the original order of his minor prophecies. He uses material from *America* in pages 91–95 of his manuscript, and material from *Europe* in pages 95–98.[7] The first arrangement thus remains true to Blake's earlier vision of history, in which revolution leads to reaction. The American and French Revolutions shake up the European dynasties, and in particular lead to conflict between England and France, which will presumably result in Orc overthrowing Urizen. In Blake's first arrangement of the manuscript pages, the action culminates in a call to war which has a distinctly apocalyptic ring to it (98:30–31). The implication of the original order of the pages is that the political violence in Europe is leading to the liberation Blake seeks. By rearranging VIIb into the sequence pp. 95–98, 91–95, Blake broke with the pattern of his minor prophecies, and, more importantly, broke with the idea that European warfare could lead to positive results. The stirring call to arms with which the first arrangement ends becomes buried in the middle of the new arrangement, which now builds up to a call for patience (95:8). Blake seems to be losing faith that the conflict between Orc and Urizen can solve man's problems, and sees them instead locked in a never-ending and ultimately pointless contest for dominion over each other.

Blake carried on his rethinking of the path to salvation in the later version of Night VII. He retains the confrontation of Orc and Urizen in VIIa, and their initial exchanges still have some of the fierceness of their encounters in *America*.[8] But the conflict of Orc and Urizen reaches a dead end about a third of the way into Night VIIa, as Orc repeats Fuzon's error, becoming a mirror image of his foe, rather than displacing him:[9]

> And Orc began to Organize a Serpent body
> Despising Urizens light & turning it into flaming fire
> Receiving as a poisoned Cup Receives the heavenly wine
> And turning affection into fury & thought into abstraction
> A Self consuming dark devourer rising into the heavens
>
> (80:44–48)

Despite Orc's avowed contempt for Urizen, organizing a body is the Urizenic activity par excellence, and the description of Orc in l. 48 clearly calls to mind the description of his arch enemy at the beginning of *The Book of Urizen*. "Turning affection into fury & thought into abstraction" may be Blake's epitaph for the ideals of the French Revolution. Noble goals like brotherhood became the excuse for murder once they began to function as abstract slogans, with no regard for their concrete human meaning. Blake came to question the French Revolution because of its origins in philosophical doctrines which allowed its leaders to claim to love man in the abstract, while hating him in the concrete form of the so-called enemies of the Revolution.

Having shown the futility of Orc's rebellion against Urizen, Blake loses interest in their conflict and turns his attention for the remainder of VIIa to Los, Enitharmon, and a new character in his mythology, the Spectre of Urthona, who evidently represents an aspect of Los's psyche.[10] The drama of these characters gradually replaces the struggles between Orc and Urizen as the focus of Blake's myth, as is particularly evident in *Jerusalem*, which begins with Los and the Spectre of Urthona in conflict and cannot reach a resolution until Los gets his Spectre under control. The turn from the Orc–Urizen conflict to the Los–Spectre conflict marks a shift in Blake's interest from external political action to internal psychological action.

More specifically, the way Los gradually replaces Orc as the hero of Blake's later prophecies reflects the poet's growing disillusionment with armed rebellion and his increasing sense that only art can save mankind. As we have seen, Los represents the artist, and he serves as Blake's alter ego in the major prophecies. Blake rejected Orc as the agent of apocalyptic change because he came to believe that the force of passion by itself cannot restore the balance in man's soul. Suddenly released from the restraints of reason, passion is likely to become a force for disorder, as events in revolutionary France quickly proved. Blake turns to Los as the one figure who can exert control over both Orc and Urizen, for, as we have seen, the imagination can mediate between reason and passion. The most hopeful sign at the end of VIIa is that Los effects a reconciliation with these ancient enemies one at a time.[11] By seeking "to comfort Orc in his divine sufferings," Los re-establishes contact with the passionate element in his own soul: "look my fires enlume afresh /

Before my face ascending with delight as in ancient times"
(90:13–14). As we saw in *The Book of Urizen*, Los initially
ruined his chances of regaining Eternity by allowing "his fires to
decay," and thus losing his prophetic energy to his offspring Orc.
Here in *The Four Zoas*, Los takes the first step toward the
apocalypse by in effect reabsorbing Orc's fires.

But in Los, unlike Orc, passion does not rage out of control.
Blake stresses the reasonableness of Los's energy, as Los turns it
to a formative purpose in works of art. As Enitharmon tells Los:
"Thy works are all my joy. & in thy fires my soul delights / If mild
they burn in just proportion" (90:17–18). In his "sweet mod-
erated fury" (90:22), Los provides the synthesis that neither Orc
nor Urizen could achieve alone. By learning to channel passion
into artistic activity, Los is able to lead men away from the
destructiveness of corporeal warfare to the creativity of mental
strife:

> Los his hands divine inspired began
> To modulate his fires studious the loud roaring flames
> He vanquishd with the strength of Art bending their iron points
> And drawing them forth delighted upon the winds of Golgonooza
> From out the ranks of Urizens war & from the fiery lake
> Of Orc bending down as the binder of the Sheaves follows
> The reaper in both arms embracing the furious raging flames
> Los drew them forth out of the deeps   (90:25–32)

One can see how Los's form of liberation differs from Fuzon's or
Orc's in his ability to embrace his supposed enemy:

> Startled was Los he found his Enemy Urizen now
> In his hands. he wondered that he felt love & not hate
> His whole soul loved him he beheld him an infant.
>   (90:64–66)

The loving sympathy of Los seems to restore Urizen to his
childhood form and hence to point the way to the only true
revolution: the recovery of man's innocence.[12]

In the end, then, Blake turned to art itself to accomplish what
he no longer thought politics capable of bringing about. Blake's
rejection of politics reaches its peak in a relatively late prose work,
the *Public Address* (1810), which is perhaps the most bitter of his
writings. It is difficult to recognize the early partisan of the French
Revolution in this total rejection of any form of political activity:

I am really sorry to see my Countrymen trouble themselves about Politics. If Men were Wise the Most arbitrary Princes could not hurt them If they are not Wise the Freest Government is compelld to be a Tyranny. Princes appear to me to be Fools Houses of Commons & Houses of Lords appear to me to be fools they seem to me to be something Else besides Human Life. (p. 18; E, 80)

If forms of government are irrelevant to human happiness, Blake turns to forms of art as the focus of civilization: "Let us teach Buonoparte & whomsoever else it may concern That it is not Arts that follow & attend upon Empire but Empire that attends upon & follows The Arts" (p. 66; E, 77). Originally Blake had looked to political revolution to liberate the artistic potential within man. But he eventually reversed his position to the point where he saw artistic freedom as the necessary prelude to any improvement in man's political condition: "Poetry Fetter'd, Fetters the Human Race! Nations are Destroy'd, or Flourish, in proportion as Their Poetry Painting and Music, are Destroy'd or Flourish!" (*Jerusalem*, Pl. 3).[13]

In Blake's most mature and poetically most extraordinary rendering of man's redemption, the final plates of *Jerusalem*, art becomes an integral part of the apocalypse. The reintegration of man and his community comes about through the mediation of artistic forms:

> And they conversed together in Visionary forms dramatic
> which bright
> Redounded from their Tongues in thunderous majesty, in Visions
> In new Expanses, creating exemplars of Memory and of Intellect
> Creating Space, Creating Time according to the wonders Divine
> Of Human Imagination.   (98:28–32)

In this vision of the apocalypse, man cannot simply be returning to an uncivilized beginning, because language is so deeply involved in the final moment: "every Word & Every Character / Was Human" (98:35–36). The immediacy of man's original experience can be recaptured only through the mediation of artistic symbols. For Blake, art, as the highest of man's civilized accomplishments, eventually proves to be the one means for overcoming the Rousseauian antinomy between nature and civilization. Blake's apocalyptic moment combines the unity and harmony of man's original state with the complexity and development of his experience in civil society.

III

When Blake set out to write *The Four Zoas*, he was trying to find a way to incorporate the historical events of his own time into a cosmic mythic framework. But as he worked on the poem, his changing view of the role of politics in human life made the form of his myth less and less appropriate to the vision he wished to express. Once Blake no longer saw the French Revolution as opening the way back to paradise, he no longer had to worry about connecting his account of man's origins with the political events of the late eighteenth century. By turning to the new mythic patterns of *Milton* and *Jerusalem*, Blake was freer to concentrate on the drama that came to concern him more, the struggles going on within the artist's own soul.[14]

In rethinking the path from the creation to the apocalypse, Blake found himself rethinking the nature of the two poles of his myth as well. While Blake conceived of the apocalypse as resulting from political events, he pictured it as a specific moment in history, and hence a state that could be reached once and for all, like the Biblical Last Judgment. If history has a definite end, then it is plausible to think of it as having a definite beginning too. In short, the focus on political–historical events in Blake's original conception of his myth gave it a neat structure, a linear narrative shape similar to the Bible's. But as Blake's conception of his myth became increasingly psychological, the linear shape of his narrative began to break down. Instead of dealing with unique historical events, Blake found himself dealing with recurrent psychological patterns. The French Revolution originally functioned in Blake's thought as a privileged moment in history, the one great turning point which would usher in the end of history. But in switching his attention from Orc to Los, Blake started dealing with processes and developments which all artists go through at all times. As a result, Blake gradually ceased thinking of the apocalypse as a final state and began to view it as an ongoing activity.[15]

This dynamic rather than static conception of the apocalypse made it harder for Blake to remain content with a simple view of man's beginning. Blake's open-ended vision of the apocalypse led him to an equally open-ended view of the creation and the fall. The way Blake kept adding material at the beginning of *The Four Zoas*, pushing back the origin of the fall to earlier and earlier events, makes it impossible to think of the fall as one specific event in the past anymore. Like the apocalypse, the fall becomes in effect an ongoing process in *The Four Zoas*. Blake's hesitancy about limiting man's future options by pinning him down to a definitive end of history led him to keep his account of man's beginning indeterminate as well.

IV

The version of the apocalypse in Night IX of *The Four Zoas* retains many traditional elements, and thus at first sight seems compatible with a linear view of history. Blake uses the familiar apocalyptic imagery from the Bible, and he also tends to portray the final events in overtly political terms.[16] The Biblical and political strains often run together:

> The heavens are shaken & the Earth removed from its place
> The foundations of the Eternal hills discoverd
> The thrones of Kings are shaken they have lost their robes & crowns
> The poor smite their oppressors they awake up to the harvest
> The naked warriors rush together down to the sea shore
> Trembling before the multitudes of slaves now set at liberty
>
> (117:16–21)

Here Blake still seems to be viewing the apocalypse on the model of the French Revolution. Events quickly reach a climax in a confrontation between Albion and Urizen. Albion puts the blame for all man's trouble squarely on Urizen's shoulders, and one might think that all that is needed for universal redemption is for Urizen to admit his past errors and reform his misguided ways. As in early works like *America*, the focus of the apocalypse seems to be on undoing Urizen's interference with the free expression of man's impulses, a comparatively straightforward resolution of historical conflict.[17]

But Urizen does everything Albion demands of him, renouncing the control he tried to exercise over the other Zoas, and he still does not bring history to an end. Even Urizen's outright reversal of his original position: "lo futurity is in this moment" (121:22) is not enough to undo the fall. We soon realize that Blake's apocalypse is not going to be accomplished in a single stroke. As Night IX unfolds, we see that the apocalypse is going to involve a lot of hard work:

The noise of rural work resounded thro the heavens of heavens
The horse[s] neigh from the battle the wild bulls from the sultry waste
The tygers from the forests & the lions from the sandy desarts
They Sing they sieze the instruments of harmony they throw away
The spear the bow the gun the mortar they level the fortifications
They beat the iron engines of destruction into wedges
They give them to Urthonas Sons ringing the hammers sound
In dens of death to forge the spade the mattock & the ax
The heavy roller to break the clods to pass over the nations

(124:14–22)

Gradually one begins to understand that the apocalypse is not being ushered in by this work. This work is the apocalypse itself, a heightening and refining of man's productive energies. For Blake, Eden is not defined by the absence of labor. That is why, contrary to the popular view of Blake, he does not see the return to Eden as requiring man to renounce the technology he has developed in civilization. Taking a hint from Isaiah, Blake sees the key to redemption in man transforming the nature of his tools, making them serve creative rather than destructive purposes.

The apocalyptic work of Night IX is so strenuous that soon Urizen and his sons must rest from their exertions. The episode that follows is our most important clue for understanding how and why Blake remakes the traditional notion of the apocalypse. Blake's characters enter a state he calls Beulah, a "land of doubts & shadows sweet delusions unformed hopes" (126:22), a place where man can take a vacation from reality, and put the strife of the world out of his mind (126:23–27).[18] Man recuperates from the strain of his creative labor precisely by dreaming of a paradise which requires no effort at all on his part. Blake traces the perennial vision of the "ancient golden age renewed" (126:29) to man's inability to pursue his creative activity without some hope of someday being able to relax from his seemingly ceaseless strivings.

At the center of Night IX, Blake's characters dream the traditional dream of paradise. In their sleep, they picture the apocalypse as a literal return to man's simple pastoral beginnings, and Blake accordingly recreates the mood and tone of his *Songs of Innocence*.[19] The strenuous chanting of the prophet suddenly relaxes into the gentle accents of a child. Almost magically, we find ourselves back in the world of Blake's first prophecy, *The Book of Thel*:

Eternally thou must have slept nor have felt the morning dew
But for yon nourishing sun tis that by which thou art arisen
The birds adore the sun the beasts rise up & play in his beams
And every flower & every leaf rejoices in his light
Then O thou fair one sit thee down for thou art as the grass
Thou risest in the dew of morning & at night art folded up

Alas am I but as a flower then will I sit me down
Then will I weep then Ill complain & sigh for immortality
And chide my maker thee O Sun that raisedst me to fall

(127:10–18)

Blake finds a brilliant way of portraying man's recovery of innocence: he himself returns to one of his earlier poetic modes. Blake's latter-day Thel finds the answer to the doubts which troubled her predecessor (127:24–27) and thus is able to live in total harmony with the world of nature (128:13–15).[20] Blake emphasizes the restfulness of this paradise, whose peace takes the form of sleep: "And soft sleep fell upon her eyelids in the silent noon of day" (128:27).

The dream of paradise regained culminates in a vision of childhood recaptured:

And now her feet step on the grassy bosom of the ground
Among her flocks & she turnd her eyes toward her pleasant house
And saw in the door way beneath the trees two little children playing
She drew near to her house & her flocks followd her footsteps
The Children clung around her knees she embracd them & wept over
    them

Thou little Boy art Tharmas & thou bright Girl Enion
How are ye thus renewd & brought into the Gardens of Vala

(130:2–8)

The interlude of Tharmas and Enion reclaiming the joys of childhood provides a charming relief from the strain of Blake's normally fiery apocalyptic verse. But if this vision had to serve as the true climax of *The Four Zoas*, we would surely have to regard it as an anti-climax. Has all the titanic warfare in Blake's universe, all the heaven-storming and earth-shattering conflict, resulted in no more than this, a little boy and a little girl playing in a meadow? One cannot help feeling a let-down in the thought that the agonies of history have only succeeded in restoring man to the "Eternal Childhood" (131:16) he might have enjoyed if he had never left paradise in the first place. Tharmas himself is dissatisfied with his seeming paradise:

I am sick & all this garden of Pleasure
Swims like a dream before my eyes but the sweet smelling fruit
Revives me to new deaths I fade even like a water lilly
In the suns heat till in the night on the couch of Enion
I drink new life & feel the breath of sleeping Enion
But in the morning she arises to avoid my Eyes
Then my loins fade & in the house I sit me down & weep

(131:1-7)

In Tharmas's complaint, we once again hear the voice of Thel, and he expresses a similar frustration, the inability to fulfill himself sexually on the level of innocence. If his image of his loins fading is to be taken literally, then evidently he has had to give up his mature sexuality in order to return to the joys of childhood, a questionable exchange which sufficiently accounts for his unhappiness with paradise.

Blake uses the dream interlude of Night IX to remind us of the original lesson of the fall: man is not meant to dwell in childhood forever and the unchanging calm of nature spells stagnation for the human spirit. Ironically, when man is left to dream of paradise, he envisions a state which cannot satisfy his deep need to change and grow. In the midst of all his labors, man tends to image paradise as a perfectly static state. Man yearns to escape from his constant struggles, to leave all his anxiety behind and indulge himself in total peace. But Blake baulked at the idea that man should aspire to a state virtually indistinguishable from sleep. He recognized the paradox in most progressive views of history: the striving for the end of history is a more interesting, creative, and soul-satisfying condition for mankind than the end itself.

Thus, although Blake allows the sons of Urizen their dream of paradise, in his view Beulah is clearly a "lower Paradise" (128:30). The sons of Urizen must awake refreshed from their dreams and resume their apocalyptic labors (131:20-21, 132:2-9). The higher paradise for Blake involves energetic activity. He almost immediately corrects the dream vision of the union of Tharmas and Enion with a true one:

Joy thrilld thro all the Furious form of Tharmas humanizing
Mild he Embracd her whom he sought he raisd her thro the heavens
Sounding his trumpet to awake the dead on high he soard
Over the ruind worlds the smoking tomb of the Eternal Prophet

(132:36-39)

The mature passion involved in this union of Tharmas and Enion allows them to reach greater heights than they ever could in their childhood forms and thus raises their love to a more truly apocalyptic pitch.

The events of Night IX fall into a distinctive rhythm: activity, followed by repose, followed by renewed and presumably invigorated activity.[21] This pattern anticipates the more fully developed notion of the Eden–Beulah dialectic in Blake's *Milton* and *Jerusalem*.[22] Blake came to picture man alternating between a higher and a lower paradise, a state of fiery creativity and a state of cool repose.[23] This division of paradise reflects Blake's conviction that no artist can function continually at the highest pitch of his creativity without burning himself out. Hence the artist needs to find ways of refreshing his energies in the more ordinary pleasures and comforts of life, which Blake images in the land of Beulah. The creator in man has to make allowances for the needs of the creature.

Blake thus breaks with the traditional notion of paradise as a single unchanging state. He finally learned to apply to paradise itself the central principle by which he analyzed human history: "Without contraries is no progression."[24] It would indeed be strange if paradise turned out to be a less complex and interesting state than all the stages undergone to reach it. Blake reformulated the notion of paradise so that it allows for an alternation of states, inspiration and recuperation, and hence continued movement and continued creativity. *The Four Zoas* ends with a sense, not of finality, but of a new beginning:

> Urthona is arisen in his strength no longer now
> Divided from Enitharmon no longer the Spectre Los
> Where is the Spectre of Prophecy where the delusive Phantom
> Departed & Urthona rises from the ruinous walls
> In all his ancient strength to form the golden armour of science
> For intellectual War The war of swords departed now
> The dark Religions are departed & sweet Science reigns.
>
> (139:4–10)

Traditionally the apocalypse should end with a vision of peace, but Blake pointedly ends his poem with a vision of war. Of course, by this time the corporeal war of Urizen and Orc has been transformed into the intellectual war of Los.

For Blake, man's mistake is to conceive of the apocalypse as the recovery of a static mythic state rather than of a dynamic mythic power. Blake reverses the traditional understanding of end and means in his conception of the apocalypse.[25] What had been thought of as the end, the perfect state of rest, becomes for Blake merely in effect the means. Man's dream of a final paradise is what gives him the hope needed to sustain his striving. By the same token, what had been thought of as the means, the fight for paradise, becomes for Blake the end itself. The only legitimate aim for human striving is a continual state of striving, exertions "that end in endless Strife," to use a paradoxical formulation from *For the Sexes: The Gates of Paradise* (no. 5; E, 262). Contrary to the implications of the prefatory poem in *Milton*, Blake does not promise a cessation of "Mental Fight." For Blake, the spiritual Jerusalem is not something which can ever be built once and for all; it requires continual renewal in human creativity.[26]

V

It is only fitting that we end our discussion of *The Four Zoas* by examining its beginning. We cannot hope to clear up the confusions of the opening Nights, confusions which one might in fact regard as strangely functional. Certainly no creation myth has ever done a better job of conveying a sense of the initial chaos out of which the world began. The fact that Blake's own uncertainty as to where exactly to begin his poem is responsible for the impression of flux he creates does not lessen the appropriateness of the opening. *The Four Zoas* ends with a sense that wherever one chooses to conclude one's account of the development of the human spirit, more remains to be said and man will go on changing and growing. Similarly the poem begins with a sense that wherever one chooses to pick up the story, something has already happened. Blake's line: "Begin with Tharmas Parent power" (4:6) sounds like an admission of the arbitrariness of his starting point. When Tharmas begins to speak, a fall has already occurred: "Lost! Lost! Lost! are my Emanations" (4:7). The beginning of *The Four Zoas* is no more absolute than the end. One must begin somewhere, but one could always find an earlier starting point for the action.[27]

In all the confusion of the opening Nights, only one thing is clear: in Blake's new account of the creation, he pictures all the components of the psyche implicated in the fall from the beginning, and not just Reason, as in *The Book of Urizen*.[28] As the various accounts of the fall accumulate, we learn that every faculty had a role to play in the disintegration of man's original wholeness. Above all, we see that Luvah, the unfallen form of Orc, may well have been just as responsible for the original psychic catastrophe as Urizen. Blake's disenchantment with revolutionary passions evidently led him to suggest that Luvah conspired with Urizen in the beginning to overthrow Albion. If Luvah and Urizen began as co-conspirators, we should not be surprised that in his fallen form of Orc, Luvah eventually reunites with his seeming antagonist and ends up doing Urizen's work for him.

What is most peculiar about the various accounts of the fall in *The Four Zoas* is that there are so many of them, and no two agree as to the basic facts of the story.[29] Did Urizen and Luvah begin the fall, or is Vala responsible, or is Albion himself at fault? Trying to reconcile the mutually contradictory views, one begins to sense that Blake is no longer trying to come up with a definitive account of the fall.[30] No one of the creation myths in *The Four Zoas* can simply be accepted as Blake's own. Blake seems in fact to be portraying how and why creation myths come into being.[31] Everyone who offers an account of the fall in *The Four Zoas* has an axe to grind.[32] In the hands of Blake's generally self-righteous characters, the creation myth becomes a means of self-justification. Usually the Zoas try to fix responsibility for the fall on someone else, and thereby justify their own claims to rule. Whichever element in the psyche can clear itself of any blame for the fall can then assert its right to pre-eminence within the human whole.

Blake's Zoas look to the past to establish their power in the present. Each tailors his understanding of earlier events to suit his need to seem godlike to his fellows, and to stake out the boundaries of his authority. Urizen seeks to share power with Los on the basis of his understanding of the misdeeds of Luvah and Vala:

> Thou art the Lord of Luvah into thine hands I give
> The prince of Love the murderer his soul is in thine hands
> Pity not Vala for she pitied not the Eternal Man
> Nor pity thou the cries of Luvah. Lo these starry hosts
> They are thy servants if thou wilt obey my awful Law

> Los answerd furious art thou one of those who when most complacent
> Mean mischief most. If you are such Lo! I am also such

One must be master. try thy Arts I also will try mine
For I perceive Thou hast Abundance which I claim as mine

Urizen startled stood not Long soon he cried
Obey my voice young Demon I am God from Eternity to Eternity

(12:13–23)

Later Los himself uses cosmic history to lay claim to his own
territory and to set limits to his fellow Zoa, Tharmas:[33]

Los answerd in his furious pride sparks issuing from his hair
Hitherto shalt thou come. no further. here thy proud waves cease
We have drunk up the Eternal Man by our unbounded power
Beware lest we also drink up thee rough demon of the waters
Our God is Urizen the King. King of the Heavenly hosts
We have no other God but he thou father of worms & clay
And he is fallen into the Deep rough Demon of the waters
And Los remains God over all. weak father of worms & clay
I know I was Urthona keeper of the gates of heaven
But now I am all powerful Los & Urthona is but my shadow.

(48:11–20)

But Tharmas has his own account of the fall, one which he
hopes will put him in a favorable light and lead to an alliance with
Los:

Tharmas replied. Art thou Urthona my friend my old companion,
With whom I livd in happiness before that deadly night
When Urizen gave the horses of Light into the hands of Luvah
Thou knowest not what Tharmas knows. O I could tell thee tales
That would enrage thee as it has Enraged me even
From Death in wrath & fury.   (50:28–33)

Tharmas's friendly nostalgia soon turns into his own claim to
rule:

Now all comes into the power of Tharmas. Urizen is falln
And Luvah hidden in the Elemental forms of Life & Death
Urthona is My Son O Los thou art Urthona & Tharmas
Is God. The Eternal Man is seald never to be deliverd
I roll my floods over his body my billows & waves pass over him
The sea encompasses him & monsters of the deep are his companions
Dreamer of furious oceans cold sleeper of weeds & shells
Thy Eternal form shall never renew my uncertain prevails against thee

(51:12–19)

Tharmas can tell Los tales indeed, tales to bring him under
Tharmas's control.

The speeches of Los and Tharmas reveal a peculiar tendency among the Zoas. Their will to power is so strong that each is willing to accept the fallen world as long as he can come up with an account of the fall that entitles him to rule in it. As Rousseau writes of men in civil society: "domination becomes dearer to them than independence, and they consent to wear chains in order to give them to others in turn" (SD, 173). One begins to suspect a connection in *The Four Zoas* between establishing a definitive account of creation and establishing property rights. Both involve basing a claim on a genealogy: each Zoa wants to inherit godlike power as if he were the favorite son in Albion's will. Perhaps Blake came to suspect something inherently Urizenic in the very act of staking out the one true myth of creation.

At the beginning, Blake has Tharmas sound a warning against probing too deeply into the human soul and trying to pin it down to some kind of fixed pattern:

> Why wilt thou Examine every little fibre of my soul
> Spreading them out before the Sun like Stalks of flax to dry
> The infant joy is beautiful but its anatomy
> Horrible Ghast & Deadly nought shalt thou find in it
> But Death Despair & Everlasting brooding Melancholy
>
> Thou wilt go mad with horror if thou dost Examine thus
> Every moment of my secret hours Yea I know
> That I have sinnd & that my Emanations are become harlots
> I am already distracted at their deeds & if I look
> Upon them more Despair will bring self murder on my soul
>
> (4:29–38)

Tharmas senses that man's obsession with the past can become a self-destructive passion. He does not want Enion prying into his secret deeds just to be able to feel morally superior to him. He suspects that the Zoas' fascination with origins is part of their continuing power struggle, in which cosmic history becomes a tool of domination.

In the opening of *The Four Zoas*, Blake presents the search for an authentic account of creation in the context of a quarrel between two jealous lovers. To fix the blame for the fall on one element of the psyche is just like one lover trying to blame the other for all their troubles. We know that in the strife of lovers, looking to the past will not solve anything, and in fact may merely serve to keep the conflict going. Perhaps the Zoas as a whole might learn something from the fruitless bickering of Tharmas and Enion. As long as the Zoas keep on arguing about the past, they cannot do anything about their future. Each must learn to accept part of the responsibility for the fall, or rather to drop the whole issue of responsibility. The important question is not who caused the fall, but how to overcome it, and quarreling over past deeds may obscure that fact.[34] The lesson of *The Four Zoas* seems to be that the quest for the definitive history of creation is itself a potentially divisive enterprise.

In that sense, *The Four Zoas* might be regarded as a kind of anti-creation-myth.[35] What we see in Blake's process of revising the poem is a poet working his way out of a form he only gradually realized was unsuitable to his deepest purposes. To establish a definitive account of man's beginning would set limits on him just as much as a definitive account of his end. One might even have to infer his end from his beginning. If one could know with certainty what man's original state was like, and also exactly what force or combination of forces disturbed his initial wholeness, then one could define a particular model of human nature. By fixing blame for the fall on one aspect of human nature, a creation myth could work to exalt the others, and thus to narrow the range of human possibilities. Blake's uncertainty about how to begin *The Four Zoas* may reflect his dissatisfaction with the implications of the creation myth as a form. To come up with a single account of creation is to uphold a single idea of what man should be.

The initially clear outlines of the Romantic creation myth come to be blurred in *The Four Zoas*, as the stages of the Romantic dialectic no longer fall neatly into a linear sequence. Instead of the fall as a distinct moment in history, Blake offers several competing and perhaps even incompatible accounts of the fall. As for getting from the fallen world to the apocalypse, Blake never settled on a single path, but left several different versions of the transition in Night VII. Finally, Blake's apocalypse itself does not bring history to a definitive conclusion, but opens up new possibilities for human development. As he worked on his myth in *The Four Zoas*, Blake came closer and closer to Rousseau's strategy in the *Second Discourse*. Rousseau provides a deliberately hazy view of man's beginnings in order not to pin him down to a single course of development.[36] Rousseau comes up with the vaguest definition possible of human nature. He defines man as a cipher at the beginning, a creature who only develops his characteristics in history. Moreover, Rousseau stresses that the particular course of human development he sketches out is hypothetical (SD, 140–41). Men may have developed along a variety of paths. Rousseau's vagueness about man's beginning is necessary to support his vagueness about man's end. The Rousseau of the *Reveries*, who wishes to wander wherever he wants through the world, refused to limit man to a single course in life by giving him a definitive history.

Similar considerations account for the way Blake virtually dismantles the framework of his myth before our eyes in *The Four Zoas*, shaping a narrative with an end that is not final and a beginning that is not fixed. Blake breaks out of the potentially rigid mould of the linear paradise–fall–paradise pattern because it implies an overly rigid conception of human nature. Blake's ideal of freedom eventually required him to free himself even from the constraints of a particular mythic form. As we shall see, this movement from closed to open forms of myth characterizes the development of the creation myth as a genre throughout the Romantic period.[37]

PART TWO

The Romantic Prometheus

CHAPTER 3

The Prelude to Apocalypse

I

Like certain early Gnostics,[1] the Romantics made a hero out of Prometheus by glossing over those aspects of the original legends which cast him in a bad light, particularly the stories which portray him as a trickster, responsible for bringing Zeus's wrath down upon man's head.[2] By concentrating instead on those stories which show Prometheus as a courageous rebel against divine tyranny and as the would-be benefactor of mankind, the Romantics turned the Titan into a symbol of their own aspirations. Shelley carries the rehabilitation of Prometheus's reputation further than any other Romantic. By taking up his story centuries after his enchainment, Shelley allows Prometheus's original transgressions to fade into the background. Redeemed by years of suffering, Prometheus becomes for Shelley "the type of the highest perfection of moral and intellectual nature, impelled by the purest and truest motives to the best and noblest ends."[3]

Because Shelley focuses on the glorious conclusion of the Titan's story, rather than the morally ambiguous beginning, *Prometheus Unbound* may seem out of place in a study of Romantic myths of creation. Compared to *The Book of Urizen*, *Prometheus Unbound* is sketchy in its account of how the cosmos originated. Nevertheless, Shelley does glance back to the source of Prometheus's situation, and of the human condition as a whole, drawing upon Hesiod's account of creation in the process. And since Shelley views the apocalypse as a new creation, or recreation, of the world, *Prometheus Unbound* makes a major contribution to the Romantic understanding of creativity. Moreover, as a myth about myth-making itself, *Prometheus Unbound* is central to any understanding of Romantic creation myths.

Finally, *Prometheus Unbound* attempts to correct *Paradise Lost* in the characteristic gnostic fashion of Romantic myth. Like Blake, Shelley inverts Milton's values, portraying the ruling god as a demonic tyrant, while treating the rebel-figure in his story sympathetically. In his *A Defence of Poetry*, Shelley developed a reading of *Paradise Lost* remarkably similar to Blake's, claiming that Milton secretly sides with his devil:

Milton's poem contains within itself a philosophical refutation of that system of which, by a strange and natural antithesis, it has been a chief popular support. Nothing can exceed the energy and magnificence of the character of Satan as expressed in Paradise Lost. It is a mistake to suppose that he could ever have been intended for the popular personification of evil ... Milton's Devil as a moral being is as far superior to his God as one who perseveres in some purpose which he has conceived to be excellent in spite of adversity and torture, is to one who in the cold security of undoubted triumph inflicts the most horrible revenge upon his enemy, not from any mistaken notion of inducing him to repent of a perseverance in enmity, but with the alleged design of exasperating him to deserve new torments. Milton has so far violated the popular creed (if this shall be judged to be a violation) as to have alleged no superiority of moral virtue to his God over his Devil.[4]

In his Preface, Shelley points to the link between his Prometheus and Milton's Satan, and claims that his creation improves upon Milton's:

The only imaginary being resembling in any degree Prometheus is Satan; and Prometheus is, in my judgment, a more poetical character than Satan because, in addition to courage and majesty and firm and patient opposition to omnipotent force, he is susceptible of being described as exempt from the taints of ambition, envy, revenge, and a desire for personal aggrandisement, which in the Hero of *Paradise Lost*, interfere with the interest. (R & P, 133)

One way Shelley creates a more sympathetic character in Prometheus is to associate him with Christ, remaking the Titan's torture on the model of the Crucifixion, and thus gnostically turning the demonic rebel of orthodoxy into a savior.[5] At the same time, Shelley associates his Jupiter with the God of the Old Testament. Prometheus's curse of Jupiter, for example, echoes the opening lines of Genesis, though with a turn of phrase that casts God's motives in a sinister light: "Let thy malignant spirit move / In darkness over those I love" (I.i.276–77). To blacken his portrait of Prometheus's antagonist further, Shelley transfers to his God some of the negative qualities Milton gives to Satan. Like Satan, Jupiter finds that it is his fate to be "damned, beholding good" (I.i.293).[6] Although Shelley does not follow the outline and details of Milton's myth as closely as Blake does, the spirit of his assault on *Paradise Lost* is the same.

For a drama, even a lyrical drama, *Prometheus Unbound* is singularly lacking in action. The entire first act deals with one event, Prometheus's calling back his curse on Jupiter, and in a sense the rest of the work merely unfolds the consequences of this single deed.[7] As the work opens, Prometheus has been enduring Jupiter's tortures for centuries, remaining defiant and refusing to submit to the Olympian regime. But almost at the very beginning, Prometheus expresses a desire to renounce his curse on Jupiter, because he feels his hate is gone (I.i.57) and he wishes "no living thing to suffer pain" (I.i.305). His change of heart puzzles his friends and allies, who regard it as a defeat for Prometheus and a sign that he has at long last yielded to his divine foe (I.i.306–11). To understand why calling back the curse is actually a form of triumph for Prometheus, it is helpful to turn to a work Shelley was writing at the same time as *Prometheus Unbound*, his verse tragedy *The Cenci*.[8] Because it presents a nightmarish inversion of the dream world of *Prometheus Unbound, The Cenci* illuminates Shelley's visionary intention.

The play deals with an innocent young maiden, Beatrice Cenci, who has her father murdered because he raped her. For Shelley, the act of father–daughter incest symbolizes the old regime's oppression. As a parent trying to dominate his child completely, unwilling to release his hold on her or to share her in any way with another, Count Cenci stands for an entire dying aristocracy, trying to crush, rather than nurture, the fresh life in the new generation to which it has given birth. Thus Cenci's daughter becomes a symbol of innocence, but an innocence defiled. Once Beatrice decides to take action in the world that holds her in bondage, she begins to participate in its corruption. Like Fuzon rebelling against Urizen, she can only answer her father's violence with more violence in return.[9] Though at her trial she flatly denies her complicity in the crime and claims to have maintained her innocence, she defends herself with something of the same casuistical skill her father once displayed in justifying the way he tormented her.

In the end, Beatrice fails to liberate herself from her father's spirit. Instead, she becomes subject to it in a new, and vastly expanded, form, as, shortly before her death, she has a nightmare vision:

> If there should be
> No God, no Heaven, no Earth in the void world;
> The wide, grey, lampless, deep, unpeopled world!

If all things then should be . . . my father's spirit
His eye, his voice, his touch surrounding me;
The atmosphere and breath of my dead life!
If sometimes as a shape more like himself,
Even the form which tortured me on earth,
Masked in grey hairs and wrinkles, he should come
And wind me in his hellish arms, and fix
His eyes on mine, and drag me down, down, down!
For was he not alone omnipotent
On Earth, and ever present?   (V.iv.57–69)

In her efforts to exorcize her father's hellish spirit, Beatrice only succeeds in elevating him to the stature of a god. She feels she has nowhere left to turn to escape from his power, which now fills every corner of the universe. In that sense, Cenci finally accomplishes his incestuous purposes only after his death. Once he exists only in his daughter's imagination, his spirit expands to become the whole world in her eyes.[10]

Beatrice's final vision of her father serves to introduce an important idea in Shelley's thought, what one might call a psychology of mythology. For Shelley a fundamental reason why myths arise is that human beings feel a need to see a person behind the evil they suffer in the world. Beatrice's speech actually begins with a far more frightening vision than that with which it ends: "If there should be / No God, no Heaven, no Earth in the void world; / The wide, grey, lampless, deep, unpeopled world!" As she begins to lose her faith that God exists, Beatrice glimpses into a nihilistic abyss. Everything that has happened to her should in fact shake her belief that the universe is ordered by a morally good force. But at the last minute, Beatrice pulls back from the void that has opened up before her eyes, and suddenly starts seeing her demonic father in the place of the traditional God. If she cannot find God in her world, she can at least create an image of the Devil. Evidently she would rather believe that an evil being rules the universe than that no being at all is in charge.[11] What she cannot accept is the idea that the universe is simply indifferent to her and to man in general. She feels more at home in a universe dominated by a human will. Even though she sees that will as hostile to her, at least it is a force with which she is familiar (a point effectively made by her seeing the universe dominated specifically by her own father).

The way Beatrice projects her father as the ruling spirit of the universe provides a model of Prometheus's relation to Jupiter. Like

Beatrice, Prometheus is imprisoned by his own need to find a single person responsible for all the evil he has suffered, a convenient focus for all his frustration and hatred. As long as Prometheus has Jupiter to curse, his potentially creative energies are dissipated in sterile hatred. His defiance of Jupiter is not a true rebellion against his rule, a means of liberating Prometheus's spirit. On the contrary, Prometheus's hate actually binds him to Jupiter: it in effect creates the god. To hate Jupiter is to accept his existence and thus to play into his hands.[12] The most powerful weapon against the gods' tyranny is not hatred, but indifference.

Prometheus must avoid Beatrice Cenci's error; he must not let the force of his hatred turn him into a mirror image of what he hates. When confronted by the hideous Furies sent by Jupiter, Prometheus becomes aware of the danger of taking on the characteristics of the very beings he despises:

> Whilst I behold such execrable shapes,
> Methinks I grow like what I contemplate
> And laugh and stare in loathsome sympathy.
>
> (I.i.449–51)

The Furies torment Prometheus with visions of the pointlessness of human history, specifically of how idealistic impulses become frustrated and perverted. They show Prometheus how man's efforts to win freedom have only led to new forms of oppression, as the rebels turn into the very tyrants they rebelled against:

> SEMICHORUS I
> See! a disenchanted nation
> Springs like day from desolation;
> To truth its state, is dedicate,
> And freedom leads it forth, her mate;
> A legioned band of linked brothers
> Whom love calls children –
> SEMICHORUS II
>   'Tis another's –
> See how kindred murder kin!
> 'Tis the vantage-time for Death and Sin:
> Blood, like new wine, bubbles within
>   Till Despair smothers
> The struggling World, which slaves and tyrants win.
>
> (I.i.567–77)

This vision makes a deep impression upon Prometheus, who begins to question the value of destroying one tyrant only to install another:

The nations thronged around, and cried aloud
As with one voice, "Truth, liberty and love!"
Suddenly fierce confusion fell from Heaven
Among them — there was strife, deceit and fear;
Tyrants rushed in, and did divide the spoil.   (I.i.650–54)

In portraying Prometheus's reaction to the Furies' vision, Shelley shows the way a whole generation of Romantic artists was threatened with despair, once the Reign of Terror and Napoleon's rise to power ended the concrete hopes for political liberation raised by the overthrow of the old regime in France.[13]

In order to avoid the frustration the French revolutionaries experienced, Prometheus must learn the lesson of their failure, a lesson Shelley read in the fate of Beatrice Cenci:

The fit return to make to the most enormous injuries is kindness and forbearance, and a resolution to convert the injurer from his dark passions by peace and love. Revenge, retaliation, atonement, are pernicious mistakes.[14]

The rebel can easily take his cause too personally, fighting against the individual who happens to be tyrant, rather than against the idea and institution of tyranny itself. If one identifies the tyrant with the tyranny, one ends up assuming that one man is responsible for all the evil in the world and that all that is necessary is to remove that one man from the throne. But if one overthrows the tyrant, not the tyranny, one is simply preparing the way for a new tyrant to take his place.

Hatred narrows and distorts the soul by restricting perception. The rebel loses sight of the humanity of the tyrant he opposes, gradually destroying the very power of sympathy he most needs to undo the tyrant's evil. For Shelley, as for Blake, what has to be unbound in man is his perception. The "loathsome sympathy," which turns the rebel into the tyrant, has to be exchanged for a loving sympathy, which creates new possibilities for man: "As a lover or chameleon / Grows like what it looks upon" (IV.i. 483–84). Only a rebellion guided by a poetic idea of what man can become has any hope of improving the human condition. For Shelley, again as for Blake, the artist, as the man of broad sympathies and imaginative vision, becomes the type of the redeemed human being, and the leader of man's struggle for liberation.

On the deepest level of interpretation, Prometheus symbolizes the way man has created gods like Jupiter to account for his suffering. Because he forgets their source, man ends up subjected to the divine images he has projected out of his own brain.[15] The fundamental human error in Shelley's view is to see evil, not as something arbitrary or accidental in the universe, but as part of some grand cosmic scheme.[16] What men have a hard time coping with is the chanciness of evil. They do not like to think that their suffering is merely the result of their happening to be at the wrong place at the wrong time. They would rather believe that their misfortunes result from someone's will, even if that means positing an evil will behind the working of the universe. A universe governed by personal will seems more comprehensible to man, and offers the possibility of forestalling evil by somehow placating the ruling spirit.[17] But in creating the gods to explain his suffering, man gradually accepts the idea that they are independent and superior beings, who have the right to tell him how to act. Moreover, by trying to understand evil as part of a divine plan, man begins to view evil as inherent in the fabric of the universe and hence unremediable by human efforts. To recover his freedom, man must realize that the gods are his own creation. This is where the artist has a central role to play for Shelley. By recreating the old myths, he can shatter the hold they have on men's minds and point the way to a recovery of man's original freedom of imagination.

III

Though Prometheus's recognition of the impotence of hatred as a revolutionary force and his decision to rescind his curse on Jupiter are necessary for his unbinding, what happens in Act I does not in itself release the Titan from his chains. Until Asia makes her journey to Demogorgon's cave in Act II, Jupiter cannot be overthrown. Evidently Asia is needed to complete the process begun by Prometheus.[18] One way of understanding the relationship of Prometheus and Asia is to view them on the model of Blake's Los and Enitharmon. In Blake's terms, Asia is Prometheus's Emanation, the feminine half, as it were, of the total being of which Prometheus is the masculine half.[19] As in Blake's mythology, one of the conceptual difficulties in analyzing *Prometheus Unbound* is that the mythical figures function at one and the same time as independent, self-subsistent characters and as fragments of an original, larger unity.

As we discover in Act II, perhaps the fundamental aspect of Prometheus's fall is his division from the feminine side of his being, and his consequent loss of all its positive qualities. Shelley does not portray as elaborate a dividing up of the cosmos as Blake does. Nevertheless, Shelley's fall does involve the shattering of an original unity:

> The good want power, but to weep barren tears.
> The powerful goodness want: worse need for them.
> The wise want love; and those who love want wisdom;
> And all best things are thus confused to ill.   (I.i.625–28)

Shelley states abstractly what Blake portrays concretely and mythically when he shows Enitharmon torn from Los's side in what is the beginning of a painful division of the originally creative unity of man's wrath and pity into warring opposites. Shelley shares with Blake the idea that in man's fallen condition his faculties no longer work together, but are instead at odds, and tend to cancel each other out.

Denied the physical presence of Asia, Prometheus loses his ability to love, and becomes absorbed in his all-consuming and sterile hatred of Jupiter. What happens in Act I is only the intellectual realization on the part of Prometheus of why he must renounce hate. For Shelley, that purely mental event does not suffice; the Titan cannot undo centuries of lovelessness in one moment of insight. His recognition on the level of the mind requires a corresponding movement on the level of the heart. That is what Asia supplies in Act II.[20] Her dialogue with Panthea at the beginning of the act emphasizes feeling as opposed to reason. The two sisters are led, not by any guidance from their conscious minds, but by the passions sweeping through them:

> I saw not – heard not – moved not – only felt
> His presence flow and mingle through my blood
> Till it became his life and his grew mine
> And I was thus absorbed – . . .
> I always knew what I desired before
> Nor ever found delight to wish in vain.
> But now I cannot tell thee what I seek;
> I know not–   (II.i.79–82, 95–98)

By allowing themselves to be swept along unthinking on the current of their emotions (II.ii.41–63), Asia and Panthea provide a perfect complement to the role of Prometheus, whose name, after all, means forethought.

Like Blake, then, Shelley looks forward to a reintegration of man's self-divided faculties as a prelude to the apocalyptic release of his long-imprisoned creative powers. One way of interpreting the course of action in *Prometheus Unbound* is to view Shelley as portraying in mythic terms what is needed to awaken the poetic faculty in man. Shelley's *A Defence of Poetry* supplies an important gloss on the symbolic action of his myth:

Poetry is not like reasoning, a power to be exerted according to the determination of the will. A man cannot say, "I will compose poetry." The greatest poet even cannot say it: for the mind in creation is as a fading coal which some invisible influence, like an inconstant wind, awakens to transitory brightness: this power arises from within, like the colour of a flower which fades and changes as it is developed, and the conscious portions of our natures are unprophetic either of its approach or its departure. (R & P, 503–4)

Shelley's belief that the power to write poetry is not within the conscious control of the mind explains why Prometheus's conscious determination to cease hating Jupiter cannot in itself free him from the image of Jupiter he has created. The Prometheus of Act I resembles a poet who has reached the decision: "I will compose a new Jupiter."[21] He still must await the unconscious current of feeling necessary to set his creative powers in motion, mythically represented by Asia's descent to Demogorgon's cave, an apt symbol of man getting in touch with the deep, subconscious sources of his inspiration. The conjunction of Acts I and II of *Prometheus Unbound*, the partnership of Prometheus and Asia in liberating the human spirit, reflects Shelley's fundamental belief that, not the conscious mind alone, but the whole soul is at work in poetic creation. Only when both the intellect and the emotions are ready can the power of the imagination be mysteriously released. Again as for Blake, for Shelley the imagination, when functioning properly, mediates between reason and passion, providing a synthesis of the two forces normally at odds in the fallen world.

When Shelley speaks of poetry in the *Defence* as a power which "arises from within . . . and the conscious portions of our natures are unprophetic . . . of its approach," he might well be describing the way Demogorgon takes Jupiter by surprise at the beginning of Act III. Many interpretations have been offered of Demogorgon's role in *Prometheus Unbound*, and one must grant that such a shadowy figure can never be precisely pinned down to a single meaning.[22] But whatever one chooses to make Demogorgon himself represent, the significance of his arrival at Jupiter's court is clear. The overthrow of Jupiter is essentially the dethronement of an image, in effect the writing of the new god-poem Prometheus wills in Act I.[23]

The action of *Prometheus Unbound* can be summed up rather simply: Prometheus takes back his curse on Jupiter and Asia journeys to the cave of Demogorgon. As a result, the power of Demogorgon is set in motion, Jupiter is overthrown, and Prometheus is liberated from his chains. But this simple action is a complex mythic representation of how the forces in man's soul might combine to release his creative power and restore his imaginative freedom. One takes nothing away from the mystery of Demogorgon by comparing his arrival at Jupiter's court to the sudden onset of poetic inspiration, for in Shelley's view this power is itself the greatest mystery in the world. As a drama, *Prometheus Unbound* lacks the inevitability of plot one expects in a well-made play. There is no reason why any of the events should take place precisely when they do: why Prometheus, for example, should choose just this day to renounce his curse, why Asia should set off on her journey at about the same time, above all, why Demogorgon should rise against Jupiter at this one moment and not another. But the logic of Shelley's plot is the logic of a mental universe, and hence not conventional dramatic logic at all. One can no more determine the precise moment when Demogorgon's power will be released than one can predict the day and hour when a great poem will be written. Even when Asia arrives at Demogorgon's cave and begins to question him, she finds it impossible to penetrate the mystery of his being.

The dialogue between Asia and Demogorgon develops the familiar gnostic contrast between the benighted god of this world, who attempts to imprison the human spirit, and a higher, transmundane god, who is somehow the goal of man's true spiritual yearnings. Given Shelley's idealism, Asia's question concerning "who made the living world" turns out to be a question concerning the origin, not of the physical universe, as one might have expected, but of man's spiritual faculties, "thought, passion, reason, will, / Imagination" (II.iv.9–10). Asia wonders, not who created the material creation, but who created man's creative energies.

When Asia turns to the god of this world, we learn that all he creates are forces which inhibit man's creativity: "terror, madness, crime, remorse," "abandoned hope," "love that turns to hate," "self-contempt," and "pain," all the aspects of man's existence that "drag heavily" upon his spirit, and weigh down his aspirations (II.iv.19–28). Discriminating between the good god who supports creativity and the evil god who undermines it should ultimately free man's spirit. But at this point something strange happens. Though Demogorgon is willing to speak of the good force in the universe in conventional terms, referring to "Almighty God" and "Merciful God" (II.iv.11, 18), when it comes to the evil force, he refuses to use a name, and instead confines himself to the vague and non-committal expression "He reigns" (II.iv.28, 31). This behavior is all the more puzzling, because ever since the beginning of the play we have become accustomed to calling the god of this world by the name of Jupiter, and cannot help wondering why Demogorgon tries to conceal a fact which everyone already knows. Asia herself is frustrated by Demogorgon's coyness: "Utter his name – a world pining in pain / Asks but his name; curses shall drag him down" (II.iv.29–30).

Asia's desire to learn the name of her oppressor is perfectly understandable, but the fact that she intends to bring him down with curses should be a clue that something has gone wrong with her thinking.[24] Asia is apparently falling into Prometheus's original error, believing that the evils of man's condition can be traced to a single hostile will in the universe, and that the one thing needful is to discover this being's identity and overthrow him. Asia's encounter with Demogorgon thus dramatizes once more how man's mythic impulses can lead him astray. Bewildered by Demogorgon's answers, Asia embarks upon the one fully developed myth of creation in *Prometheus Unbound*. Evidently Asia believes that the only way to comprehend how the human spirit has been imprisoned is to go back in time and tell the story of man's fall.

Asia's speech develops in mythic terms Rousseau's contrast between the state of nature and the state of civil society. Shelley adapts Hesiod's Golden Age under Saturn's rule to symbolize man's original (and subhuman) condition according to Rousseau:

> such the state
> Of the earth's primal spirits beneath his sway
> As the calm joy of flowers and living leaves
> Before the wind or sun has withered them
> And semivital worms, but he refused
> The birthright of their being, knowledge, power,
> The skill which wields the elements, the thought
> Which pierces this dim Universe like light,
> Self-empire and the majesty of love,
> For thirst of which they fainted.   (II.iv.34–43)

As Asia portrays Saturn's Golden Age, it embodies the combination of positive and negative qualities characteristic of Rousseau's state of nature. Men are innocent under Saturn's rule, and they enjoy the happiness of animals, or rather the untroubled peace of vegetables. But according to Asia, they are denied their birthright. They are not allowed to develop their specifically human faculties, and above all they lack "self-empire," the right to govern their own lives.[25]

For the sake of developing man's freedom, Prometheus brings about what amounts to a fortunate fall. He gives Jupiter the throne of heaven on the condition: "Let man be free" (II.iv.45).[26] But Jupiter proves faithless and creates a world hostile to man:

> on the race of man
> First famine and then toil and then disease,
> Strife, wounds, and ghastly death unseen before,
> Fell; and the unseasonable seasons drove,
> With alternating shafts of frost and fire,
> Their shelterless, pale tribes to mountain caves.
>   (II.iv.49–54)

The condition of man in Jupiter's reign corresponds to Rousseau's state of civil society or Blake's state of Experience.[27] Man endures misery, but at least he develops his human faculties. Trying to compensate for the defects of Jupiter's creation, Prometheus gives man fire and teaches him the various productive arts and theoretical sciences. In Asia's myth, man's talents do not come to him "naturally," that is, they come to him against the will of the gods. Prometheus is even necessary to give "man speech, and speech created thought" (II.iv.72). Evidently Shelley follows Rousseau in the idea that natural man lacked language and reason.[28]

Asia's myth serves the function of a theodicy. By showing that man's suffering is what brings about the development of his faculties, it justifies his loss of his primeval happiness. But Asia is

88

not satisified by her own myth. In her account, the arts and sciences
Prometheus has given man ought to enable him to rebuild paradise
for himself, and Asia is left wondering what still stands in the way
of complete human happiness. Unable to deal satisfactorily with
the problem of evil, her myth fails to answer her most disturbing
questions:

> but who rains down
> Evil, the immedicable plague . . .? –
> Not Jove: while yet his frown shook Heaven, aye when
> His adversary from adamantine chains
> Cursed him, he trembled like a slave. Declare
> Who is his master? Is he too a slave? (II.iv.100–101, 106–9)

At this point, faced with the heart of the mystery of human
suffering, *Prometheus Unbound* passes into the realm of oracular
brevity and opaqueness. The elliptical quality of the dialogue
would seem to forestall forever any efforts to expound Shelley's
meaning fully.[29] The central point of the exchange between Asia
and Demogorgon seems in fact to be the necessary inadequacy of
myth, or any other means of expression, for dealing with the
problem of evil. Demogorgon darkly hints that the human way of
speaking about things is itself responsible for man's missing the
truth he seeks:

> DEMOGORGON
> All spirits are enslaved who serve things evil:
> Thou knowest if Jupiter be such or no.
> ASIA
> Whom callst thou God?
> DEMOGORGON
> I spoke but as you speak –
> For Jove is the supreme of living things. (II.iv.110–13)

Demogorgon resists Asia's demand for anthropomorphic explana-
tions. As long as he must name a person responsible for the evil in
the universe, he is forced to fall back on conventional mythology,
and refer to whatever god men worship at the moment.

Pressed further by Asia, Demogorgon tries to break her of the
habit of personifying evil:

> – If the Abysm
> Could vomit forth its secrets: – but a voice
> Is wanting, the deep truth is imageless:
> For what would it avail to bid thee gaze

On the revolving world? what to bid speak
Fate, Time, Occasion, Chance and Change? To these
All things are subject but eternal Love.   (II.iv.114–20)

"The deep truth is imageless" – that is at once the reason why
Demogorgon cannot answer Asia's questions and the only answer
he can give her. From the beginning, she has been seeking an image
to resolve all her difficulties, an anthropomorphic deity who would
conveniently explain away all the problems that disturb her. The
image of Jupiter, a domineering god in the sky, who rules man's
destiny and is responsible for the good and evil in his life, is a
comforting idea. It puts all doubts to rest, and also relieves man of
the duty of charting his own destiny. Demogorgon wants Asia to
give up her quest for an anthropomorphic answer to her questions,
and to realize that abstract, impersonal forces are what thwart
human desires.[30] Even at this point, human language fails Demogorgon, for it is difficult not to read "Fate, Time, Occasion, Chance
and Change" as mythical personifications. But to do so would be to
misread Demogorgon's message completely. What he is trying to
say is precisely that the evil in the world cannot be personified. It is
not the result of some cosmic will ranged against man's, but largely
the product of the fact that events happen by chance and often turn
out contrary to man's hopes and wishes. Only because man is a
person in an impersonal universe can his spirit triumph over any
obstacle. His aspirations may be thwarted by the laws of the
physical universe, but his unique ability to aspire makes him
superior to the blind forces which frustrate him.[31] That at least is
one way of making sense out of Demogorgon's final claim that "to
these / All things are subject but eternal Love."

Apparently, Demogorgon succeeds in communicating his message to Asia, for she achieves a recognition which leads in turn
directly to the overthrow of Jupiter:

So much I asked before, and my heart gave
The response thou hast given; and of such truths
Each to itself must be the oracle.   (II.iv.121–23)

The force of Asia's realization seems to be something along these
lines: she has learned that she must not seek intellectual answers to
her questions, but must trust her own feelings;[32] and she has
learned that she must not turn to institutionalized, communal
answers, but must seek the truth on her own, and in an individual
form.[33] In her resolve to serve as her own oracle, Asia has in effect

decided to reject the myths she has inherited, and thus her actions in Act II precipitate the fall of Jupiter, the overturning of the established image of god. Asia has learned to do without the mental crutch of traditional myth.[34]

In that sense, the real turning point for Asia occurs just before her meeting with Demogorgon, when she has a strikingly original and unconventional vision of the power behind nature:

> Fit throne for such a Power! Magnificent!
> How glorious art thou, Earth! and if thou be
> The shadow of some Spirit lovelier still,
> Though evil stain its work and it should be
> Like its creation, weak yet beautiful,
> I would fall down and worship that and thee.
>
> (II.iii.11–16)

Asia is not looking to nature to find some all-powerful force, which can give absolute support and security to her values. On the contrary, she admits that the spirit behind nature may be weak, perhaps in need of support itself, and yet she is willing to worship its beauty. She thus anticipates Demogorgon's notion that the true spiritual principle might not be able to realize its goals fully in the material world, and still represent the highest value in the universe.[35]

In her vision of nature, Asia reverses Beatrice Cenci's view. Reluctant to assume that the universe is not fully controlled by a single hand, Beatrice projects a malevolent will behind all events. Asia, by contrast, is more concerned with asserting the good will of the supreme spirit, even if that means she has to live with a certain chanciness in the cosmos, the uncertainty that any will is powerful enough to accomplish all its purposes. In short, faced with the impossibility of maintaining both benevolence and omnipotence in the divine nature, Beatrice sacrifices the former attribute, Asia the latter. In Shelley's view, Beatrice's position is closer to that of conventional religion, which leaves man believing that the evil in the universe is divinely willed, and therefore something he must learn to live with. Asia's view of the divine does not offer the security of Beatrice's, but it leaves man free to evaluate the world order according to his own standards, and to decide for himself whether or not to tolerate existing evils. As Asia shows, to break with conventional notions of divinity requires a struggle. But the alternative is to remain the prisoner of traditional myths, which destroy man's freedom to think and act.

IV

The way man is tempted to rest content with inherited myths is a special case of the mental inertia Shelley saw constantly threatening the imagination.[36] Myths, like all images, are originally an expression of human creativity, but once they confront man as ready-made objects, seemingly self-subsistent in the external world, they weigh down man's spirit, rather than giving it flight.[37] Striving to remind man of how his myths originate, Shelley hoped to keep man's imagination active, and prevent it from coming to rest with its finished products. He saw the highest function of poetry as breaking man out of the mental ruts into which he routinely falls:

> Poetry defeats the curse which binds us to be subjected to the accident of surrounding impressions . . . It purges from our inward sight the film of familiarity which obscures from us the wonder of our being. It compels us to feel that which we perceive, and to imagine that which we know. It creates anew the universe after it has been annihilated in our minds by the recurrence of impressions blunted by reiteration. (R & P, 505–6)

The chains which bind Shelley's Prometheus are habits of thought and feeling, ingrained ways of imaging the universe which lead him to accept his condition and blind him to the fact that his prison is of his own making. The purely mental character of Prometheus's chains is what makes his unbinding at once so difficult to set in motion and so easy to accomplish.

For Shelley, the fundamental fall is the collapse of imaginative vision into fixed form, in particular the degeneration of expressive poetic utterance into everyday speech. Man's imagination is vital and expansive in its movement, but the attempt to embody visions in permanent form necessarily drains the life out of them, contracting and rigidifying their meaning. In discussing poetry, Shelley reveals a remarkable ability to separate the imaginative content of literature from the specific form in which it is expressed. For Shelley, the execution of an artistic idea never lives up to the grandeur of the original vision:

> When composition begins, inspiration is already on the decline, and the most glorious poetry that has ever been communicated to the world is probably a feeble shadow of the original conception of the poet. (R & P, 504)

Shelley's belief that inspiration necessarily outruns composition reflects his more general sense that spiritual values are inevitably compromised when they take material form. This attitude explains why he felt that the deepest truths are distorted when we try to express them in the concrete form of images. Thus, for Shelley the history of mankind is a history of recurrent "falls." Man seeks out the openness of imaginative vision, only to lose it once his living creations harden into lifeless forms, which await the power of a new vision to bring them back to life and start the process all over again.[38]

The idea of a fall is central to Shelley's view of the history of poetry, and particularly his understanding of the role of poets in the primeval life of man:

Their language is vitally metaphorical; that is, it names the before unapprehended relations of things, and perpetuates their apprehension, until the words which represent them, become through time signs for portions or classes of thoughts instead of pictures of integral thoughts; and then if no new poets should arise to create afresh the associations which have been thus disorganized, language will be dead to all the nobler purposes of human intercourse . . . In the infancy of society every author is necessarily a poet, because language itself is poetry . . . Every original language near to its source is in itself the chaos of a cyclic poem: the copiousness of lexicography and the distinctions of grammar are the works of a later age, and are merely the catalogue and the form of the creations of Poetry.[39]

In this reworking of the Garden of Eden story, the original paradise is the state of imaginative freedom man enjoys when he first tries to translate his visions into words, and the fall is the gradual loss of energy these primal words undergo as they become the common-place counters of everyday communication.[40] The history of European poetry Shelley tells in his *Defence* is a history of poets struggling against the tendency of words to lose their vitality and go dead.[41] For Shelley, poets are the saviors of language:

But, as Machiavelli says of political institutions, [social] life may be preserved and renewed, if men should arise capable of bringing back the drama to its principles. And this is true with respect to poetry in its most extended sense: all language, institution and form, require not only to be produced but to be maintained: the office and character of a poet participates in the divine nature as regards providence, no less than as regards creation. (R & P, 492)

In the *Defence*, the great danger Shelley sees throughout the history of poetry is the tendency of visionary poetry, such as Dante's or Milton's, to harden into a new orthodoxy, and become the very opposite of the liberating force it was originally meant to be. When the iconoclastic creator is himself elevated into an idol, it is time for a new poet to come along and smash the old idols, thus reviving the prophetic spirit in poetry. *Prometheus Unbound* portrays this process mythically. Prometheus is the poet, and Jupiter his creation, an image of the divine which seeks to capture spiritual and transcedent truth in palpable form. When this image begins to imprison the human mind, Asia, who symbolizes the poet's muse, the subconscious source of his inspiration, must restore his power to create freely and displace the old ways of thinking that stand in his way.

Prometheus Unbound is an anti-mythic myth. Shelley uses the form of myth to suggest how myths distort man's view of the world, and to show the need to break through their rigidity of meaning. Thus form and content are fundamentally at odds in *Prometheus Unbound*.[42] Shelley has to use myth, but he distrusts its power. In particular, as a dramatist Shelley must make his mythic figures behave like characters in a play, with a life of their own. But he also feels it necessary to undermine the literal reality of his creations, suggesting that Prometheus, Asia, Jupiter, and Demogorgon are only imperfect embodiments of a deeper spiritual truth which will always elude concrete expression. Shelley's dissatisfaction with his medium of expression is one of his distinguishing features as a poet. He is always struggling against the limits of language, seeking to express precisely what he feels words cannot express.[43] His linguistic skepticism is a basic tenet of his philosophy:

The words *I*, and *you* and *they* are grammatical devices invented simply for arrangement and totally devoid of the intense and exclusive sense usually attached to them. It is difficult to find terms adequately to express so subtle a conception as that to which the intellectual philosophy has conducted us. We are on that verge where words abandon us, and what wonder if we grow dizzy to look down the dark abyss of – how little we know.[44]

Shelley presents the paradox of a poet who believes that "the deep truth is imageless," and yet can only work through images to try to convey that truth.[45]

Shelley's straining against his medium is particularly evident in *Prometheus Unbound*. For example, his plot requires Panthea and Asia to meet Demogorgon face-to-face, but in Shelley's paradoxical visualization, nothing can be seen:

> I see a mighty Darkness
> Filling the seat of power; and rays of gloom
> Dart round, as light from the meridian Sun,
> Ungazed upon and shapeless – neither limb
> Nor form – nor outline; yet we feel it is
> A living spirit.   (II.iv.2–7)

When Demogorgon meets Jupiter, he seems to sense that they are only mental abstractions acting out a symbolic drama. But he somewhat condescendingly allows Jupiter to play at being a real character in a real drama, with a will of his own, and the means to execute it:

> The tyranny of Heaven none may retain,
> Or reassume, or hold succeeding thee . . .
> Yet if thou wilt – as 'tis the destiny
> Of trodden worms to writhe till they are dead –
> Put forth thy might.   (III.i.57–61)

Jupiter's reply is probably the most extreme example of how the action in Shelley's play tends to become hollow when thematic considerations override dramatic:

> Detested prodigy!
> Even thus beneath the deep Titanian prisons
> I trample thee! . . . Thou lingerest?   (III.i.61–63)

"Thou lingerest?" is almost comic in its lameness. A good drama would have built up to a climactic confrontation between Demogorgon and Jupiter, with the sky-god genuinely fighting to hold on to his throne in heaven. But Shelley's scene is deliberately anti-climactic, for his conception of Jupiter as a mental projection dictates that he vanish with as little physical struggle as possible.[46]

The peculiar elusiveness of *Prometheus Unbound* can be traced to the fact that Shelley's figures are constantly wavering between two planes of reality. Sometimes they must act like rounded characters, with distinct personalities and dramatic motivations; at other times, they become purely symbolic figures, following a logic of idea rather than of plot.[47] This vacillation between literal and symbolic meanings should not, however, be viewed as an artistic failing. In a sense, the central aim of *Prometheus Unbound* is to suggest the limitations of literal meaning, to show that however much we try to embody our visions in the concrete form of myth, something is always left over which transcends the images we create. Shelley wants us to be dissatisfied with the myth he creates in *Prometheus Unbound* because he does not want us to be tempted to rest content with any particular and limited formulation of eternal truth. But our uncertainty as to how much of the play's action should be taken literally poses special problems for interpreting its conclusion. When it comes to Shelley's portrayal of the apocalypse, we feel a need to separate the literal from the symbolic. In short, we want to know how much of this promised paradise is real, and how much is only in the eye of the beholder.

V

Acts III and IV of *Prometheus Unbound* unfold the consequences of restoring man's creative freedom, and thus provide the most extensive account of the Romantic apocalypse in English poetry, with the possible exception of Night IX of *The Four Zoas*. But in trying to show man recapturing paradise, Shelley risks becoming the captive of his own mythic mode. He views the apocalypse as a purely spiritual event, an inner transformation of consciousness. But given the requirements of myth, he ends up showing a literal transformation of the external world. Shelley threatens to compromise the ideality of his vision by casting it in material terms. As Northrop Frye writes: "It is no good rejecting a tyrannical Jupiter merely to fall into the childish belief that God has really designed nature for our convenience."[48] As a result of the ambiguous nature of Shelley's apocalypse, it becomes especially difficult to know exactly how to take some of the claims concerning human nature he makes toward the end of the work.

Shelley's apocalypse begins with many of the traditional images for the return of the Golden Age, such as the rising of the island Atlantis (III.ii).[49] Shelley presents the apocalypse as basically an undoing of the fall. The seasons, for example, are henceforth to become mild again and no longer trouble man with alternating freezing cold and burning heat (III.iii.114–23). The apocalypse thus ushers in the third stage of the Romantic dialectic, when man can combine the wisdom he has gained by means of his painful experience with the happiness he originally possessed in his ignorant innocence.[50] Shelley appropriately symbolizes this achievement by a wise child, the Spirit of the Earth:

> Mother, I am grown wiser, though a child
> Cannot be like thee, within this day
> And happier too, happier and wiser both.   (III.iv.33–35)

As the Spirit of the Earth catalogues the changes that have occurred in the world, we learn that everything that had once plagued man's existence now seems beautiful: "All things had put their evil natures off" (III.iv.77). But Shelley shows that this transformation is largely a matter of changing mental perspectives:

> Those ugly human shapes and visages
> Of which I spoke as having wrought me pain,
> Past floating through the air, and fading still
> Into the winds that scattered them; and those
> From which they past seemed mild and lovely forms
> After some foul disguise had fallen – and all
> Were somewhat changed, and after brief surprise
> And greetings of delighted wonder, all
> Went to sleep again: and when the dawn
> Came – wouldst thou think that toads and snakes and efts
> Could e'er be beautiful? – yet so they were
> And that with little change of shape or hue.   (III.iv.65–76)

Shelley's imagery of masks and foul disguises falling off suggests that the apocalyptic change involves, not so much the inner nature of things, as the way they appear to us. The moment when the Spirit of the Earth sees the toads and snakes and efts in a new light and suddenly appreciates their beauty should remind us of the moment when the transfiguring power of the moonlight leads Coleridge's Ancient Mariner to bless the water snakes unaware.[51] In both cases, we feel that the reptiles have hardly altered, if at all. The real change is in the eye of the beholder, and, as Blake says, "the Eye altering alters all."[52] Shelley minimizes the degree of objective change in his apocalypse. The humans are only "somewhat" changed, and the reptiles become beautiful "with little change of shape or hue."

Shelley emphasizes the subjective character of the change to suggest that much of what we see as miserable and evil in nature is only the result of our projecting our own emotions into nature.[53] Once we restore the harmony in our own souls, nature will seem harmonious to us, and not a hostile world:

> Man, one harmonious Soul of many a soul
> Whose nature is its own divine controul
> Where all things flow to all, as rivers to the sea;
> Familiar acts are beautiful through love;
> Labour and Pain and Grief in life's green grove
> Sport like tame beasts – none knew how gentle they could be!
> (IV.i.400–405)

The idea that labor, pain, and grief will suddenly reveal how gentle they can be has a simplistic ring to it. To make sense out of Shelley's claims, we must turn to the long speech by the Spirit of the Hours which concludes Act III. The Spirit first notes that the objective change in the world has not been as great as he expected:

> I wandering went
> Among the haunts and dwellings of mankind
> And first was disappointed not to see
> Such mighty change as I had felt within
> Expressed in outward things.   (III.iv.126–30)

The focus of the change turns out to be political:

> but soon I looked,
> And behold! thrones were kingless, and men walked
> One with the other even as spirits do,
> None fawned, none trampled.   (III.iv.130–33)

Political change provides the point at which the subjective and the objective intersect for Shelley. In politics, a change in mental attitude can have very real consequences in the material world. If man's political condition were fundamentally transformed, nature itself would look radically different to him.

In particular, what makes providence look defective is the scarcity of resources in the world. Because there never seems to be enough of any good to go around, man thinks of nature as failing to provide adequately for him. But for Shelley, this scarcity is less a physical fact than a political. It is a result, not of the immutable laws of nature as most men think, but of the accidental course human history has taken. The faulty and inequitable distribution of natural goods in society is largely responsible for the fact that some men have to go without adequate provisions.[54] Drawing upon the *Second Discourse*, Shelley believes that the inequalities of wealth which have developed over the centuries are the cause of man's seeing evil intentions in nature where none in fact exist. If man could reform and improve the political order under which he lives, the natural order would suddenly look better to him, too. Man is too easily tempted to confuse the political with the natural order, mistaking what his own society has created for the eternal decree of God.[55] Shelley hoped that by learning to distinguish those human evils which are the product of man's own actions from those which are actually inherent in the frame of nature, man could learn to see the world as basically suited to his happiness, and in that sense a paradise.

The speech of the Spirit of the Hour culminates in a vision of man's transformation:

> The loathsome mask has fallen, the man remains
> Sceptreless, free, uncircumscribed – but man:
> Equal, unclassed, tribeless and nationless,
> Exempt from awe, worship, degree, – the King
> Over himself; just, gentle, wise – but man:
> Passionless? no – yet free from guilt or pain
> Which were, for his will made, or suffered them,
> Nor yet exempt, though ruling them like slaves,
> From chance and death and mutability,
> The clogs of that which else might oversoar
> The loftiest star of unascended Heaven
> Pinnacled dim in the intense inane.   (III.iv.193–204)

Again following the lead of Rousseau, Shelley believed that the only way to see the true nature of man is to strip him of everything society has given him, to view him removed from any social context.[56] Shelley's ideal man has the cardinal virtue of Rousseau's natural man: he is autonomous, "the King / Over himself." He also has some of the traditional virtues: he is "just, gentle, wise" (notice that Shelley has substituted gentleness for the Greek virtues of courage and temperance). At this point, sensing that conventional ethics would have something to say about keeping the passions in check, Shelley is quick to point out that his ideal man would not be passionless. But he would be free from guilt and pain, forms of suffering which man imposes upon himself.

For Shelley, then, man's ultimate triumph is over his own mind, with a strong suggestion that the physical constraints on his happiness will be lessened as well. Man will not be "exempt . . . from chance and death and mutability," the impersonal forces Demogorgon referred Asia to in her quest for the source of human evil. Evidently Shelley cannot bring himself to assert that man's power will be completely unlimited. But he blurs the question of its limits by saying that, although man will not be free of physical constraints, he will rule over them "like slaves."[57] Shelley seems to be trying to have the best of both worlds. He does not want to seem like a naive utopian dreamer, who totally forgets the limits of the material world. But he does not want to acknowledge that material factors might check the flight of the human spirit. In the end,

Shelley is reduced to justifying man's material existence as a kind of ballast, which prevents his spirit from floating off into the outer reaches of space and evaporating into infinity.[58]

Shelley's suggestion at the end of Act III that man has finally conquered chance is, however, undermined by the end of Act IV. Though earlier Demogorgon explicitly stated that Jupiter was to be the last tyrant in heaven (III.i.57–58), his concluding speech implies that man could fall under the yoke of divine tyranny again:[59]

> And if, with infirm hand, Eternity,
> Mother of many acts and hours, should free
>   The serpent that would clasp her with his length –
> These are the spells by which to reassume
> An empire o'er the disentangled Doom.   (IV.i.565–69)

This speech introduces a discordant note into the otherwise triumphantly harmonious ending of *Prometheus Unbound*. Suddenly it sounds as if the apocalypse is not the once-and-for-all event it had seemed to be. Eternity may have an "infirm hand," unable to accomplish its purposes with finality. Man may be faced with an eternal cycle of tyranny, liberation, the return of tyranny, and the renewal of liberation. The rule of Jupiter may recur, although undoubtedly under a different name, requiring a new Prometheus to free mankind. The possibility of such a cycle is demanded by Shelley's desire to keep the apocalypse a purely human phenomenon. If man is to have the power to save himself, then he must have the power to damn himself as well. In traditional religion, the apocalypse has true finality, because a force beyond man's power brings it about and guarantees the permanence of the transformation.[60] But if the apocalypse has its source in forces immanent in human life, it becomes an event in human history, and cannot be said to transcend time. The power by which man liberated himself may someday fail and plunge him back into an enslaved condition.

Demogorgon's concluding speech reveals a deep ambiguity in *Prometheus Unbound*. For much of the work, Shelley appears to be working within a traditional mythic framework, a linear vision of cosmic history. His myth seems to demand a one-way sequence of unique events: an initial paradise, a single moment of fall, and an apocalypse that is truly a Last Judgment, bringing history to an end (IV.i.14). But Demogorgon's talk of Eternity's "infirm hand" suggests a cyclical view of history, with man's creative power continually rising and falling, bursting into sun-like brightness and then undergoing eclipse. This view of human history is closer to that of *A Defence of Poetry*, which could be regarded as a prosaic account of what is presented poetically in *Prometheus Unbound*. In the *Defence*, no poetic achievement is portrayed as final. Since even the most revolutionary poetry eventually hardens into ortho-doxy, the creative process must go on forever, with each new generation having to begin anew. Shelley presents no evidence for the idea that man will ever transcend the need to renew his creative energies from their continual fall into the fixity of form. We have seen Shelley at odds with the demands of his mythic medium at several points in *Prometheus Unbound*. The most fundamental tension in the work is that between a literal and a symbolic conception of the apocalypse. The traditional Prome-theus myth projects a genuine culmination to history. But Shelley may be using the myth to symbolize an ongoing process of artistic creation, with no more finality than we have seen in *The Four Zoas*.[61]

This wavering between the literal and the symbolic is basic to Shelley's poetry. He always fears being trapped by the literal meaning of words, having his ideal visions pinned down to specific images. On the other hand, he understands that to retreat from literal meaning would be to lose touch with ordinary reality, and leave his visions floating in the air, disembodied, without all grounding in the concrete world. The contradictions in Shelley's understanding of his poetic medium mirror the contradictions in his understandng of human nature, specifically of the relation of soul and body. Shelley would like to free man's soul from the limitations of his body, for he believes that the material world corrupts the purity of the spiritual. And yet he sees the problem in completely separating the soul from the body. The soul needs the "clogs" of the body to give it substance, to prevent it from melting away into thin air, "pinnacled dim in the intense inane." This last phrase, oddly enough, captures perfectly what is most problematic about Shelley's poetry. In his hesitation at embodying his visions, his reluctance to see the deep truth imprisoned in images, he sometimes leaves the reader adrift in a sea of half-realized symbols and vague ideas.[62] In a letter, Shelley found a remarkably concrete image for the abstractness of his poetry: "as to real flesh and blood, you know that I do not deal in those articles; you might as well go to a gin-shop for a leg of mutton, as expect anything human or earthly from me."[63] For the nightmare of an idealistic creator confronted by the flesh-and-blood embodiment of his imaginative vision, we turn to Mary Shelley's *Frankenstein*.

CHAPTER 4

The Nightmare of Romantic Idealism

I

Frankenstein has as much claim to mythic status as any story ever invented by a single author. The original novel continues to be read by a wide audience, and has of course spawned innumerable adaptations, imitations, and sequels.[1] Through its cinematic incarnations, the Frankenstein story has ingrained itself on the popular imagination. Although no one believes in the literal truth of the story, it has all the other earmarks of a genuine myth, above all, the fact that men keep returning to it to find ways of imaging their deepest fears. But as original as the Frankenstein myth is, Mary Shelley did not create her story out of thin air. Much of the power of her book can be traced to the ways she found of drawing upon traditional mythic patterns. A glance at the title-page shows that in composing the book she had two of the central creation myths in the Western tradition in mind. The subtitle of *Frankenstein*, "The Modern Prometheus," points to the myth of the Greek Titan. The epigraph from *Paradise Lost* suggests that the story refers to Milton's creation account, and by extension to Genesis. But if one tries to align the characters in *Frankenstein* with traditional mythic archetypes, one runs into difficulties. Although *Frankenstein* at first seems to offer a potentially confusing array of mythic correspondences, by trying to sort out the mythic roles assigned to the central characters, we can approach the thematic heart of the book.

We can begin by asking: who is the modern Prometheus referred to in the subtitle? The obvious answer is Victor Frankenstein, and many critics have pointed to the Promethean elements in Frankenstein's character.[2] Victor wants to be the benefactor of mankind, rebels against the divinely established order, steals, as it were, the spark of life from heaven, and creates a living being. But like Prometheus he ends up bringing disaster and destruction down upon those he was trying to help. In many respects, however, the monster Frankenstein creates is an equally good candidate for the role of Prometheus in the story. It is the monster who literally discovers fire, and in a sense steals it (99–100). Moreover, the monster tantalizes Frankenstein with a mysterious secret concerning what will happen on his wedding night. Frankenstein's blindness to the real meaning of the monster's prophecy (182) associates him with the role of Zeus, particularly if one looks ahead to Percy Shelley's version of the Prometheus myth, in which the story of the secret concerning Jupiter's wedding hour is central to the plot. The fact that both Frankenstein and the monster have their Promethean aspects should not be surprising, since the original Prometheus archetype is ambiguous. With respect to man, he appears as a creator and thus as a divine figure; with respect to Zeus, he takes on the role of a rebel against divine authority and eventually of a tortured creature, thus becoming a symbol of human suffering at the hands of the gods.

The same sort of ambiguity of mythic archetypes is evident when one considers the Miltonic analogues to the Frankenstein story.[3] As the creator of a man, Frankenstein plays the role of God. But Frankenstein also compares himself to Satan: "All my speculations and hopes are as nothing, and like the archangel who aspired to omnipotence, I am chained in an eternal hell" (200). The narrator Walton describes Frankenstein in terms that clearly recall the fallen Lucifer of *Paradise Lost*: "What a glorious creature must he have been in the days of his prosperity, when he is thus noble and godlike in ruin! He seems to feel his own worth and the greatness of his fall" (200).

The monster similarly compares himself to two Miltonic roles. He is both Adam and Satan, as he tells his creator: "Remember that I am thy creature; I ought to be thy Adam, but I am rather the fallen angel, whom thou drivest from joy for no misdeed" (95). Later, while reflecting on his reading of *Paradise Lost*, the monster develops this idea:

I often referred the several situations, as their similarity struck me, to my own. Like Adam, I was apparently united by no link to any other being in existence; but his state was far different from mine in every other respect. He had come forth from the hands of God a perfect creature, happy and prosperous, guarded by the especial care of his Creator; ... but I was wretched, helpless, and alone. Many times I considered Satan as the fitter emblem of my condition, for often, like him, when I viewed the bliss of my protectors, the bitter gall of envy rose within me. (124)

The Nightmare of Romantic Idealism

The apparent difficulty in aligning the characters of *Frankenstein* with their Miltonic archetypes is that the two main characters, Frankenstein and the monster, must be correlated with three figures from *Paradise Lost*: God, Satan, and Adam. In reducing three characters to two, Mary Shelley has in effect eliminated the middle term, taking some elements from the role of Satan and giving them to her god-figure, Frankenstein, and taking other elements from Satan and giving them to her Adam-figure, the monster. The result is to make both characters in her story, both creator and creature, in some sense Satanic. Satan's role in the traditional story is to take all of the blame for the evil in the world away from God and some of the blame away from man. In Milton's account, God intended the world to be perfectly good; only Satan's willfulness perverted the creator's plan. And although man is responsible for his fall, he was in a sense the victim of a clever enemy's machinations. The third term in Milton's story allows him to grant a greater purity of intention and motive to both his creator and his creature.

Without a separate Satan-figure to mediate between her creator and creature, Mary Shelley gives a gnostic twist to her creation myth: in her version the creation becomes identified with the fall. Frankenstein does God's work, creating a man, but he has the devil's motives: pride and the will to power. He is himself a rebel, rejecting divine prohibitions and, like Satan, aspiring to become a god himself. But Victor's act of rebellion is to create a man, and what he seeks out of creation is the glory of ruling over a new race of beings. Mary Shelley thus achieves a daring compression of Milton's story. *Frankenstein* retells *Paradise Lost* as if the being who fell from heaven and the being who created the world of man were one and the same. In *Frankenstein* one can no longer speak of an original divine plan of creation which is perverted by a demonic being; the plans of Mary Shelley's creator-figure are both divine and demonic from the beginning.

If the creator's motives in *Frankenstein* are suspect, one might at first suppose that the rebellion of his creature must be unequivocally good. One could in fact attempt a straightforward gnostic reading of *Frankenstein*.[4] The story suggests that the original creation of man was defective; therefore man owes nothing to his creator; his wisest course is then to rebel against what he has always been told is the divine order. But in *Frankenstein* our sympathies are not this simply allied with the creature against his creator. The creature's rebellion does not lead to liberation. On the contrary, it results in the creator and creature becoming locked in a life-and-death struggle that eventually destroys them both. Rebelling against Frankenstein's tyranny, the monster threatens to become a tyrant himself, seeking to turn the tables on his master, to the point where Frankenstein actually speaks of "the whole period during which I was the slave of my creature" (146). Thus although the monster has something of Adam's innocence, he is also impelled to his rebellion by Satan's motives: envy and the thirst for revenge. The monster carries his tempting serpent within his own breast. Instead of being passively seduced into rebellion like Adam, he actively pursues rebellion like Satan.

The mythic ambiguity of the central figures in *Frankenstein* points to an underlying moral ambiguity. What is characteristic of Mary Shelley's creation account is that neither her creator in his creation nor her creature in his rebellion have morally pure motives. In this respect, her myth contrasts sharply with that of her husband in *Prometheus Unbound*. Percy Shelley rejected the figure of Satan as a poetic paradigm precisely because of the moral ambiguity of his nature. In explaining in his preface why his Prometheus is a fitter subject for a poem than Satan, Shelley suggests that Satan has both good and bad sides. He has "courage," "majesty," and "firm and patient opposition to omnipotent force," but he also is moved by "ambition, envy, revenge, and a desire for personal aggrandisement" (R & P, 133). In creating his own myth, Shelley as we have seen divided up these qualities between his Prometheus and his Jupiter, keeping the one wholly pure in his motives and the other thoroughly corrupt and ripe for overthrow. Even Shelley realized that it would take a struggle for Prometheus to overcome his desire for revenge and become purely good. But Mary Shelley displays a deeper sense of the complexity of human nature. She was unwilling to divide up the character of Satan in the same way, parcelling out all his good qualities to the rebellious monster and leaving the creator-god, Frankenstein, with all the bad. She maintains the same moral ambiguity in both characters, and in virtually the same proportions.[5]

In *Frankenstein*, the creature is truly made in the image of his creator: Frankenstein and the monster are mirror images of each other. As many readers have sensed, they are the same being, viewed in different aspects, as creator and as creature.[6] As creator this being feels an exhilarating sense of power, an ability to transgress all the limits traditionally set to man and realize his desires and dreams. But as creature, this being feels his impotence, feels himself alone in a world that fails to provide for him or care for him, a world in which he is doomed to wander without companions to a solitary death. It is important to realize that both Frankenstein and the monster experience both these sets of feelings. It might at first seem logical for one to feel like the creator and the other to feel like the creature. But the book does not fall into that simple pattern. Although Victor obviously has his moments of triumph and the monster his moments of despair, the two characters reverse their roles as the book proceeds, until it becomes difficult to tell one's voice from the other's. Consider the following passage:

> I abhorred the face of man. Oh, not abhorred! They were my brethren, my fellow beings, and I felt attracted even to the most repulsive among them, as to creatures of an angelic nature and celestial mechanism. But I felt I had no right to share their intercourse ... How they would, each and all, abhor me and hunt me from the world did they know my unhallowed acts and the crimes which had their source in me! (176)

Reading this passage out of context, one would guess it was the monster speaking, but it is actually Frankenstein. Victor at times feels cut off from all mankind, denied human sympathies as if he himself were the monster: "I walked about the isle like a restless spectre, separated from all it loved and miserable in its separation" (162).

By the same token, the monster has moments when he glories in his strength, when he even feels himself more powerful than his creator:

> Slave, I before reasoned with you, but you have proved yourself unworthy of my condescension. Remember that I have power; you believe yourself miserable, but I can make you so wretched that the light of day will be hateful to you. You are my creator, but I am your master; obey! (160)

When the monster murders Victor's younger brother, he triumphantly proclaims his own creativity:

> I gazed on my victim, and my heart swelled with exultation and hellish triumph; clapping my hands, I exclaimed "I too can create desolation; my enemy is not invulnerable; this death will carry despair to him, and a thousand other miseries shall torment and destroy him." (136)

The statement "I too can create desolation" reveals the heart of the monster's tragedy. He can imitate his creator only in creating suffering and misery.

Both Frankenstein and the monster experience feelings of triumph and despair; each has his "creative" and his "creaturely" moments, though obviously Frankenstein emphasizes the creative side of man, and the monster the creaturely. *Frankenstein* deals with the tension in human existence basic to the Romantic understanding of man, the tension between man's visionary powers as a creator and his spiritual limits as a creature. The alternation between feelings of power and impotence is in fact characteristic of nothing so much as the Romantic poets themselves. Consider the case of Percy Shelley: as a poetic visionary he thinks that his power to remake the world is unlimited, culminating in his triumphant claim in *A Defence of Poetry* that "poets are the unacknowledged legislators of the World" (R & P, 508). But Shelley also has a debilitating sense of himself as a creature, his creative spark trapped in the "loathsome mask" of the flesh (*Prometheus Unbound*, III.iv.193). One need not claim that Mary Shelley was trying specifically to give a portrait of her husband in *Frankenstein*, although there is evidence that her personal experiences did play a role in the genesis of the book.[7] In any case, in seeking to portray a creator Mary Shelley could not help being influenced by her most direct experience of what creative spirits are like, and that means her observations of her husband (and Byron as well). As a result, by whatever process of imaginative recreation, she has captured in the composite figure of Frankenstein and the monster the complex duality of the Romantic soul, the dark as well as the bright side, the violent as well as the benevolent impulses, the destructive as well as the creative urges. On the one hand, she portrays the sympathetic reaching out to other human beings; on the other hand, a merciless and brutal turning in upon the self, a willful sundering of all bonds that tie a man to the rest of humanity. *Frankenstein* is not simply an example of Romantic myth; it is also on the deepest level of interpretation a myth about Romanticism, a mythic dramatization of the dangers of an unbridled idealism.

At first sight, *Frankenstein* seems to provide a clear case of a Romantic creation myth, since its explicit theme is remaking man. The scientist becomes a metaphor for the poet[8] – Frankenstein's physical attempt to reconstruct the human frame serves as an image for the goal of Romantic artists: the spiritual regeneration of man. But somehow, put into practice, this process fails to have the glorious results it was supposed to have. The creation itself is portrayed as a filthy and disgusting process, and the creator is revealed to be seized by a will to power. Originally the creation myth served Romantic artists as a vehicle for criticizing the established order, for exposing the corrupt foundations of religious and political authority. But Mary Shelley seems to have turned the creation myth back upon Romanticism, making Romantic creativity itself, in all its problematic character, her subject. Although certain revolutionary elements can be found in *Frankenstein*, the work seems basically conservative in its implications. Human creativity appears to be dangerous in *Frankenstein*, because it is unpredictable and uncontrollable in its results. *Frankenstein* remains what it was when the idea for it first came to Mary Shelley: a nightmare, the nightmare of Romantic idealism, revealing the dark underside to all the visionary dreams of remaking man that fired the imagination of Romantic myth-makers.[9] If one wonders why of all Romantic myths it is the Frankenstein story that has caught on with the popular imagination, perhaps the reason is that the understanding of creativity embodied in *Frankenstein* is close to the common sense understanding: while creativity can be exhilarating, it can also be dangerous, and passes over easily into destructiveness.

II

Given the link between creator and creature in *Frankenstein*, discussions of Frankenstein as a character and of the monster as a character tend to shade into each other, that is, one can approach either character through analyzing the other. In studying Frankenstein, one readily sees how the monster can be regarded as an extension of his creator, in a sense as a projection of Frankenstein's psyche. The more difficult task is to show in analyzing the monster's character how in a strange sense Frankenstein can be regarded as a projection of the creature's psyche.

The key to understanding Frankenstein's character can be found in the detailed portrait of his childhood Mary Shelley creates. Victor himself sees a connection between his idealistic pursuit of science and his childhood aggressiveness: "My temper was sometimes violent, and my passions vehement; but by some law in my temperature they were turned not towards childish pursuits but to an eager desire to learn" (37). Given the eventual results of

Frankenstein's experiments, we should not be surprised to hear that his interest in science was originally a sublimation of his violent impulses.[10] But the most important fact we learn about Frankenstein's youth is his attitude toward Elizabeth, the little orphan girl his family takes in. Here Mary Shelley introduces a displaced incest motif, a familiar device in Romantic fiction.[11] Victor calls Elizabeth his "more than sister" (35), and indeed their relationship has all the potential for incest except the blood tie.[12] They grow up in the same household, share the same childhood experiences, and have a secret bond of sympathy, much as do Catherine and Heathcliff in *Wuthering Heights*. Even when presented in displaced form, an incestuous relationship involves an inward-turning of energies, a refusal to leave the self-contained world of childhood desires and dreams, that is the central impulse in Frankenstein's life.[13]

The other trait that Victor's attitude toward Elizabeth reveals is his possessiveness. Elizabeth is introduced to him as a present, and he persists in regarding her that way, as something given to him to hold on to as his private possession:

On the evening previous to her being brought to my house, my mother had said playfully, "I have a pretty present for my Victor – tomorrow he shall have it." And when, on the morrow, she presented Elizabeth to me as her promised gift, I, with childish seriousness, interpreted her words literally and looked upon Elizabeth as mine – mine to protect, love, and cherish. All praises bestowed on her I received as made to a possession of my own. We called each other familiarly by the name of cousin. No word, no expression could body forth the kind of relation in which she stood to me – my more than sister, since till death she was to be mine only. (35)

This possessiveness turns out to be the root of Frankenstein's activity as a creator. He creates a being because he wants someone to worship him with complete devotion: "A new species would bless me as its creator and source; many happy and excellent natures would owe their being to me. No father could claim the gratitude of his child so completely as I should deserve theirs" (52). Victor views his experiment as a way of becoming a father, obviously an alternative to becoming a father in the ordinary sense in view of the way the experiment poisons his relationship to Elizabeth. The irony of Frankenstein's story is that he is obsessed with the idea of creating human life, and yet seems to do everything in his power to avoid creating life in the easiest fashion. As Robert Kiely writes of *Frankenstein*:

Stripped of rhetoric and ideological decoration, the situation presented is that of a handsome young scientist, engaged to a beautiful woman, who goes off to the mountains alone to create a new human life. When he confesses to Walton that he has "worked hard for nearly two years" to achieve his aim, we may wonder why he does not marry Elizabeth, and, with her cooperation, finish the job more quickly and pleasurably.[14]

Victor's hope for his creations — "no father could claim the gratitude of his child so completely as I should deserve theirs" — shows why he rejects the conventional role of a parent. A father must share the gratitude of his children with their mother. As a true Romantic creator, Victor wants total responsibility — and total credit — for any of his creations. In the image of Victor Frankenstein going to any lengths to avoid being indebted to nature, Mary Shelley's myth embodies a profound understanding of the character of modern creativity. Frankenstein rejects a natural means of creativity, fatherhood, which would prevent him from calling his creation wholly his own, in favor of an artificial means of creativity, which allows him to regard his creation as solely a projection of his self. But to produce a creature with its origin in his self and his self alone, Frankenstein must draw upon every resource within his self. He ends up cannibalizing his life for the sake of his experiment, sacrificing all his everyday human concerns to his single-minded aim of creating a living being:

I pursued my undertaking with unremitting ardour. My cheek had grown pale with study, and my person had become emaciated with confinement ... My eyes were insensible to the charms of nature. And the same feelings which made me neglect the scenes around me caused me also to forget those friends who were so many miles absent, and whom I had not seen for so long a time ... I wished, as it were, to procrastinate all that related to my feelings of affection until the great object, which swallowed up every habit of my nature, should be completed. (53–54)

In psychological terms, Frankenstein is a classic case of sublimation; he uses the energy he derives from repressing his normal feelings, especially his sexual desires, to fuel his intellectual and scientific pursuits.[15] Victor's loneliness and isolation is thus not accidental to his creativity. He must cut himself off from the rest of humanity to achieve his goals, and his goals require that he do everything alone.

Frankenstein's urge to create life by himself shows his titanism, his longing to do something never before attempted by man. But it also suggests a less heroic side to his character, a fear of growing up, a hesitation at taking his place in the world of adult responsibility.

That this fear is in part sexual in nature is shown by the fact that Frankenstein's anxieties eventually come to focus on his wedding night. Though on the literal level of plot, the monster's threats concerning this night give Victor sufficient cause to be afraid, certain details of the narrative make one wonder what exactly is the "dreadful secret" (183) Frankenstein is worried about revealing to his innocent bride. The description of Frankenstein on his wedding night suggests an immature and nervous bridegroom, looking for anything to divert him from consummating his marriage. When Victor speaks of the struggle he anticipates, though he clearly has the monster in mind as his adversary, he is inadvertently revealing the subconscious, childish fears that have long delayed his union with Elizabeth, whom he in some sense regards as his real enemy:

> I had been calm during the day, but so soon as night obscured the shapes of objects, a thousand fears arose in my mind. I was anxious and watchful, while my right hand grasped a pistol which was hidden in my bosom; every sound terrified me, but I resolved that I would sell my life dearly and not shrink from the conflict until my own life or that of my adversary was extinguished.
>
> Elizabeth observed my agitation for some time in timid and fearful silence, but there was something in my glance which communicated terror to her, and trembling, she asked, "What is it that agitates you, my dear Victor? What is it you fear?"
>
> "Oh! Peace, peace, my love," replied I, "this night, and all will be safe; but this night is dreadful, very dreadful."
>
> I passed an hour in this state of mind, when suddenly I reflected how fearful the combat which I momentarily expected would be to my wife, and I earnestly entreated her to retire, resolving not to join her until I had obtained some knowledge as to the situation of my enemy. (185–86)

Noting "the language of anxiety, phallic inference, and imagery of conflict," Kiely writes of this passage: "the immediate situation and the ambiguity of the language contribute to the impression that the young groom's dread of the monster is mixed with his fear of sexual union as a physical struggle which poses a threat to his independence, integrity, and delicacy of character."[16] When Frankenstein's monster succeeds in turning his bridal bed into a "bridal bier" (186), one might read the episode in psychological terms as indicating that Frankenstein's marriage is destroyed by his fear that sexuality is something monstrous, a force that turns men and women into something other than human beings.

But Frankenstein's fear of getting married and having a family like any ordinary man is not simply sexual. He regards family life as dull and conventional, potentially stifling to his creativity. When he reflects upon his father's career, he sees a disjunction between the path of glory and the path of raising a family:

My father had filled several public situations with honour and reputation ... He passed his younger days perpetually occupied by the affairs of his country; a variety of circumstances had prevented him from marrying early, nor was it until the decline of life that he became a husband and the father of a family. (31)

The 1818 edition of *Frankenstein* contains a further suggestion that Victor has reason to fear that a family will limit his creativity: "When my father became a husband and a parent, he found his time so occupied by the duties of his new situation, that he relinquished his public employments, and devoted himself to the education of his children."[17] Victor reveals another defect of becoming a father in the conventional way: it carries a sense of responsibility to one's children, to care for them and raise them properly. Victor does not want to be burdened by such time-consuming ties to other human beings. He was spoiled as a child, and as he grows older he does not want to relinquish the situation of having everything go his way, without his having to make any concessions to the needs of others. He says of his childhood:

My mother's tender caresses and my father's smile of benevolent pleasure while regarding me are my first recollections. I was their plaything and their idol, and something better – their child, the innocent and helpless creature bestowed on them by heaven, whom to bring up to good, and whose future lot it was in their hands to direct to happiness or misery, according as they fulfilled their duties towards me. (33)

When Frankenstein comes to be a father in his special way, he conveniently forgets these duties of parents to their offspring. The one quality he most conspicuously lacks as a creator is the quality he most praises his own parents for: "the deep consciousness of what they owed towards the being to which they had given life" (33). What ultimately turns Frankenstein's creation into the improvident, even bungled work of a gnostic demiurge is the fact that from the start he seeks out this form of creativity precisely as a way of escaping the responsibilities of ordinary parenthood.

From one point of view, Frankenstein appears as a Faustian figure, daring to undertake a superhuman task; from another, he seems like a little boy, hoping to prolong forever the situation of his childhood, in which he can live within the private world of his own fantasies, unburdened by the duties of adult life. In particular, he seems to fear the entanglements of mature sexuality, and one senses that his experiment has in part the purpose of finding a way for him to reproduce without his own body having to become directly involved in the process. Frankenstein wishes that human beings could create life with their minds alone. He is most fundamentally a Romantic in his faith in the power of the imagination to shape a world in accord with man's dreams and visions, although ironically his attempt to realize his dreams only draws him deeper and deeper into contact with the corrupt material world he is seeking to avoid. In the end, one cannot distinguish the heroic from the childish side of Frankenstein. All his strengths and weaknesses are bound up with his refusal to accept an adult role in life. By clinging to his childhood dreams, he retains a power of vision that lifts his imagination above that of ordinary men, and gives him the power to create. But at the same time, he is thoroughly irresponsible in his creativity and lacks the courage to face up to the consequences of his deeds.

Like many Romantic works, *Frankenstein* suggests a link between the creator and the child. But Mary Shelley portrays this relation much more equivocally than most Romantics do, for she senses the childish, as well as the childlike, aspects to Frankenstein's "innocence." What from one angle appears as a visionary refusal to rest content with the way things are and always have been, from another angle appears as an immature unwillingness to come to terms with the facts of the human condition. At the core of Frankenstein's scientific enterprise is a partly heroic, partly childish, refusal to accept the fact of death. Victor's departure for the University of Ingolstadt, where his researches begin, is immediately preceded by the death of his mother. His reaction to this event perhaps supplies the deepest motive for his experiments:

I need not describe the feelings of those whose dearest ties are rent by that most irreparable evil, the void that presents itself to the soul, and the despair that is exhibited on the countenance. It is so long before the mind can persuade itself that she whom we saw every day and whose very existence appeared a part of our own can have departed forever . . . The time at length arrives when grief is rather an indulgence than a necessity . . . My mother was dead, but we had still duties which we ought to perform. (43)

For once Victor speaks with the sober voice of experience. But beneath his adult reflections on the need to accept death and carry on with the day-to-day business of life, one can hear the accents of his uncompromising idealism, his hope that the mind could somehow triumph over the brute fact of death. That becomes the goal of his scientific experiments:

Life and death appeared to me ideal bounds, which I should first break through, and pour a torrent of light into our dark world ... I thought that if I could bestow animation upon lifeless matter, I might in process of time ... renew life where death had apparently devoted the body to corruption. (52–53)

If to be a Romantic is to deny the limits on human creative power, then Frankenstein's project becomes the ultimate test of Romantic vision. With the eagerness, the confidence, and the willfulness of a child, he sets out to challenge the one seemingly indisputable fact of man's nature, his mortality.

III

Frankenstein's activity as a creator presents such a mixture of idealistic and self-serving motives that evaluating it in moral terms becomes difficult. But whatever Frankenstein's intentions may be, he clearly does not plan his creation with the interests of his creature in mind. He is too concerned about his own glory to take the safer, surer course in creation:

I doubted at first whether I should attempt the creation of a being like myself, or one of simpler organization; but my imagination was too much exalted by my first success to permit me to doubt of my ability to give life to an animal as complex and wonderful as man. (52)

Frankenstein's talk of his "exalted imagination" makes one think of a poet, and indeed he thinks he can become a poet of material reality, immediately embodying his most ideal visions in physical form. The narrator Walton, who admits to being a failed poet himself (16), displays the same fault as Frankenstein: "I am too ardent in execution and too impatient of difficulties" (18). In his haste and lack of attention to details, Frankenstein adopts a course guaranteed to satisfy his eagerness but at the same time to make his creature miserable:

The materials at present within my command hardly appeared adequate to so arduous an undertaking, but I doubted not that I should ultimately succeed ... Nor could I consider the magnitude and complexity of my plan as any argument of its impracticability ... As the minuteness of the parts formed a great hindrance to my speed, I resolved, contrary to my first intention, to make the being of a gigantic stature, that is to say, about eight feet in height, and proportionably large. (52)

Frankenstein casually revises his plans at the last moment, solely to make things easier for himself, without the slightest thought of how this "gigantic stature" will affect his creature's life. His idealistic unwillingness to compromise with the limits of human nature evidently passes over easily into total disregard for practical considerations of the physical needs of man.

As a result, Mary Shelley's myth takes us back to the world of the demonic creator. Frankenstein resembles a gnostic demiurge, struggling to infuse the spark of life into dead matter:

In a solitary chamber, or rather cell, at the top of my home, and separated from all the other apartments by a gallery and staircase, I kept my workshop of filthy creation; my eyeballs were starting from their sockets in attending to the details of my employment. The dissecting room and the slaughterhouse furnished many of my materials; and often did my human nature turn with loathing from my occupation. (53)

From the way Frankenstein secludes himself, one begins to suspect that he is ashamed of what he is doing. By his own admission, Frankenstein's creation is a "filthy" process, and he dwells upon its disgusting physical aspects. He is clearly not the benevolent, all-powerful creator of Genesis, who could stand back from his creative activity and see that it was good. On the contrary, Frankenstein has to struggle with his materials and with himself to go on with the creation, and the whole process makes him ill.

It comes as no surprise, then, that Frankenstein is repulsed by the end-product of his creativity:

His limbs were in proportion, and I had selected his features as beautiful. Beautiful! Great God! His yellow skin scarcely covered the work of muscles and arteries beneath; his hair was of a lustrous black, and flowing; his teeth of a pearly whiteness; but these luxuriances only formed a more horrid contrast with his watery eyes, that seemed almost of the same colour as the dun-white sockets in which they were set, his shrivelled complexion and straight black lips ... Now that I had finished, the beauty of the dream vanished, and breathless horror and disgust filled my heart. (56)

Mary Shelley provides a nightmarish counterpart to her husband's experience as a poet of the gap between inspiration and composition: "When composition begins, inspiration is already on the decline, and the most glorious poetry that has ever been communicated to the world is probably a feeble shadow of the original conceptions of the poet" (R & P, 504). Frankenstein beholding his creature is like a Shelleyan poet, disgusted by the fixed form into which his imaginative inspiration has sunk.[18] The corrupting medium of human flesh has distorted Frankenstein's creation into a grotesque mockery of his original vision. When forced to confront his creation later, Frankenstein rejects him completely. Having created for the sake of his own glory, Frankenstein is ready to take out his frustrations on his creature for not living up to his expectations. His first thought is to destroy the evidence of his own limitations and failings as a creator, not to try to make up for the defects of his creation.

But the monster survives and as a result, Frankenstein's will to power does not stop with the act of creation. The monster becomes Frankenstein's *Doppelgänger,* his double or shadow, acting out the deepest, darkest urges of his soul, his aggressive impulses, and working to murder one by one everybody close to his creator.[19] As we have seen, Frankenstein thinks that his violent side has been harmlessly sublimated into his scientific pursuits. But the result of his experiments is to set free the aggressive emotions his conscious mind refuses to acknowledge. In particular, Victor's possessiveness as a lover ultimately requires the death of his beloved, for only death can turn her into an object instead of an independent human being, and thus into something he can call his own. Immediately after creating the monster, Victor dreams of Elizabeth's death:

I thought I saw Elizabeth in the bloom of health, walking in the streets of Ingolstadt. Delighted and surprised, I embraced her, but as I imprinted the first kiss on her lips, they became livid with the hue of death; her features appeared to change, and I thought that I held the corpse of my dead mother in my arms; a shroud enveloped her form, and I saw the grave-worms crawling in the folds of the flannel. (57)

In addition to vividly expressing Victor's Oedipal longings, this dream shows that he somehow associates Elizabeth with the death of his mother.[20] His mother contracted her fatal illness while taking care of Elizabeth and died instructing her: "Elizabeth, my love, you must supply my place to my younger children" (42). Perhaps Victor does not believe that Elizabeth has adequately supplied the place of the woman she "killed," and harbors repressed anger against her that can reach the surface of his mind only in the distorted form of a dream, in which Elizabeth dies and then is replaced by Victor's mother, thus reversing and righting her original "crime." Finally, the dream reveals how closely linked the ideas of love and death are in Frankenstein's mind. In his subconscious, the kiss of love is ultimately the kiss of death, and one can possess one's beloved only in a shroud.

The timing of Victor's dream – his passing out at this point results in setting the monster loose – suggests that the monster is the agent for bringing about Frankenstein's equation of love and death. He himself sees that the monster serves his own destructive urges:

I considered the being whom I had cast among mankind and endowed with the will and power to effect purposes of horror, such as the deed which he had now done, nearly in the light of my own vampire, my own spirit let loose from the grave and forced to destroy all that was dear to me. (74)

Accordingly, Frankenstein seems to know intuitively what the monster has done, even before he receives confirmation of the facts: "Could he be (I shuddered at the conception) the murderer of my brother? No sooner did that idea cross my imagination than I became convinced of its truth" (73). Frankenstein even seems able to anticipate the monster's intentions:

Sometimes I thought that the fiend followed me and might expedite my remissions by murdering my companion. When these thoughts possessed me, I would not quit Henry for a moment, but followed him as his shadow, to protect him from the fancied rage of his destroyer. (155)

Frankenstein knows the monster's intentions because deep down they are his own. Something in Frankenstein wants to kill anyone who comes close to him so that he can maintain his willful isolation. Once the monster has succeeded in cutting Victor off from all the ties that bind him to the rest of humanity, only one task remains: to see that Frankenstein himself is destroyed. From the beginning, Victor's aggressive impulses have the potential of being directed inward. If the monster is truly his double, then Frankenstein's destructiveness is finally revealed to have been self-destructiveness.[21]

As we have seen, from the start Frankenstein's experiments serve the purpose of avoiding marriage and banishing him from the ranks of ordinary mankind. His idealism provides him with a noble-sounding excuse for not facing up to his immediate responsibilities. Frankenstein is characterized by a kind of abstract benevolence. He is willing to see himself and anyone else he knows suffer in the name of a visionary dream of aiding mankind as a whole. We see how his mind operates when he rejects the idea of creating a mate for the monster, despite the threat to his loved ones:

A race of devils would be propagated upon the earth who might make the very existence of the species of man a condition precarious and full of terror. Had I right, for my own benefit, to inflict this curse upon everlasting generations? ... I shuddered to think that future ages might curse me as their pest, whose selfishness had not hesitated to buy its own peace at the price, perhaps, of the existence of the whole human race. (158–59)

Later Victor tells his father of the monster's victims: "A thousand times would I have shed my own blood, drop by drop, to have saved their lives; but I could not, my father, indeed I could not sacrifice the whole human race" (177). Frankenstein may well be correct in his assessment of the dangers of allowing a race of monsters to propagate, and his self-sacrifice in acting to prevent that outcome is noble. Nevertheless, it is significant how quickly his mind moves from the immediate and concrete threat against his friends and family to the more remote and vaguer threat against humanity in general. Frankenstein readily leaps from his specific situation to visions of distant lands and future ages, and he shows the reformer's mentality in his willingness to sacrifice individual men and women for the sake of mankind. As he himself senses, there is even something of the religious zealot in his character:

I trembled with excess of agitation as I said this; there was a frenzy in my manner, and something, I doubt not, of that haughty fierceness which the martyrs of old are said to have possessed. But to a German magistrate, whose mind was occupied by far other ideas than those of devotion and heroism, this elevation of mind had much the appearance of madness. He endeavored to soothe me as a nurse does a child and reverted to my tale as the effects of delirium. (191)

In its equation of religious martyrdom with madness, and of heroism and elevation of mind with the delusions of a child, this passage sums up the complex character of Frankenstein, who forever presents two sides to us, no matter how we look at him.

IV

As fruitful as it is to study the monster as an extension of his creator, one cannot fully appreciate the significance of the character until one studies his story from his point of view. In portraying the monster, Mary Shelley, whether directly or indirectly, drew upon Rousseau's conception of natural man.[22] Thus at the same time as *Frankenstein* involves a retelling of *Paradise Lost*, it also undertakes an imaginative recreation of the *Second Discourse*, blending Milton and Rousseau just as the poetic creation myths we have studied do.

One could undertake a fairly simple interpretation of the monster's story in Rousseauian terms. The monster as originally created corresponds to natural man; his fall is his fatal attraction to civil society; and his attempt to join the ranks of social men leads to his misery. The story would then show how civilization corrupts an essentially benevolent being into a demon. Society is shown as being based on the will to power, and therefore rejects the outward-turning sympathies of natural man. The civilized world brutalizes the monster, awakening his lust to dominate by thwarting his impulse to love.[23] One can almost hear the voice of the monster in Rousseau's comment on himself in the *Reveries*:

If I had remained free, obscure, and isolated as I was made to be, I would have done only good; for I do not have the seed of any harmful passion in my heart. If I had been invisible and all-powerful like God, I would have been beneficent and good like Him. (R, 82)

The fact that the representative of natural man in *Frankenstein* appears as monstrous to those he meets could be a telling commentary on a society that has lost touch with its origins and thus lost its ability to distinguish true humanity from the veneer of civilization.

One can find elements of social commentary in *Frankenstein*, and one should not neglect the ways in which the novel is a plea for social justice and benevolence among men. The story exposes the decadence and corruption of sophisticated society, while portraying the virtues and benefits of a simple life. This dimension of the novel is particularly evident in the long De Lacey episode, which contrasts the injustice of the French monarchy with the rustic simplicity and harmony of the Swiss republic, thus moving between the two poles of Rousseau's life and thought: Paris and Geneva. But a straightforward social–political reading of *Frankenstein* is ultimately inadequate. To be sure, on one level Mary Shelley is saying that a little more kindness and understanding in the world would improve the lot of man. But she senses a profounder tension in human existence than mere social conflicts. Thus her novel is truer than most Romantic works to the complexities of Rousseau's thought. Like the *Second Discourse*, *Frankenstein* is a story of a being's fall from an original unity with nature into a state of painful separation. But, also like the *Second Discourse*, *Frankenstein* does not offer a way to overcome this separation. In Mary Shelley's myth, isolation from nature seems to be the permanent price man pays for his consciousness and his creativity. The monster moves through the first two stages of the Romantic dialectic, but never achieves any third or higher stage which would allow him to transcend the contradictions of his existence.

Like Rousseau's natural man, the monster begins his life in a solitary state, living in the woods by himself with only accidental contact with other beings. This solitariness gives him the freedom of Rousseau's natural man: "I was dependent on none and related to none" (123). His life is uncomplicated by social relations, and also uncomplicated by the sophisticated and decadent wants men acquire in the process of civilization as Rousseau portrays it. At first the monster need only fulfill his basic animal desires, which he finds simple enough to do, since he is not attached to any given locale and can move on whenever he runs out of food:

Food, however, became scarce, and I often spent the whole day searching in vain for a few acorns to assuage the pangs of hunger. When I found this, I resolved to quit the place that I had hitherto inhabited, to seek for one where the few wants I experienced could be more easily satisfied. (100)

In accord with Rousseau's speculation that natural man did not eat meat,[24] the monster is a vegetarian: "My food is not that of man; I do not destroy the lamb and kid to glut my appetite; acorns and berries afford me sufficient nourishment" (139). With his simple diet and easily satisfied wants, the monster begins life in animal contentment. Like Rousseau, he at times longs for this original state: "Oh, that I had forever remained in my native wood, nor known nor felt beyond the sensations of hunger, thirst, and heat!" (115).

But the monster's innocent state has its limitations, even if he eventually comes to regret having left it. Again like Rousseau's natural man, he originally lacks speech or fully developed powers of reasoning. The world presents itself to him right after his creation as a mass of undifferentiated sensations, which he only gradually learns to distinguish:

A strange multiplicity of sensations seized me, and I saw, felt, heard, and smelt at the same time; and it was, indeed, a long time before I learned to distinguish between the operations of my various senses ... No distinct ideas occupied my mind; all was confused. I felt light, and hunger, and thirst, and on all sides various scents saluted me ... Sometimes I wished to express my sensations in my own mode, but the uncouth and inarticulate sounds which broke from me frightened me into silence again ... My eyes became accustomed to the light and to perceive objects in their right forms; I distinguished the insect from the herb, and by degrees, one herb from another. (98–99)

This account of the development of the monster's consciousness resembles Rousseau's speculations on the origins of speech and reasoning, particularly in the characterization of the monster's mental growth as a process of learning to differentiate an originally unarticulated whole (SD, 123). The monster's mental progress is, however, considerably faster than that of Rousseau's natural man, largely because he is able to acquire language from already civilized men.

But the monster's reaction to his education is much like Caliban's to his teacher Prospero: "You taught me language, and my profit on't / Is, I know how to curse" (*The Tempest*, I.ii.363–64). The monster's loss of innocence and growing experience of the world only make him progressively more miserable: "sorrow only increased with knowledge" (115). At times he longs to reject his learning and return to his original state of virtual unconsciousness: "Of what a strange nature is knowledge! It clings to the mind when it has once seized on it like a lichen on the rock. I wished sometimes to shake off all thought and feeling" (115). Frankenstein expresses the same sentiments in a passage that reads like pure Rousseau:

Alas! Why does man boast of sensibilities superior to those apparent in the brute; it only renders them more necessary beings. If our impulses were confined to hunger, thirst, and desire, we might be nearly free; but now we are moved by every wind that blows and a chance word or scene that that word may convey to us. (93)

In *Frankenstein* both creature and creator end up seeking freedom from the burden of consciousness. But in the bleak world of Mary Shelley's myth, no way to achieve this freedom can be found, no means of combining the happiness and unity of man's original state with the consciousness and developed power of his civilized state.

Thus the monster has a tragic vision of the direction in which his story is headed: "I learned that there was but one means to overcome the sensation of pain, and that was death" (115). In the absence of a means of retaining the gains of experience while recapturing man's lost innocence, death becomes desirable as the only way of annihilating the painful divisions of consciousness. The monster's story culminates in the promise of an apocalyptic moment of death, which, in its symbolism of a funeral pyre and drowning waters, is reminiscent of the climax of Wagner's *Götterdämmerung*:

I shall die, and what I now feel be no longer felt. Soon these burning miseries will be extinct. I shall mount my funeral pile triumphantly and exult in the agony of the torturing flames. The light of that conflagration will fade away; my ashes will be swept into the sea by the winds. My spirit will sleep in peace, or if it thinks, it will not surely think thus. (211)

The monster's Immolation scene centers on a common Romantic image for consciousness: a fire rapidly consuming itself which gives off blinding light but eventually burns itself out.[25] The monster expects his ashes to be swept out to sea, where, dissolving into the primeval waters, he can at last be reunited with nature. Death conceived as physical dissolution becomes a way of recapturing the primal unity man lost when he first departed from his natural state. This motif of undoing the fall by means of a catastrophic dissolution into nature is the mythic equivalent of the more familiar Romantic notion of the healing powers of nature. Frankenstein knows that when he is feeling depressed, he ought to seek out sublime scenery:

Sometimes the whirlwind passions of my soul drove me to seek, by bodily exercise and by change of place, some relief from my intolerable sensations. It was during an access of this kind that I suddenly left my home, and bending my steps towards the near Alpine valleys, sought in the magnificence, the eternity of such scenes, to forget myself and my ephemeral, because human, sorrows. (89–90)

Achieving some form of unity with nature helps Victor overcome the divisions within his own soul, until he is able to achieve a momentary peace and release from suffering: "The same lulling sounds acted as a lullaby to my too keen sensations; when I placed my head upon my pillow, sleep crept over me; I felt it as it came and blessed the giver of oblivion" (91). But sleep is only temporary, and like the monster, Frankenstein eventually can find relief from the intolerable pain of his consciousness only in death.

One interpretation of the original Prometheus myth is that it embodies man's awareness of the equivocal value of his consciousness.[26] According to this view, the spark Prometheus steals for man is the spark of consciousness. Prometheus awakens man from his animal ignorance, thereby making him conscious of the threatening aspects of his existence, above all, his mortality. *Frankenstein* is true to its central Prometheus archetype in suggesting that man's fall results from his attempt to rise above his animal nature, for in developing his specifically human potential, his creative powers, he brings a greater awareness of pain and suffering upon himself. Frankenstein expresses the feeling of being trapped within his own consciousness in a passage that suggests the image of Prometheus Bound: "For an instant I dared to shake off my chains and look around me with a free and lofty spirit, but the iron had eaten into my flesh, and I sank again, trembling and hopeless, into my miserable self" (153). Having sought to create solely out of his own self, Frankenstein succeeds in destroying everything he loves, everything that might threaten his independence, until he is left alone with only a creation of his own hands, an extension of his self. But under these circumstances, his self becomes a prison to him. Frankenstein banished with his creature to the Arctic waste-lands becomes an emblem of the dangerous solipsistic tendency inherent in the Romantic concept of the imagination.[27] If man creates the world through the power of his own consciousness, then man is threatened with having to exist alone in that world, or, worse, to be confronted only by an externalization of his own desires that horrifies him in its hideousness. To be the sole creator of one's world seems like a glorious prospect, until one realizes the consequences of seeing one's self mirrored everywhere one turns.

V

Is there any way out of the Romantic prison of the self? Paradoxi-cally the monster pursues a solution to this problem with a greater sense of urgency than his human creator does. Frankenstein usually expresses a longing for another human being only when that person has been placed out of reach by death. The monster by contrast truly desires a living companion. In depicting the monster's sympa-thetic reaching out for human beings, Mary Shelley draws upon another trait of natural man in Rousseau's view, his compassion (SD, 130–33). From the beginning, the monster experiences fellow feeling for all living creatures. He even applies Rousseau's formula for natural man to himself, claiming that he was naturally good until human society made him otherwise: "Everywhere I see bliss, from which I alone am irrevocably excluded. I was benevolent and good; misery made me a fiend. Make me happy, and I shall again be virtuous" (95–96). Longing for some form of love, the monster reaches out for any human being he sees, and of course his one request of his creator is to provide him with a mate. The monster exhibits all the natural sympathies Frankenstein had to repress in order to create him.

But there is a dark side to the monster's reaching out for sympathy. When he is rejected, he lashes back with fierce hatred, most often with murderous fury:

All, save I, were at rest or in enjoyment; I, like the arch-fiend, bore a hell within me, and finding myself unsympathized with, wished to tear up the trees, spread havoc and destruction around me, and then to have sat down and enjoyed the ruin. (130)

The monster has inherited a deep ambivalence of emotions from his creator: his love is never far from hate. He is most demonic – even quoting Milton's Satan – when he vents the sum of his frustrations in his final revenge upon his creator:

When I discovered that he, the author at once of my existence and of its unspeakable torments, dared to hope for happiness, that while he accumulated wretchedness and despair upon me he sought his own enjoyment in feelings and passions from the indulgence of which I was forever barred, then impotent envy and bitter indignation filled me with an insatiable thirst for vengeance ... Evil thenceforth became my good. (208–9)

The monster certainly has reasons for hating humanity, but in one sense he may be treating men as unfairly as they treat him. For all his fellow feeling, the monster is not sympathetic to others in one respect, for he fails to understand fully their difficulty in accepting him. They judge him by appearances, and his looks are hardly calculated to inspire warmth and affection.

This problem calls our attention to the one decisive respect in which the monster differs from natural man in Rousseau. Natural man is of course in the state of nature, that is, everybody around him is in more or less the same condition and thus nobody stands out. But the monster's state more closely resembles that of a natural man in the midst of civil society. One can compare his situation to that of the savages brought to Europe whom Rousseau discusses in the *Second Discourse*. His situation is even worse, since the people who meet the monster will not even acknowledge his common humanity. They all think that he is some form of beast, an inferior being. None of the characters in *Frankenstein* acknowledges the ways in which the monster is superior to them, the fact that he is physically stronger, can endure the elements better, can survive in places which would destroy them, and is all in all the more independent being.[28] The monster's tragedy is that he is forced to accept the civilized world's view of him as inferior, for he has no other standard to go by. Rousseau's savages can reject Europe and return to their own people, as the Frontispiece of the *Second Discourse* reminds us: "He goes back to his equals" (76). Possessing an independent standard for judging themselves, these savages can remain convinced of their own worth, no matter what the Europeans think of them. But having no equals and hence no standards of his own, the monster is forced to accept the opinion of the only beings he has ever known and they all think that he is hideously ugly. He must accept the same conclusion:

I had admired the perfect forms of my cottagers – their grace, beauty, and delicate complexions; but how was I terrified when I viewed myself in a transparent pool! At first I started back, unable to believe that it was indeed I who was reflected in the mirror; and when I became fully convinced that I was in reality the monster that I am, I was filled with the bitterest sensations of despondence and mortification. Alas! I did not yet entirely know the fatal effects of this miserable deformity. (108)

The reason the monster desperately desires a mate is to have someone who would deny his ugliness, if only because she shared it. In demanding a creature as "hideous" as himself, the monster clearly has this consideration in mind:

I am alone and miserable; man will not associate with me; but one as deformed and horrible as myself would not deny herself to me. My companion must be of the same species and have the same defects ... It is true, we shall be monsters, cut off from all the world; but on that account we shall be more attracted to one another. (137, 139)

When Frankenstein fails to fulfill the monster's request, he destroys his one hope of achieving any form of self-satisfaction.

The deepest source of the monster's troubles is that he is alienated from himself, doomed to see himself as others see him. In that respect, he is not free to be a natural man in Rousseau's terms: "The savage lives within himself; the sociable man, always outside of himself, knows how to live only in the opinion of others; and it is, so to speak, from their judgment alone that he draws the sentiment of his own existence" (SD, 179). Tragically, the monster is forced to endure the isolation of natural man, but is denied his independence of judgment. His socially derived sense of his own ugliness, and hence of his unworthiness, ultimately thwarts all his benevolent impulses. Convinced that his creation was defective, the monster is filled with an "impotent envy and bitter indignation" that awakens his "insatiable thirst for vengeance" (208). Thus he lays all the blame for his crimes at the feet of his creator, since Frankenstein is responsible for his being ugly: "Unfeeling, heartless creator! You had endowed me with perceptions and passions and then cast me abroad an object for the scorn and horror of mankind" (133). In this reproach we begin to get a glimpse of how Frankenstein can be regarded as a projection of the monster's psyche. The monster is undoubtedly placed in unusual circumstances by his objective ugliness and he clearly has just cause for complaint against his creator. And yet his situation is not unique the way he claims; his experience is not entirely remote from that of ordinary men. All men have moments when they feel different, when they feel themselves inadequate to mixing in society, when they sense some form of ugliness standing between themselves and other human beings. The monster's fear of not being accepted because of being different is, paradoxically, a very human fear.[29] But the monster also has a very human response to this fear: he claims that he is not really different – inside he is just like any human being – only his outward form makes him seem different,[30] and for that his creator is to blame. In making a distinction between inner being and outward form, the monster is trying to turn what differentiates him from others into a principle external to his self, projecting onto his creator the total responsibility for his alien character.

In this way, the monster is strangely like a Romantic myth-maker, picturing for himself an incompetent, power-mad creator, who is wholly to blame for the misery of his situation. The monster gets to act out the scene many a Romantic poet dreamed of: the opportunity to confront his creator and tell him how thoroughly he bungled the job of creation. The idea of a demonic creator allows man to evade responsibility for his condition in the thought that, given the chance, he would have made himself better. We see this tendency toward evasion in the monster, even though he is more justified than most in criticizing his creator. "Victor Frankenstein" becomes his answer to all his nagging questions concerning why he fails to fit into the world. The monster continually consoles himself with the idea that if he had only been made with more skill and forethought, he would have been a morally better being. His repeated argument is that any ugliness in his soul is purely the result of the ugliness of his body; he is in no way responsible for his self because his self is the product of someone else's creativity; he was not given the freedom to create his self once he was placed in a warped body. Mary Shelley's epigraph from *Paradise Lost* sums up the monster's charges:

> Did I request thee, Maker, from my clay
> To mould me Man, did I solicit thee
> From darkness to promote me?   (X.743–45)

These lines express what came to be a widespread Romantic experience: the protest against the lack of autonomy in the human condition.[31] Milton's Adam speaks for many Romantics when he complains: "my will / Concurred not to my being" (X.746–47).[32] The desire to remake man's being until it becomes entirely the product of his own will, or at least to reject a situation not of his own making and choosing, is what is expressed in the gnostic pattern of Romantic creation myths. Though they express it in different ways, both the monster and Frankenstein share this attitude. Convinced that only a defective providence denied him happiness, and armed with hard and fast evidence of the limitations of his creator, the monster expresses the Romantic sense of man as a creature. Confident in his ability to remake human nature, Frankenstein expresses the Romantic hope in man as a creator. One of the profound ironies of Mary Shelley's myth is that the visionary creator can only produce a heightened version of human creaturely dependence.

VI

No matter what line we pursue in *Frankenstein*, we keep coming back to the fundamental identity of Victor and the monster, of the creator and the creature. The story of the monster seems to take up what it would be like for a lower, or more primitive, being to fall into civilized society. But at the same time, it takes up what it would be like for a higher, or more advanced, being to move among the ranks of ordinary men, if we bear in mind the ways in which the monster exceeds normal human capabilities. Conventional society cannot tell if the monster is an inferior or a superior being, for it cannot fully understand him. All it really knows is that he is somehow different from ordinary men. In this respect, the monster's story is the same as Frankenstein's. As Victor suspects (and as several movies have proven), if the common people knew of his experiments, they would hunt him down like a beast. Any man with an unconventional vision runs the risk of being regarded as inhuman by conventional society. Rousseau expresses this idea in a passage that sounds as if it came right out of the pages of *Frankenstein*:

> Could I in my good sense have supposed that one day I, the same man that I was, the same that I still am, would – without the slightest doubt – pass for and be taken as a monster, a poisoner, an assassin; that I would become the horror of the human race, the plaything of the rabble. (R, 2)

Frankenstein is in a very real sense a higher being than those around him: he is more imaginative and has greater creative powers. But for that very reason he can no more fit into conventional society than his monster can.

In dramatizing the position of an alien being in an uncomprehending community, *Frankenstein* embodies what gradually emerged as the Romantic conception of the artist's relation to society. Victor is the epitome of the isolated Romantic genius: a man with a special power of insight, a rebel against convention, living on the fringes of society, losing touch with his fellow men even as he works to transform their existence. Both Frankenstein and the monster stand out from the ranks of ordinary men. What distinguishes the creator from the creature is that he glories in his sense of being different: "I could not rank myself with the herd of common projectors" (200). The monster, by contrast, does not like to dwell upon the ways in which he excels ordinary men, but only craves their acceptance in normal life. Frankenstein, who evidently could enjoy a successful family life with Elizabeth, gives it up for the sake of his creativity, while the monster, who is free of all ties and could, for example, achieve success as an Arctic explorer beyond Robert Walton's wildest dreams, longs for nothing more than lingering by the sort of family hearth both Frankenstein and Walton despise. Deep down, the creator and the creature in *Frankenstein* yearn to exchange roles: the monster craves the home life Frankenstein rejects, and Frankenstein covets the freedom from personal bonds which the monster views as his curse.

Perhaps then we can view the monster's attitude toward Frankenstein as the creature in man rebelling against the creator in man. The monster expresses the resentment of man's creaturely instincts against his creative impulses, which cause him to suffer and be lonely in his life. Reduced to its essentials, the monster's charge against Frankenstein is: "You've made me miserable for the sake of your creativity." One can think of this reproach as the human half of a poet saying to the artistic half: "For the sake of your art, you've ruined my life." If we take seriously the idea of Frankenstein and the monster as a composite being, we see that in portraying the conflict of creator and creature, Mary Shelley's novel begins to explore the tension between art and life that became such a central theme in nineteenth-century literature.

If one thinks of the creator-half as the real essence of man, then the monster is his nightmare image of his human, all-too-human limitations.[33] To an idealistic visionary like Percy Shelley, his creaturely aspects as a human being can seem monstrous. Anxious to soar into the heaven of his own imagination, he would like to be free of the weight of his own body, which he regards as ill-made because it is not the creation of his own mind. But in trying to reject his creaturely impulses, to distance himself from them, the artist runs the risk of perverting them, of letting his darkest urges work below the level of consciousness toward destructive ends because he refuses to recognize them for what they are. Frankenstein is much like Blake's Urizen:[34] he tries to reject his emotions, to separate himself from them by shunting them off into his creation. But as a result Frankenstein's emotions run wild in the externalized form of his monster.[35] His story suggests that the worst thing that can happen to an artistic visionary is to let his concern for his art and his vision thwart his ordinary human sympathies. Frankenstein himself rather heavy-handedly points the moral of his tale:

If the study to which you apply yourself has a tendency to weaken your affections and to destroy your taste for those simple pleasures in which no alloy can possibly mix, then that study is certainly unlawful, that is to say, not befitting the human mind. (54)

If the creature-half is the real essence of man, then an obsessed creator-god is his nightmare image of the artist in him. He sees this force as ruining all his chances for acceptance in life and thereby making him miserable. The danger of this form of projection is that it provides an excuse for not facing up to the challenges of life.

The thought that only his creator could improve his condition relieves the monster of the task of trying to make something of his ugliness, of creating something out of his admittedly defective existence. It is perhaps asking too much to expect the monster to accept his solitary situation and learn to sublimate his energies into some form of creative endeavor. But if he did, it would not be the first time that a curse proved to be a blessing, and the creaturely defects of man turned out to be a spur to his creativity. Because of his resentment against his creator, the monster ensures that his difference from others can never become a creative difference. Only once does he force himself to leave his creaturely doubts behind him:

I felt emotions of gentleness and pleasure, that had long appeared dead, revive within me. Half surprised by the novelty of these sensations, I allowed myself to be borne away by them, and forgetting my solitude and deformity, dared to be happy. (134)

Here the monster achieves an important insight: for him happiness requires daring. Pursuing the life of a Rousseauian solitary walker and rejecting the artificial standards of civilization in order to achieve communion with nature, the monster is able for the moment to forget his "deformity." But as he says, this path requires the courage to set his own standards and be his own judge. Once the monster turns to Frankenstein to give him happiness, assuming that Frankenstein knows what is best for him and is the only one who has creative power, the monster seals his fate. One begins to suspect that Frankenstein plays the role of God for the monster in a deeper sense than at first appears.[36]

The psychological projections Frankenstein and the monster attempt can, then, be viewed as ways of evading responsibility for their deeds.[37] Each becomes the other's all-purpose excuse. One must not be misled by the tendency of Frankenstein and the monster to wallow in self-accusations. Their admissions always take the form: "I am the greatest of criminals, but –." Each always has some way of disclaiming ultimate responsibility for his actions. *Frankenstein* builds up to what promises to be a climactic scene of mutual confession from Victor and the monster. But what starts out in the *mea culpa* mode passes imperceptibly into a final round of self-justifications. Somehow Frankenstein finds it possible to conclude: "During these last days I have been occupied in examining my past conduct; nor do I find it blamable" (206). And the monster returns to his favorite theme: "Am I to be thought the only criminal, when all mankind sinned against me? ... Even now my blood boils at the recollection of this injustice" (210). In their conviction of the original purity of their intentions, and their belief that only material circumstances thwarted their benevolent impulses, both Frankenstein and the monster maintain to the end the idealist's moral composure in the face of even his most disastrous attempts to act in the real world. The source of this self-assurance is in the nightmare images Frankenstein and the monster have of each other, which allow them to project their faults and failings onto something external to their selves.

Understanding the psychological functions which Frankenstein and the monster serve for each other helps in understanding why they become locked in a life-and-death struggle of mutual flight and pursuit. The creator can never get entirely free of the creature in man, and the creature would be lost without the creative power that is his only hope for making something better of himself. Yet somehow the creative and creaturely principles cannot get together and they remain at war with each other. *Frankenstein* embodies the two images of man that are the imaginative core of Romantic creation myths, but it relates them differently than do most Romantic works. The monster stands for man as suffering creature, poorly provided for by an indifferent world order. Frankenstein stands for man as powerful creator, hoping to claim his long-sought happiness by making himself anew. But in Mary Shelley's myth, the deformed is not transformed, the monster is not the prelude to Frankenstein, the suffering creature is not on the verge of turning himself into the powerful creator in an apocalyptic metamorphosis of the human condition. For Mary Shelley, the two sides of man coexist, and apparently can never achieve a simple harmony. Both Frankenstein and the monster are symbols of the Romantic revolt against the human condition, the idealistic refusal to accept the facts of human nature. In portraying the disastrous consequences of this revolt, Mary Shelley wrote one of the few truly tragic stories in Romantic literature, perhaps because she was dramatizing the tragedy of Romanticism itself. For another attempt to portray the Romantic tragedy, to show the twisting of idealistic thoughts into murderous impulses, we turn to Byron's *Cain*.

PART THREE

The Loss of Eternity

CHAPTER 5

The Metaphysical Rebel

I

In the continuing Romantic war with *Paradise Lost*, Byron's *Cain* attempts the most direct attack. Byron criticizes Jehovah Himself, not his surrogates Jupiter or Urizen. As a result, the heretical and even blasphemous character of Byron's work was readily apparent to his contemporaries. *Cain* created a furor when it was published in 1821; the controversy even got as far as Chancery Court.[1] The many clergymen who took up their pens to refute Byron testify to *Cain*'s original impact, an impact greater than that of any other Romantic attempt at revolutionary myth-making.

But the subject of Cain had more to offer Byron than religious shock-value. The mere act of turning from Adam and Eve to Cain and Abel suggests that Milton did not tell the story of the real fall. The act of eating the Forbidden Fruit was a crime only because God prohibited it. The murder of Abel, on the other hand, strikes us as an inherently criminal act. In other words, because Cain violates what we think of as a natural, rather than a revealed, law, his story tells us much more about the nature of human evil. Moreover, Cain completes the fall, because his crime leads to the fragmenting of the human race, which otherwise might have remained literally one great big happy family. Finally, Cain is the one who actually brings death into the world, thereby completing what Adam and Eve only began. Their knowledge of death was at first purely abstract. They do not feel it in their bones until they see Abel lying lifeless at Cain's feet.

For Byron, then, coming to terms with the story of Cain is more fundamental to understanding the human condition than coming to terms with the story of Adam and Eve. Not having grown up in a typical human setting, they can never be truly typical of mankind. Cain's wife, Adah, points out how Eve's experience differs from that of all her children:

> Thou at least hast passed
> Thy youth in Paradise, in innocent

And happy intercourse with happy spirits.
But we, thy children, ignorant of Eden,
Are girt about by demons.   (I.i.397–401)

Cain is the first human being, because he is the first to be raised in
what have come to be human circumstances, particularly in view of
his consciousness of man's mortality.[2] Byron's choice of subject
thus embodies a polemical thrust: Cain is a more fitting emblem of
the human condition than Adam and Eve, because his story shows
more radically that the human condition is one of exile and
alienation.

In developing his version of the Cain story, Byron follows the
gnostic pattern of Romantic creation myths.[3] He treats sympathetically two of the principal rebels in the Biblical tradition, Lucifer
and Cain, and he allows some very negative views to be expressed
concerning the creator-god of Genesis. Stressing the solitariness of
the creator, Lucifer raises doubts about the benevolence of a God
who must forever remain frustrated because he is forever alone:

<blockquote>

He is great,
But in his greatness is no happier than
We in our conflict. Goodness would not make
Evil, and what else hath he made? But let him
Sit on his vast and solitary throne,
Creating worlds, to make eternity
Less burthensome to his immense existence
And unparticipated solitude.
Let him crowd orb on orb, he is alone
Indefinite, indissoluble tyrant.
Could he but crush himself, 'twere the best boon
He ever granted. But let him reign on
And multiply himself in misery.
Spirits and Men, at least we sympathise
And, suffering in concert, make our pangs
Innumerable, more endurable
By the unbounded sympathy of all
With all! But *He*, so wretched in his height,
So restless in his wretchedness, must still
Create, and re-create.   (I.i.144–63)
</blockquote>

For Lucifer, God creates out of personal emptiness, not as orthodoxy would have it out of fullness. One can therefore trace the
defects in creation to a fundamental lack in the creator which led
Him to create in the first place. In Lucifer's eyes, God becomes a
bored tyrant, making worlds to relieve the tedium of His unending

existence. Lucifer's view of God leads to the idea of the superiority of the creature to his creator, since the creature can feel sympathy and love in a way that the creator cannot, a theme we have just seen in *Frankenstein*. As a result, God's creativity is not far from destructiveness, or as Lucifer says: "he makes but to destroy" (I.i.267).

The most gnostic element in *Cain* is the repeated rejection of Eden as a state in which man was to be kept innocent through ignorance. On this basis, both Cain and Lucifer defend the serpent, who tried to lead man to freedom from a divinely imposed ignorance:

> The snake spoke truth. It *was* the tree of knowledge;
> It *was* the tree of life. Knowledge is good,
> And life is good, and how can both be evil?　　　(I.i.36–38)[4]

The attack on human ignorance in *Cain* takes the specific form of an attack on blind reliance on divine revelation. Both Cain and Lucifer argue that if we do not accept revelation at face value, but try to evaluate God on the basis of the evidence at hand, then He does not seem to have had man's interest in mind in creating the world. Cain finds many reasons to question God's justice in handling Adam and Eve in Eden. He wonders about his father's actions:

> 　　　　　　　　　　　　　　Why did he
> Yield to the serpent and the woman? Or
> Yielding, why suffer? What was there in this?
> The tree was planted, and why not for him?
> If not, why place him near it, where it grew
> The fairest in the centre? They have but
> One answer to all questions, "'Twas *his* will,
> And he is good." How know I that? Because
> He is all pow'rful, must all-good, too, follow?
> I judge but by the fruits – and they are bitter –
> Which I must feed on for a fault not mine.　　　(I.i.69–79)

Cain rejects the orthodox approach to the problem of evil. The conventional believer starts from the assumption that God is omnipotent and benevolent and then tries to reconcile this assumption with the observed facts of God's treatment of man. Cain, by contrast, proceeds inductively, starting from the facts of man's situation and inferring from them what kind of creator is responsible for the human condition. This procedure yields an image of

God very different from that produced by the orthodox approach. As Cain says: "I never could / Reconcile what I saw with what I heard" (I.i.168–69).

The attempt to use human standards to judge God, instead of divine standards to judge man, becomes the key to Lucifer's attack on orthodoxy at the end of Act II. In Lucifer's view, only by accepting God's standards uncritically have men been able to worship Him as good, or rather only by accepting God's actions as self-validating. God is superior to Lucifer only by virtue of His victory, not by virtue of His virtue. As Lucifer says:

> I have a victor, true, but no superior.
>
> . . .
>
> He as a conqueror will call the conquered
> Evil, but what will be the good he gives?
> Were I the victor, his works would be deemed
> The only evil ones.   (II.ii.429, 443–46)

God's deeds, in themselves indistinguishable from Lucifer's, provide no basis for proclaiming Him the moral superior. He seems in fact as vindictive as any tyrant in humbling a defeated rival. According to Lucifer, all we have is God's word that He stands for the good. Take that away and the moral issue between God and Lucifer seems wide open for debate. Lucifer wants men to reject God's will as the standard of the good, and instead to judge God's actions by an independent standard of what things are in themselves:

> Evil and good are things in their own essence
> And not made good or evil by the giver;
> But if he gives you good, so call him. If
> Evil springs from him, do not name it mine,
> Till ye know better its true fount; and judge
> Not by words, though of spirits, but the fruits
> Of your existence, such as it must be.   (II.ii.452–58)

Lucifer's exhortation to mankind culminates in a plea for reliance on reason rather than faith:

> One good gift has the fatal apple giv'n –
> Your reason; let it not be over-swayed
> By tyrannous threats to force you into faith
> 'Gainst all external sense and inward feelings.
> Think and endure and form an inner world
> In your own bosom, where the outward fails.

So shall you nearer be the spiritual
Nature, and war triumphant with your own.

(II.ii.459–66)

Lucifer's "inner world / In your own bosom" clearly echoes the "paradise within thee, happier far" that Michael speaks of to Adam at the end of *Paradise Lost*.[5] But the echo only underlines the difference between Byron and Milton. Whereas Milton's angel is telling man to limit his quest for knowledge in humble submission to God, Byron's devil wants man to rely on his own mind to decide moral issues and thus to question, and, if need be, defy the ways of God to men, rather than seek to justify them.

In exploring the problem of evil, *Cain* quickly cuts the Gordian knot of theological speculation. There is evil in the world because its creator is not good, at least in any human sense of *good*. Byron realized that he would be accused of some form of gnosticism in *Cain*, specifically the Manichean heresy: the belief that the principles of Good and Evil are coeternal and divide up the universe between them.[6] By identifying the orthodox God with the principle of evil, Byron seems to justify revolution against established authority, and *Cain* accordingly centers on the theme of the rebel against the divine order. In the story of the practiced revolutionary, Lucifer, seeking to win over the novice, Cain, Byron takes up an aspect of the problem of evil that interested him more than the cosmological formulation, the problem of the origin of human evil, the problem of evil as the Romantics formulated it: If man is naturally good, how does he become evil, or at least how does he come to commit evil? In Byron's presentation, Cain is by no means a criminal type from birth. On the contrary, he is the noblest character in the play, with high ideals and a deep-seated abhorrence of human suffering. And yet Cain ends up committing the foulest of crimes, fratricide. The practical problem Byron faced as a dramatist – how to present sympathetically the inherently horrible crime of killing Abel – became the poet's theoretical problem as well. How could Cain's noble thoughts ever have been perverted into murderous impulses?

Byron seems to have a very peculiar answer to his question: science leads to murder. The cause of Cain's killing Abel appears to be the planetarium show Lucifer stages for Cain's benefit in Act II. In addition to expressing a gnostic world-view, Byron portrays the unsettling and unbalancing effects of that world-view. *Cain* is similar to *Frankenstein* in its ambivalence, showing a world order ripe for rebellion, and yet at the same time suggesting that rebellion is somehow self-defeating. In revolt, Cain plays right into the hands of the tyrannical creator, accomplishing God's purposes in the very act of defying Him. Cain himself recognizes the irony in the fact that he who hated death is responsible for bringing death into the world:

> I, who abhor
> The name of death so deeply that the thought
> Empoisoned all my life before I knew
> His aspect, I have led him here and giv'n
> My brother to his cold and still embrace.   (III.i.371–75)

Like the Frankenstein monster, Cain becomes a murderer in rebellion, and hence something of a tyrant himself in his willingness to take the power over human life and death into his own hands. Seemingly against his will, Cain finds himself turning into a parody or mirror image of the God he hates: isolated, discontented, and destroying others to relieve his own frustration.[7]

Through Lucifer's help, Cain gains greater awareness of his place in the universe. But the price he pays for that understanding is that he feels less and less at home in the universe, a realization which in turn awakens his destructive impulses, perhaps even his self-destructive impulses. In the remarkable second act of *Cain*, set in "the Abyss of Space," Byron symbolically portrays the revolutionary impact of nineteenth-century speculative science on modern man, the disorienting effect of the vision of an infinite universe. As a result, *Cain* becomes, like *Frankenstein*, as much a myth about Romanticism as a Romantic myth, showing the dangers of gnostic rebellion, even as it provides a justification for it.

II

To understand how Lucifer influences Cain, we must immediately reject the idea that the devil works by offering his potential victim temptations, such as the chance of ruling other men. Byron does not tell a typical tale of Satanic seduction, with man cleverly duped into overestimating his powers. On the contrary, Lucifer succeeds by making Cain feel that he is nothing, thereby enticing him to strike out blindly in protest against the wretchedness of the human condition. Byron's own analysis is the key to *Cain*:

Cain is a proud man: if Lucifer promised him kingdoms, etc., it would *elate* him: the object of the Demon is to *depress* him still further in his own estimation than he was before, by showing him infinite things and his own abasement, till he falls into the frame of mind that leads to the Catastrophe, from mere *internal* irritation, *not* premeditation, or envy of *Abel* (which would have made him contemptible), but from the rage and fury against the inadequacy of his state to his conceptions, and which discharges itself rather against Life, and the Author of Life, than the mere living.[8]

Byron outlines the effect Lucifer's visions have on Cain. The sight of the vastness of the universe and of the multitude of worlds within it makes Cain feel that the earth is small and insignificant, and makes him as a dweller on the earth feel like nothing at all.

One way of understanding Act II of *Cain* is as a reply to the astronomy passages in Book VIII of *Paradise Lost*.[9] Lucifer and Cain clearly transgress the Miltonic injunction to man:

> Heav'n is for thee too high
> To know what passes there; be lowly wise:
> Think only what concerns thee and thy being;
> Dream not of other Worlds, what Creatures there
> Live, in what state, condition, or degree.   (VIII.172–76)

Whereas Raphael provides Adam with a vision of a finite world, designed to end his questioning of God's plan, Lucifer opens Cain's eyes to a cosmic infinity, leaving him wondering if there is any order to the universe at all. *Paradise Lost* is built on a comparatively neat cosmology. Although Milton hedges on the Ptolemaic–Copernican controversy, he still presents the earth and man as the center of God's concern. *Cain*, by contrast, attempts to give poetic expression to the cosmology of modern science, in which the earth has lost its privileged position in the universe. When Cain and Lucifer journey into interstellar space, we are witness to a major shift in the imaginative framework of poetry. Byron is one of the first poets to convey a sense of the tininess of the earth by cosmic standards. Cain watches the earth dwindle before his eyes:

>   As we move
> Like sunbeams onward, it grows small and smaller,
> And as it waxes little and then less,
> Gathers a halo round it like the light
> Which shone the roundest of the stars when I
> Beheld them from the skirts of Paradise.
> Methinks they both, as we recede from them,

Appear to join th' innumerable stars
Which are around us; and, as we move on
Increase their myriads.   (II.i.34–43)

Cain is at first uplifted by his superhuman vision, "proud of thought /
Which knew such things" (II.i.49–50). But it quickly makes him
dissatisfied with the earth-bound existence to which he knows he must
return, and soon he is longing for his own death to set his thoughts free
from his body's limitations (II.i.113–17).

Lucifer provides Cain with a vision of infinite time as well. Taken to
Hades, Cain views the shades of all the worlds which have existed.
Byron drew upon the latest theories of geology and paleontology
available to him, theories which had already begun the challenge to
the Biblical creation account that Darwin's work was later to
intensify.[10] Evidence from fossils and geological strata suggested that
living creatures had existed before the date at which the Bible fixed the
beginning of the world. Moreover, the fossils suggested that some of
the creatures were larger than their current counterparts on the face of
the earth. Adopting this notion, Byron allows Lucifer to reduce Cain's
self-esteem even further, particularly through the "poetical fiction" of
the Pre-Adamite men, or rather the Pre-Adamite rational beings.[11]
Lucifer shows Cain that rational beings once existed on earth who
would be to men in intelligence what dinosaurs would be to modern
reptiles in size.[12] This vision turns out to be even more unsettling than
Cain's view of the vastness of space. He has been shown that the earth
is not the jewel of the universe, but now he learns that man is not even
the jewel of the earth. Lucifer succeeds in breaking Cain out of the neat
time-frame of the Bible, in which all of cosmic history totals perhaps
some six thousand years, and events move in orderly fashion from the
Creation to the Last Judgment. Cain confronts visions of millions of
years, with no clear direction to the history of the universe. All things
seem to be created only to be eventually destroyed:

Many things will have
No end, and some which would pretend to have
Had no beginning have had one as mean
As thou; and mightier things have been extinct
To make way for much meaner than we can
Surmise, for moments only and the space
Have been and must be all unchangeable.   (II.i.156–62)

Beholding Lucifer's panorama of universal annihilation, Cain no
longer has anything secure in which he can place an absolute faith.

Faced with the infinite space and time of modern cosmology, Cain murders Abel. The visions Lucifer gives Cain make him feel alone and insignificant in a vast indifferent universe. He is therefore repelled by the piety of his brother Abel, who still talks of God as the kindly father of the human race. Worst of all, God's preference for Abel's sacrifice over Cain's seems to epitomize divine arbitrariness, confirming all that Lucifer has said about the creator. Striking out at Abel becomes the only way Cain feels he can strike at God.[13] His attitude closely resembles that of a later Byronic hero, Melville's Captain Ahab, who justifies his seemingly misdirected "vengeance on a dumb brute" in this way:

All visible objects, man, are but as pasteboard masks. But in each event – in the living act, the undoubted deed – there, some unknown but still reasoning thing puts forth the mouldings of its features from behind the unreasoning mask. If you will strike, strike through the mask! How can the prisoner reach outside except by thrusting through the wall?[14]

Unfortunately for Abel, in his brother's eyes he becomes the mask or wall standing between Cain and his creator.

The deeds of Cain and Captain Ahab are what Camus has called metaphysical rebellion, a rebellion against what is perceived as the absurdity of human existence.[15] This rebellion begins with an experience of the world order not living up to man's expectations of rationality and justice in events.[16] This disillusionment leads man to lash out against the world order in any way he can, to assert his freedom in the face of blind necessity, to substitute, if need be, the arbitrariness of his own will for God's.[17] Recall what Byron said about Cain: he murders Abel because of his "rage and fury against the inadequacy of his state to his conceptions," a feeling "which discharges itself rather against Life, and the Author of Life, than the mere living." Clearly what Byron meant to say is that the rage and fury of a man like Cain discharges itself against Life, and the Author of Life, *through* the mere living. But his wording emphasizes the important fact that God is the real target of Cain's murderous impulses, not Abel. The way Byron speaks of "the inadequacy" of Cain's "state to his conceptions" might remind us of the Shelleyan gap between inspiration and composition, or, more generally, the Romantic gap between imagination and reality. In Byron's description, Cain sounds like a frustrated artist, convinced of the inferiority of any creative power to his own desires and dreams (II.i.81–83), and hence unwilling to accept a world he himself did not make.

The notion of metaphysical rebellion suggests how *Cain* can be related to Byron's other works. For all Byron's heroes, the fundamental experience is that the world order is not a moral order. Whatever else they come to think of God, they learn that He does not support human justice in any way that man can readily understand. This recognition sets the Byronic hero free, though his freedom is clearly a burden, and threatens to become a curse. In the absence of a divinely imposed order, the Byronic hero must develop his own code to live by, if only the code of thieves. For Cain, the understanding that the world order is not a moral order comes as an epiphany. Lucifer gives him a direct vision of the nature of the universe, making it impossible for Cain to continue the life he has been leading. His crime is only a symptom of the fact that he cannot go on living in conventional society.[18] Murdering Abel becomes his way of having himself driven out into the life of solitary wandering he secretly craves.[19]

For most of Byron's heroes, the experience that triggers their life of exile is not so obviously metaphysical as Cain's. Often Byron does not spell out what the original experience was. But the outlines are at least suggested. The hero undergoes some form of disillusionment, perhaps seeing his faith in a great cause or a beautiful woman betrayed. In any case, his belief in the rationality and justice of the universe is shattered. As Byron writes of the pirate Lambro in *Don Juan*: "His country's wrong and his despair to save her / Had stung him from a slave to an enslaver" (III.liii.423–24). *Cain* is central to the understanding of Byron's poetry because it reveals what is often obscured in his earlier works: that the rebellion of his heroes is ultimately metaphysical in nature. They are pirates, bandits, or black magicians, not because of base, physical passions such as greed or lust, but because they originally aspired to something higher than ordinary men, and had their noble aspirations thwarted. Characters like the Giaour or the Corsair lash out at the world because their best impulses have been frustrated. Hence the violence Byron deals with, though it appears to be directed against other men, is ultimately directed against God. Byron's characteristic subject is the man whose crime is merely the excuse for the violence he longs to commit in protest against the absurdity of his existence.

In portraying the metaphysical criminal, Byron anticipated a theme that was to grow in importance in European literature. Among Byron's contemporaries, the best parallel to his theme of a passion for justice turning a basically honest man into a criminal can be found in

Kleist's *Michael Kohlhaas,* although the theme obviously has its roots in all the noble bandits of *Sturm und Drang* drama, beginning with Schiller's *Die Räuber.*[20] The most famous metaphysical criminal in literature is Raskolnikov in Dostoevsky's *Crime and Punishment.* Nietzsche prefigures the psychology of Raskolnikov in a fascinating passage in *Thus Spoke Zarathustra*:

Thus speaks the red judge, "Why did this criminal murder? He wanted to rob." But I say unto you: his soul wanted blood, not robbery; he thirsted after the bliss of the knife. His poor reason, however, did not comprehend this madness and persuaded him: "What matters blood?" it asked; "don't you want at least to commit a robbery with it? To take revenge?" And he listened to his poor reason: its speech lay upon him like lead; so he robbed when he murdered. He did not want to be ashamed of his madness.[21]

Byron's heroes display a similar tendency to pursue madness under the cover of reason. Conrad the Corsair, for example, adopts a seemingly rational policy of a pre-emptive strike against his enemy Seyd the Pacha. But his stratagem quickly degenerates into an insane orgy of violence, as Conrad's forces, taking on impossible odds, seem to be willing to destroy themselves, as long as they can pull down the fabric of the surrounding society with them.

III

Although *Cain* may at first appear quite different from Byron's Oriental tales, the play actually is an effort to distil into myth the range of experience he had explored in his earlier works and to expose the metaphysical basis of the dark strivings of his heroes. *Cain* provides a pathology of the consciousness of the Romantic rebel, showing how in the process of disillusionment, the good impulses of the idealistic soul can be turned to violence. *Cain* shows how the gnostic view of the world, the conviction that the world order is shot through with evil, can warp the soul. But other Romantics were as aware as Byron of how disillusionment can thwart the sympathetic impulses that make man open to his world. We have seen in *Prometheus Unbound* how in Shelley's view hate narrows perception and hence interferes with human redemption. Why does Byron give such a distinctively dark coloring to his portrayal of rebellion?

The core of the difference between Byron and Shelley or Blake is that Lucifer offers no vision of salvation to Cain, even though he is cast in the role of the gnostic emissary from another world, who usually reveals the path to redemption.[22] All Lucifer does is to ask Cain to worship him instead of God, and he goes on to say that if Cain does not worship God he is already worshipping Lucifer (I.i.317). To be sure, Lucifer gives Cain many visions of this world ordinarily denied to mortals. But he never gives Cain a vision of anything beyond or above this world, just of other worlds before this one in time, which have since passed into oblivion. What is missing, then, from *Cain* is any vision of eternity as we find it, for example, in Blake, a higher state from which man has fallen and to which he may somehow return. In Blake's terms, what Byron offers is a cycle of innocence and experience, without any possibility of reaching a higher stage. Instead of eternity, Byron portrays an unending succession of different worlds, created and destroyed and created again.[23] Byron is getting very close in *Cain* to the notion of the eternal recurrence, which was to be Nietzsche's replacement for the Romantic myth of creation. *Cain* suggests what transformed the genre of the Romantic creation myth from within: the loss of the vision of eternity that originally inspired Romantic myth-makers. *Cain* presents a view of the established world order no more negative than that of the creation myths of Blake and Shelley. But in not presenting any vision of how the world can be transformed into something better, the play fundamentally changes the character of the Romantic creation myth. It is as if Blake had written nothing but *The Book of Urizen* and *The Book of Ahania*, and never pictured a way for man to break out of the Orc cycle.

The absence of an apocalyptic vision in Byron is clear if one compares his view of Prometheus with Shelley's. Byron's "Prometheus" is of course merely a short lyric, and does not bear comparison with Shelley's long drama. But it still reveals a significant difference in emphasis.[24] Byron writes a Prometheus Bound rather than a Prometheus Unbound, focusing on the Titan's suffering, not his redemption. The only eternity Byron refers to is an eternity of pain, which perhaps explains why he calls eternity a "wretched gift" (l. 24). When Byron speaks of triumph at the end, he is not foreseeing Prometheus's triumph over Zeus, not even a reconciliation of the two. The only victory for Byron comes from enduring the continuing tyranny of this world. Death becomes the true triumph, provided one goes to the grave still defiant, the way Byron's Manfred does. The last lines of the Prometheus poems of

Shelley and Byron provide a revealing contrast: whereas Shelley equates Victory with Life, Joy, and Empire, Byron equates Victory with Death.

Instead of working in the apocalyptic mode of Romanticism, Byron develops an alternative vision: not the world transformed, but the world destroyed. His remarkable poem "Darkness" reads almost like a point-by-point refutation of the great apocalyptic speeches at the end of *Prometheus Unbound*.[25] Instead of the whole world suddenly coming to life, as happens in Shelley's poem, in Byron's, it gradually runs down and expires, as the heat and light of the sun die out. In Shelley's vision, the end of this world will mean the triumph of love and all signs of selfishness will disappear. In Byron's vision, the end of the world will involve a great increase in selfishness. Under the pressure of dwindling resources, the situation becomes one of every man for himself, as all conventional restraints on egotism drop away. "Darkness" culminates in a horrifying scene of the last two men on earth, who inevitably are enemies and finally kill each other (ll. 55–67). As "Darkness" ends, the original order of creation is reversed and the world subsides into a "chaos of hard clay" (l. 72).[26] In its vision of total annihilation, "Darkness," together with the corresponding passages in *Cain*, supplies an important counterweight to the positive prophecies of Romantic myth.[27]

In "Darkness," Byron projects the death-wish experienced by many Romantics as individuals onto a cosmic scale. In a sense, he grounds the suicidal yearnings of individuals in a vision of a universal tendency toward annihilation. If the whole universe is headed only to destruction, then the self-destructive impulses of one man no longer seem such an aberration.[28] We saw suggestions in *Frankenstein* that some Romantics give a special metaphysical status to death, sometimes viewing it as a higher state than life. Death can be viewed as an approximation to the original unity man has fallen from and hence as a means of returning to the One.[29] In "Darkness" the end of the world undoes the work of creation, and the earth ends up in an undifferentiated state – "Seasonless, herbless, treeless, manless, lifeless" (l. 71) – that overcomes the painful divisions of man's historical existence. Byron did not pursue this morbid line of Romanticism as far as certain other poets did, such as Beddoes.[30] Nevertheless, his vivid imagining of cosmic catastrophe clearly reveals a darkening of Romantic vision.

The absence of the Romantic vision of apocalypse in *Cain* contributes to the metaphysical rebellion of its hero. Cain's murderous rage is deepened by his awareness that he has not only been expelled from Paradise but also has no hope of ever returning to it. Ultimately it is Cain's fixation on Paradise, his haunting dream of a perfect state for man, that makes him, as he says, "unfit for mortal converse" (III.i.184) and turns him into a rebel and a criminal. Like Mary Shelley's characterization of Frankenstein and the monster, Byron's characterization of Cain suggests the profound connection between the bright and dark sides of Romanticism. Cain is typically Romantic in the extreme swings of his emotions, the way he quickly passes from elation to despair. One moment Cain is glorying in the power of the human mind; the next he is convinced of the nothingness of human existence. His story shows how modern idealism gives rise to modern nihilism.[31] It is in fact the height of Cain's idealistic hopes for man that leads to the depth of his nihilistic despair. Because he expects perfect rationality and justice in the world order, he is enraged by any imperfection in the divine plan.[32] The root of metaphysical rebellion is belief in an omnipotent and good creator, or rather the conviction that if there is a God, He ought to be omnipotent and good. If He fails in either respect – if He has to compromise at all with material reality or if He does not hold man's interest uppermost in mind – then He is no better than a devil. Romantic gnosticism stems from this all-or-nothing attitude, the assumption that no middle ground between a perfect and a demonic creator can be found. In this sense, Romantic myth-makers had a hard time freeing themselves from the absolutism of the religious orthodoxy against which they rebelled.

As Camus points out, metaphysical rebellion can occur only within the Biblical tradition or its descendants, because only the Biblical conception of God poses the problem of evil in all seriousness.[33] If one denies that God is omnipotent, or that He is purely benevolent from a human standpoint, or, if one goes further, and denies the existence of a single god, with a unitary plan for creation, then no reason remains to expect the world order to operate with man's welfare foremost in mind. A classical Greek, for example, would not conclude that the creator was malevolent simply because all aspects of creation do not conduce to human happiness.[34] In the classical understanding, a world order exists that on the whole works to man's benefit, but certainly not in all cases. Nature provides for man, but not perfectly. The Greek view of the cosmos does not awaken any hopes for a radical transformation of the human condition into a paradise. But Romantic myth-makers do inherit the apocalyptic expectations of the Biblical tradition, even though they no longer expect the apocalypse from the traditional source. In Romantic creation myths, man must bring about the transformation of his condition himself and not rely upon God's grace. But Romantic visions of paradise are still based on the same premise as the Biblical tradition, that a perfect world is possible for man and man may be condemned to utter misery until he finds complete happiness. Cain reveals something about the whole enterprise of Romantic myth-making in his inability to free himself from a dream of perfect happiness he inherited, even though he has learned to distrust and despise the source of that dream.

To understand this point more fully, we must examine the debate between Cain and Lucifer, which is the center of Byron's play and which gradually focuses on the issue of perfect happiness, of whether happiness must be absolute in order to be happiness at all. As part of his plan to strip Cain of everything that makes life bearable, Lucifer tries to convince him that all beauty is illusory. When Cain claims that no evil can enter into the heavens because "they are too beautiful," Lucifer replies: "Thou hast seen them from afar" (II.ii.245–46). Lucifer's reductionist mentality leads him to believe that closer inspection will reveal the hidden flaw in anything. But Cain, thinking of his beloved Adah, feels just the opposite: "The loveliest thing I know is loveliest nearest" (II.ii.251). Lucifer insists that Cain must be deluded (II.ii.252) because Adah's beauty is merely transitory:

> 'Tis fair as frail mortality,
> In the first dawn and bloom of young creation
> And earliest embraces of earth's parents,
> Can make its offspring; still it is delusion.
>
> (II.ii.269–72)

If beauty is transitory in Lucifer's eyes, then so is love, for he thinks that love is merely an appetite which lasts only as long as desire:

> Thou lovest it because 'tis beautiful,
> As was the apple in thy mother's eye;
> And when it ceases to be so, thy love
> Will cease like any other appetite.   (II.ii.323–26)

Gradually it dawns on Cain that Lucifer's scorn for anything that perishes – "Think'st thou I'd take the shape of things that die?" (I.i.228) – has made him incapable of love. This consideration may explain why earlier Lucifer suggests a disjunction between love and knowledge (I.i.423–31). Lucifer's detachment, his cool objectivity about life, which seems at first to make him superior to Cain in vision, may instead represent a willful blindness to the emotional side of life, an inability to experience beauty. Lucifer may see less of life than Cain, not, as he repeatedly insists, more.

The issue between Lucifer and Cain can be stated simply: Does the transiency of a thing undermine its value? Lucifer cannot see why anyone would fall in love with something he must eventually part with. Cain, on the other hand, cannot see why something should be any the less precious merely because it perishes. The world is poorer for the loss of the thing, but the thing does not lose the value it possessed:

> CAIN   Cease to be beautiful! how can that be?
> LUCIFER With time.
> CAIN   But time has past, and hitherto
> Ev'n Adam and my mother both are fair;
> Not like fair Adah and the seraphim;
> But very fair.
> LUCIFER   All that must pass away
> In them and her.
> CAIN   I'm sorry for it, but
> Cannot conceive my love for her the less.
> And when her beauty disappears, methinks
> He who creates all beauty will lose more
> Than me in seeing perish such a work.
>
>   (II.ii.327–36)

The whole dispute between Lucifer and Cain is summed up in two lines:

> LUCIFER I pity thee who lovest what must perish.
> CAIN   And I thee who lov'st nothing.   (II.ii.337–38)

The debate between Lucifer and Cain takes on the character of an internal dialogue. Byron allows two aspects of the self to confront each other: the principle which fights attachments to the outside world because they always involve the possibility of loss, and the principle which rejects the attempt to remain within the safe confines of the self because of the emotional impoverishment that results.

If Lucifer is voicing doubts that have at one time arisen in Cain's own mind, then we can understand why Cain is so obsessed with death, why he claims that "the thought [of death] empoisoned all [his] life" (III.i.372–73). Death threatens the value of everything he prizes because death makes everything transitory. However resolute he is when debating Lucifer, Cain cannot help remembering the tales he has been told of Paradise, of a state in which man was not to be subject to death, in which he was to enjoy what he values forever. Cain may be determined to accept the transiency of beauty, but he is haunted by the thought that once man's happiness could have been absolute and unending. Otherwise he would not lament so bitterly the fact of man's mortality. Clearly Lucifer knows the weak spot in Cain's defenses. For a brief moment during Act II, Cain has the answer to Lucifer's persistent questioning and his own persistent doubts. Death cannot change what has been; life requires an attachment to things in the here and now without an obsessed possessiveness that demands that we retain what we have forever. For a brief moment, Cain seems ripe for renouncing eternity, ready to accept human life in its mortality, without any apocalyptic hopes for absolute happiness. In Nietzsche's terms, for a moment Cain seems prepared to will the eternal recurrence. He rejects Lucifer's priestly contempt for the perishable goods of this world and claims to embrace earthly values in all their transitoriness.[35]

But as soon as Cain expresses his pity for the lovelessness of Lucifer, the devil changes the conversation to the subject of Abel. Lucifer knows that he should bring up a love in Cain that is not pure, one that is mixed with envy, with jealousy that Abel is favored by Adam and Eve, and by Jehovah as well. Lucifer subtly revives Cain's indignation and sense of cosmic injustice by speaking of "the indulgent Lord / And bounteous planter of barred Paradise" (II.ii.347–48), and reminding Cain of the arbitrariness of God's treatment of mankind, specifically his preference for Abel's sacrifices. In Act III, Cain no longer has to wrestle with the arguments of Lucifer because he carries the same doubts within his own breast. That is why Lucifer does not appear at all in Act III. In a sense, Cain's encounter with Lucifer is an externalization of a debate that has long been going on in Cain's mind.[36] As Lucifer tells him: "thou hast thought of this ere now" (II.ii.355). It is the Lucifer principle in Cain that leads him to kill Abel. For all his talk of love, Cain's soul is still filled with hate: hatred of God for not providing for him adequately, for denying him the Tree of Life. In the end Cain is not willing to accept the human condition as he finds it. He is not ready to renounce eternity but instead protests God's making man mortal by killing Abel.

V

The deepest level of Cain's tragedy is that just when he is on the verge of articulating his superiority to Lucifer, the superiority of the mortal condition to the immortal, he becomes blinded by his barely suppressed hatred of God and thereby loses his chance of becoming reconciled to his state. For all Lucifer's claims to wisdom, Cain gradually recognizes that the devil is remote from life and barred from appreciating its value. Cain pointedly replies to Lucifer's claim that Adah's beauty is only an illusion: "You think so, being not her brother" (II.ii.273), suggesting that Lucifer's lack of human ties involves a lack of human affections, and thus a lack of human insight. Although Lucifer proudly asserts the superiority of his immortal state, Cain realizes the limitations of this independence:

> LUCIFER   Mortal,
>   My brotherhood's with those who have no children.
> CAIN   Then thou canst have no fellowship with us.
> (II.ii.273–75)

Lucifer has no sister; he can have no children; he is denied human fellowship. His immortality begins to sound like a curse, rather than a blessing. Cain learns that Lucifer is no better off than the wretched Eternal God he spoke of earlier. When Lucifer claimed that God is miserable in his unending solitude, he asserted the superiority of God's creatures on the basis of their fellow-feeling: "Spirits and men, at least we sympathise" (I.i.157). But in his debate with Cain, Lucifer displays very little sympathy with the human condition. Living in a world of pure spirit, with no limits on his ability to travel through space and time, Lucifer finds it impossible to take the "narrow bounds" (I.i.243) of the human world seriously. Ultimately Lucifer cannot sympathize with a being who is a mixture of matter and spirit, and who consequently partakes of the values of both realms. Lucifer insists that "matter cannot / Comprehend spirit wholly" (II.ii.169–70). He fails to see that this lesson can be turned back upon him; spirit cannot

152

comprehend matter wholly either. At one point, even Lucifer admits that his immortality limits his knowledge: "As I know not death, / I cannot answer" (I.i.289–90). His later statement – "It may be death leads to the highest knowledge" (II.ii.164) – has interesting implications for evaluating the relative merits of the mortal and the immortal states.[37]

Cain knows two immortal beings, God and Lucifer, and from what he has seen, both are loveless. Perhaps something in their state makes it impossible for immortal beings to love. The prospect of eternity drains all the significance out of the particular moment and hence out of any finite experience such as love. When Cain asks Lucifer, "Dost thou love nothing?", the devil compares himself to God:

> thou canst not see if *I* love
> Or no, except some vast and gen'ral purpose,
> To which particular things must melt like snows.
>
> (II.ii.313–15)

In the light of the "vast and gen'ral purpose" of immortal beings like God and Lucifer, the "particular things" of this world "melt like snows." For God and Lucifer, the human horizon, within which alone all human things have their value, dissolves into a boundless world of universal space and time. Lucifer's basic strategy is to reproduce in Cain this godlike remoteness from the ordinary human world, to lift Cain out of the human framework of limited space and time in order to weaken his attachment to the goods of human life. That explains why the one force working to counteract the effect of Lucifer on Cain is not the piety of Adam, Eve, and Abel, but the love of his wife, Adah. Cain is able to resist the devil's attack to the extent he does only because his attachment to Adah works to keep his eyes fixed within a human horizon. Seeing Adah's face, he forgets the infinite reaches of space and time: "I turn from earth and heav'n / To gaze on it" (II.ii.268–69).

More absorbed in life than Cain, warmer in her sympathies and less given to intellectual doubts, Adah is aware even before her husband of the alien character of Lucifer. She first senses Lucifer's lovelessness (I.i.422) and implores Cain to "choose love" (I.i.431) over the emotionally debilitating knowledge the devil offers. She comes close to understanding how Cain's obsession with Paradise has warped his life, preventing him from enjoying what he possesses:

ADAH Dear Cain! Nay, do not whisper o'er our son
        Such melancholy yearnings o'er the past.
        Why will thou always mourn for Paradise?
        Can we not make another?
CAIN   Where?
ADAH   Here or
        Where'er thou wilt. Where'er thou art, I feel not
        The want of this much regretted Eden.   (III.i.35–40)

This is the one attitude Lucifer cannot allow to arise in Cain. All along Lucifer has been searching for a way to make Cain dissatisfied with God without letting him become satisfied with his human existence. He has to keep the thought of Eden alive in Cain, so that he will not turn his back on the whole Paradise-dream and embrace his mortality as the preferable state. Looking at his son Enoch, Cain for once has the objectivity to see that Paradise may be only an illusion:

                    He must dream –
    Of what? Of Paradise! Aye, dream of it,
    My disinherited boy. 'Tis but a dream.

                                (III.i.30–32)

This is the realization Adah is groping toward. In talking of making another paradise, she is not expressing an apocalyptic hope. She wants to make the most out of human life as she has inherited it, and above all places her faith in the power of human love. She suspects that the human condition, with all its limitations, may be more rewarding than a seemingly higher state:

    The childless cherubs well might envy thee
    The pleasures of a parent.   (III.i.153–54)[38]

Cain follows Adah's lead in recognizing that Lucifer has an alien perspective on the world and even senses at times that Lucifer is as limited in his own way in his perceptions as human beings are in theirs. Unfortunately Cain is constantly tempted to take Lucifer's difference from mortal men as a sign of superiority, with the result that he falls into the trap of adopting Lucifer's standards as his own. The deepest irony of Byron's play is that Cain persists in craving immortality, even though all the evidence he has suggests that immortality destroys the ability to enjoy life by undermining the attachment to the transitory things of this world which life requires.

154

Cain provides a dialogue between the desire to transcend the human condition and the willingness to accept life with all its limits in the here and now. In the dramatized debate, Lucifer stands for one pole and Adah for the other, with Cain caught in the middle, pulled in both directions at once.[39] Like *Frankenstein*, *Cain* sets up a dialogue between the creative and creaturely principles in man. But, again like *Frankenstein*, it does not present any resolution of the issues it raises. Byron shows the tragedy that can result from the longing for transcendence, and yet leaves us with the feeling that only an ignoble soul would be dead to that longing. Whether Byron himself was any more prepared than Cain to renounce eternity is difficult to tell. Clearly he saw the dangers in the apocalyptic dreams of Romanticism, and he refrained from developing the apocalyptic mode in his poetry. The Last Judgment was still a powerful idea in the mind of a poet like Blake. But for Byron it was reduced to the comic absurdities of his satire, *The Vision of Judgment*. Byron's active sense of humor distinguished him from most Romantics, and often enabled him to puncture the inflated dreams of Romantic fancy. And yet one senses that Byron took Cain very seriously, that he identified deeply with him, that he was not sufficiently distanced from Cain to sit back and coolly speak of where he went wrong. Like Cain, Byron did not give up his hopes for Paradise without a fight, and if he ever abandoned the Romantic vision of eternity, it was with a sense, not of Nietzschean affirmation, but of regret, or rather of defiance. For another poet's struggle with the apocalyptic dreams of Romantic myth, and perhaps a more thoroughgoing attempt to come to terms with human mortality, we turn to Keats's *Hyperion* poems.

CHAPTER 6

Romantic Myth and Tragic Vision

I

In the first version of *Hyperion*, Keats seemed to be writing in the mythic vein of Blake and Shelley, shaping a tale of cosmic and human progress. But the fact that Keats could not bring himself to complete the progressive pattern, and show it culminating in an apocalyptic moment as Blake and Shelley did, suggests that for some reason the original form of Romantic creation myth was unsuited to his poetic vision. In the process of reworking the poem as *The Fall of Hyperion*, Keats changed the nature of the myth, although he may have been merely drawing out tendencies already present in the earlier version. Turning from his original cosmic vistas to a more narrowly personal view of his theme, Keats ends up showing fallenness as the human condition itself and not just a stage in a grand historical development. Keats seems more interested in humanizing mythology than in mythologizing humanity. What is in fact most striking about Keats's divinities is their humanity.[1] Though immortal by nature, they must learn to come to terms with the basic experience of mortals, the experience of loss (*Fall*, I.440–41). Keats does not see his gods as angels or devils: they are neither raised above the limitations of humanity, nor to be held responsible for setting those limits. Keats's gods share man's fate, rather than causing it or pointing the way to transcend it.

For a Romantic myth-maker, Keats is remarkably free of gnosticism. He does not see the universe polarized between good and evil forces, and he does not view man's fate in light of the stark alternatives of salvation and damnation. That is why he is able to give such a balanced treatment of the two sides in his war in heaven, an even-handedness that distinguishes him from Blake and Shelley in their portrayals of cosmic warfare.[2] We end up sympathizing with Keats's Titans, even though presumably we are supposed to welcome the triumph of Zeus and the Olympian generation. It may even be difficult at first to see how the one

Olympian we meet in the poem, Apollo, differs from the Titans, since he seems to be undergoing the same growth through suffering that they do.[3] Though Keats's plan requires Apollo to be in some sense opposed to Hyperion, his counterpart among the Titans, we do not respond to their opposition the way we do to the conflict between Shelley's Prometheus and his Jupiter. For Shelley, Prometheus's overthrow of Jupiter is a triumphant moment, and a model of how man might liberate himself from his current suffering and attain a higher state. Keats, on the other hand, in showing one generation of gods displacing another, focuses on the feeling of loss rather than triumph, and seems to be suggesting that no state that can be reached in history is permanent and raised above the possibility of loss. Keats no longer uses myth to project a paradise beyond man's current state, an ideal to be strived for. Ultimately Keats uses myth in the *Hyperion* poems to come to terms with the human condition, not to try to change or transcend it.[4]

Keats's choice of subject matter in *Hyperion* exemplifies the Romantic search for novelty in myth which Harold Bloom and others have emphasized. Hyperion is a particularly obscure mythological character, thus giving Keats a great deal of freedom in working up his narrative, freedom to invent details concerning Hyperion or to transfer to his story details associated with other figures in Greek myth.[5] Moreover, since no poet had ever treated Hyperion as a central theme, Keats had all the advantages of being the first to address the subject. More generally, Keats's turn to the pre-Olympian deities in *Hyperion* can be understood primarily as a turn to the pre-Homeric deities. Since dealing with poetically well-established gods like Zeus or Athena invites invidious comparisons with the first of poets, it is significant that *Hyperion* breaks off just when Keats is entering Homeric territory with the turn to Apollo. As the "Ode to Psyche" shows, Keats preferred dealing with divinities as yet uncelebrated by his fellow poets. Psyche came "too late" to be hymned by the great poets of antiquity; perhaps what attracted Keats to Hyperion's generation of gods is that they came too early.

Searching out a pre-Homeric subject is one of the primary ways in which Keats imitates *Paradise Lost* in *Hyperion*. Like Milton, Keats takes pains to point out that, although he is writing later in time than Homer, the subject he is dealing with has temporal priority over Homer's.[6] Consider the description of Hyperion's consort, Thea:

> She was a goddess of the infant world,
> By her in stature the tall Amazon
> Had stood a pigmy's height; she would have ta'en
> Achilles by the hair and bent his neck,
> Or with a finger stayed Ixion's wheel.
> Her face was large as that of Memphian sphinx,
> Pedestalled haply in a palace court,
> When sages looked to Egypt for their lore.   (I.26–33)

To disparage Achilles this way is by implication to disparage Homer: belittling Achilles' size next to Thea suggests that Homer's subject matter is somehow trivial by comparison with Keats's. Keats uses Milton's tactic for compensating for any feelings of inferiority he may harbor with regard to his great predecessor. What Keats may lack in poetic greatness vis-à-vis Homer he makes up for by the comparative grandeur of his subject matter.

Furthermore, Keats stresses the antiquity of his subject, suggesting that he is in touch with primeval Egyptian lore, wisdom which predates Homer's perhaps as much as Homer's predates a nineteenth-century poet's. One can cut classical antiquity down to size by suggesting that "the ancients had their ancients," that the men we think of as embodying original wisdom looked back to more primeval times themselves.[7] Finally, by talking of the "infant world," Keats establishes the freshness of his subject. He may be writing at the end of a long epic tradition, and in that sense be threatened with stale material, but, like Milton, he claims to be dealing with the original events from which the epic tradition derives. We may have seen many bad omens before in the epics we have read, but when we come to Keats's description of Hyperion's palace, we are supposedly seeing the archetypal moment when ill-tidings first clouded the divine sky:

>   sometimes eagle's wings,
> Unseen before by gods or wondering men,
> Darkened the place, and neighing steeds were heard,
> Not heard before by gods or wondering men.   (I.182–85)

Troubled by the thought that he may be only the last in a long line of epic poets, Keats feels that he must show that at least he is dealing with the first of epic events.

The trouble with Keats's claim to priority of subject matter is of course that this tactic had itself become part of the epic tradition ever since Milton used it in *Paradise Lost*, and nothing rings more hollow than a derivative assertion of originality. Far from giving the impression of a primordial poetic utterance, *Hyperion* is if anything too literary a production. Keats may have derived the resolve he needed to attempt an epic poem from the thought that he was turning back to the earliest sources of Greek mythology, but the fact is that *Paradise Lost* had more to do with shaping *Hyperion* than anything Keats found in Hesiod or Homer. From *The Book of Urizen* to *Cain* we have seen several Romantic attempts at reworking *Paradise Lost*; *Hyperion* seems an outright effort to rewrite Milton's epic. Keats's blank verse is distinctly Miltonic in rhythm and cadence, though somewhat shorter and simpler in its periods. His handling of traditional epic devices, such as the epic simile, seems directly modelled on Milton's ways of adopting Homeric and Virgilian conventions to English.[8]

Keats derives the very structure of his poem from Milton, apparently following *Paradise Lost* book for book as he proceeds.[9] In Book I of *Hyperion*, just as in Book I of *Paradise Lost*, we see the losers of a war in heaven, reflecting on what they once were and what they have become, and searching for some means of consolation in their loss. Book II of *Hyperion* portrays a council of fallen deities trying to decide how best to cope with their fall, a scene obviously modelled on the council of fallen angels in Milton's Book II. Like Milton, Keats presents three speakers in the council. Although Keats's Oceanus, Clymene, and Enceladus cannot be exactly aligned with Milton's Moloch, Belial, and Mammon, the spectrum of opinion in Keats's debate resembles that in Milton's closely. The counsels range from accepting the fall and learning to make the best of it to openly defying the heavenly victors and renewing warfare. At the end of Book II, Keats's Titans have pinned all their remaining hopes on one of their number, just as Milton's devils turn to Satan as their champion. In Book III, Keats shifts his attention to the other camp and, in the person of Apollo, gives us our first glimpse of the triumphant Olympians, much as Milton turns from hell to heaven in his Book III, and shows us God and Christ, the victors over Satan.

II

For all the detailed parallels to *Paradise Lost*, in one respect *Hyperion* differs completely from Milton's epic. Milton tells the story of a war in heaven in which the insurgent forces are defeated, whereas Keats's rebels are victorious. *Paradise Lost* is biased against any creativity other than God's. It portrays a world order in which any change initiated by anyone other than God is necessarily for the worse. By contrast, Keats's scheme in *Hyperion* suggests the value of creativity, portraying a universe in which constant change is the only law and the replacement of the old by the new is viewed positively as a form of development. What is most fundamentally Romantic about Keats's myth in *Hyperion* is that it embodies an idea of progress.

For this reason, Oceanus's speech on cosmic development has struck many readers as the thematic heart of *Hyperion*:[10]

> As heaven and earth are fairer, fairer far
> Than chaos and blank darkness, though once chiefs;
> And as we show beyond that heaven and earth
> In form and shape compact and beautiful,
> In will, in action free, companionship
> And thousand other signs of purer life;
> So on our heels a fresh perfection treads,
> A power more strong in beauty, born of us
> And fated to excel us, as we pass
> In glory that old darkness; nor are we
> Thereby more conquered than by us the rule
> Of shapeless chaos. Say, doth the dull soil
> Quarrel with the proud forests it hath fed,
> And feedeth still, more comely than itself?
> Can it deny the chiefdom of green groves?
> Or shall the tree be envious of the dove
> Because it cooeth, and hath snowy wings
> To wander wherewithal and find its joys?
> We are such forest-trees, and our fair boughs
> Have bred forth, not pale solitary doves,
> But eagles golden-feathered, who do tower
> Above us in their beauty, and must reign
> In right thereof. For 'tis the eternal law
> That first in beauty should be first in might.   (II.206–29)

Oceanus images the increasing degree of freedom reflected in each new heavenly order. He compares the Uranian generation of gods to the soil, the Titanic gods to the trees, and the Olympian gods to birds. This hierarchy is based on the principle that active becoming is superior to static being, and the more freely one can change the better. The soil is the base of all growth, and as such is itself unmoving; the trees grow, but since they are rooted in the soil, they cannot change their places; only the birds can move freely through the skies.

Oceanus's speech closely resembles Asia's long speech in Act II, scene iv of *Prometheus Unbound,* especially since both speeches have their ultimate source in Hesiod's *Theogony* and its account of Saturn's reign. For Keats as well as for Shelley, the age of Saturn mythically embodies a Rousseauian state of nature, a time of peaceful harmony, but a time when man is not yet fully man. In painful retrospection, Saturn himself characterizes his rule as an age of

> godlike exercise
> Of influence benign on planets pale,
> Of admonitions to the winds and seas,
> Of peaceful sway above man's harvesting.　　(I.107–10)

The problem with this seeming paradise is the problem in all Romantic portrayals of the state of nature. The price man pays for being in harmony with nature is that he is locked into its cycles and unable to advance beyond them. The pre-Olympian divinities in *Hyperion* are closely associated with the forces of nature, and, although this gives them a kind of elemental grandeur, it also means that their power is strictly limited by natural law.[11]

Coelus, the one first-generation divinity we meet, is barely distinguishable from the elements themselves,[12] and sees himself as powerless in comparison with his descendant, Hyperion:

> Yet do thou strive; as thou art capable,
> As thou canst move about, an evident God,
> And canst oppose to each malignant hour
> Ethereal presence. I am but a voice;
> My life is but the life of winds and tides,
> No more than winds and tides can I avail,
> But thou canst.　　(I.337–43)

Hyperion may be more independent of nature than Coelus, but even Hyperion is powerless in the face of nature's cyclical character, as he finds when he tries to hasten the dawn:

> Fain would he have commanded, fain took throne
> And bid the day begin, if but for change.
> He might not. No, though a primeval God,
> The sacred seasons might not be disturbed.
> Therefore the operations of the dawn
> Stayed in their birth.　　(I.290–95)

During the Titans' reign, the world may be at peace, but some element of humanity is still missing in the universe, as one senses when one hears Enceladus characterized as originally "tame and mild / As grazing ox unworried in the meads" (II.66–67). The happiness of Saturn's reign is essentially the happiness of a contented cow, and thus precludes the development of man's higher potential.

Thus Keats's *Hyperion*, like many Romantic creation myths, tells the story of a fortunate fall.[13] The harmony of Saturn's reign must be shattered, and misery introduced into the universe, for the sake of progress. In the drama of the fallen Titans, Keats portrays how suffering leads to a growth of consciousness, specifically self-consciousness. As long as the Titans rule unopposed, they rule without reflecting on the basis of their rule, and hence cannot understand it. Only when they are deposed do they begin to realize what role they fulfilled in cosmic history, as Oceanus tries to tell Saturn:

> Great Saturn, thou
> Has sifted well the atom-universe;
> But for this reason, that thou art the King,
> And only blind from sheer supremacy,
> One avenue was shaded from thine eyes,
> Through which I wandered to eternal truth.　　(II.182–87)

If the king is cut off from wisdom, because in the security of his power he has no need to look deeply into things, then the chief consolation to the Titans for their loss of power is their corresponding gain in wisdom.

III

Following the common Romantic pattern, Keats's Titans move from innocence to experience, as part of an ongoing process which is developing freedom and self-consciousness. What is distinctive about *Hyperion* is the way Keats emphasizes beauty in this development. Though freedom seems to be the principle of the hierarchy Oceanus sees in the universe, he speaks of beauty more than freedom. The "fresh perfection" he talks of is "a power more strong in beauty" (II.212–13) and his speech culminates in a triumphant assertion which has a particularly Keatsian ring: "'tis the eternal law / That first in beauty should be first in might" (II.228–29). This is not how Blake or Shelley would have formulated the pattern of historical progress. They did of course think that freedom is beautiful, but the growth of freedom was their primary concern, and the resulting beauty was a kind of welcome dividend for them. Keats, on the other hand, seems primarily interested in the growth of beauty, and he prizes freedom as the means to that end.

When Blake or Shelley talk about progress, they have in view something reasonably close to what is ordinarily meant by progress, the economic and social improvement of man's condition, and when they speak of freedom, the political meaning of the word is still foremost in their minds. Keats, by contrast, seems to have lost sight of freedom as a distinctly political issue. He seems in fact to have lost interest in politics as such.[14] On the whole, Keats's poetry has less political content than that of any other English Romantic poet. In reading *Hyperion*, one is not troubled by the sort of question raised by the myths of Blake and Shelley, whether a given event is to be interpreted in political terms, and, more specifically, whether the freedom of the human spirit is to be brought about by recognizably political means. For Keats politics is not the focus of human progress. By comparison with Blake or Shelley (or Byron, for that matter), Keats's vistas are more narrowly aesthetic.

To speak of Keats's aestheticism in this context is not to disparage his achievement, but only to try to highlight his distinctive stance as a poet. The progress portrayed in Keats's epic is ultimately artistic progress. A completed *Hyperion* might well have been a contribution to a genre the eighteenth century developed, the Progress of Poetry.[15] The succession of divine generations Keats portrays may symbolize a succession of poetic dynasties. One intriguing, though highly speculative, theory of how Keats would have developed *Hyperion* after Book III is that in depicting the ascendancy of Apollo, Keats was depicting the ascendancy of Greek poetry. The poem was to go on to show the Poetic Genius passing from Greece to Rome and finally on to Britain, where Saturn was to be consoled for losing heaven by presiding over a great age of poetry.[16]

Without necessarily accepting this hypothetical reconstruction of *Hyperion*, one can make the more limited claim that the only gains made in the poem are gains in poetic power, a growth in artistic consciousness. Clymene's speech of consolation, for example, concentrates on how she learned to turn suffering into art. Telling her fellow Titans of how she made "music of our woes" (II.269), she speaks of her first encounter with the new god, Apollo, and defers to his superiority in creating a "new blissful golden melody" (II.280). The link between Apollo and poetry recurs in Book III where he appears as "the father of all verse" (III.13). Perhaps one reason Keats felt attracted to Hyperion as a subject is that the old sun-god points to the new. Apollo is the one Olympian most closely associated with the arts.[17] For Keats to focus on the growth of Apollo is to focus on the growth of poetry itself.

The idea that *Hyperion* somehow deals with the development of the poetic character is supported by an intriguing parallel between Keats's speculations on that subject in his letters and one passage in his epic.[18] Saturn, reacting to his fall, laments that he has lost his identity:

> I am gone
> Away from my own bosom; I have left
> My strong identity, my real self,
> Somewhere between the throne and where I sit
> Here on this spot of earth.   (I.112–16)

Though at the moment Saturn can see only how the loss of his "strong identity" diminishes him, the course of the poem will show that to lose one's sense of self is to gain a new power, the ability to see into the selves of others. Moments later, Saturn is already wondering whether he can still create in some manner (I.141–45), and perhaps is groping toward the idea of artistic creation as a compensation for the loss of his power to shape the external world.

When in power, Saturn was too egotistical, too absorbed in his own concerns, to be open to the world around him, and hence his insight was restricted. In that sense, loss of power might well liberate him, leading him to new powers of sympathetic insight. Oceanus and Clymene display a remarkable ability to empathize imaginatively with their successors and to appreciate the new beauty they represent. This theme in *Hyperion* seems to grow out of Keats's attempt to define the "poetical Character" in one of his most famous letters:

... it is not itself – it has no self – it is every thing and nothing – It has no character ... A Poet is the most unpoetical of any thing in existence; because he has no Identity – he is continually in for – and filling some other Body ... When I am in a room with People, ... then not myself goes home to myself: but the identity of every one in the room begins to press upon me that, I am in a very little time an[ni]hilated.[19]

The idea that one must lose one's self in order to gain insight into the selves of others explains why in both *Hyperion* poems, what looks like a loss in worldly terms turns out to be a gain in terms of poetry.

If the fullness of the poet's insight is rooted in some kind of emptiness in his self, we can begin to understand the link between suffering and wisdom in Keats's view. In searching for what distinguishes the poetic character, Keats singles out a peculiar susceptibility to running contradictory emotions together. As a result, the poet can never experience happiness totally divorced from misery. Clymene, the most artistic of the Titans we see, says that Apollo's music made her "sick / Of joy and grief at once" (II.288–89). Out of this experience of contradictory emotions in art grows a more fundamental paradox. For Clymene, listening to Apollo, "a living death was in each gush of sounds" (II.281). Apollo himself undergoes a similar experience, as he passes through a death agony to attain his power as a visionary:

> Some wild commotions shook him, and made flush
> All the immortal fairness of his limbs –
> Most like the struggle at the gate of death;
> Or liker still to one who should take leave
> Of pale immortal death, and with a pang
> As hot as death's is chill, with fierce convulse
> Die into life. So young Apollo anguished.   (III.124–30)

This positive view of death as the means to poetic vision helps explain what is probably the most peculiar feature of *Hyperion* when viewed in the context of the epic tradition: Keats's attraction to moments of defeat and suffering. Even in our one glimpse of the Olympian gods, whom we would expect to see in triumph, celebrating their victory over the Titans, we are restricted to a scene of Apollo undergoing torment, which, as we have seen, strangely reminds us of what the defeated Titans are experiencing. Though consciously writing in the epic tradition, Keats shows little or no interest in the traditional epic theme, the conquering hero, triumphing over all obstacles. Even Milton, who did his best to downgrade the classical heroic virtues by assigning them to his devil, ends up portraying Christ as an active warrior, victorious over his fallen adversaries in Book VI. But Keats's characters are curiously passive for epic figures. They are all shown in moments of defeat, or, at least in Apollo's case, suffering pain. Acted upon, rather than acting, they are essentially static figures, frozen in despair and doubt.

Hyperion, as the last of the unfallen Titans, is perhaps the closest Keats comes to a traditional epic figure. But even Hyperion is virtually paralyzed by indecision, and, uncharacteristically for an epic hero, shudders with fear (I.170).[20] Evidently Keats was not temperamentally suited to traditional epic themes. As early as *Endymion*, he explicitly rejected the subject of war in favor of the more lyric theme of love:

> The woes of Troy, towers smothering o'er their blaze,
> Stiff-holden shields, far-piercing spears, keen blades,
> Struggling, and blood, and shrieks – all dimly fades
> Into some backward corner of the brain;
> Yet in our very souls, we feel amain
> The close of Troilus and Cressid sweet,
> Hence, pageant history! Hence, gilded cheat!
>
> . . .
>
> What care, though striding Alexander passed
> The Indus with his Macedonian numbers?
> Though old Ulysees tortured from his slumbers
> The glutted Cyclops, what care? ... Juliet leaning
> Amid her window-flowers, sighing, weaning
> Tenderly her fancy from its maiden snow,
> Doth more avail than these. The silver flow
> Of Hero's tears, the swoon of Imogen,
> Fair Pastorella in the bandit's den,
> Are things to brood on with more ardency
> Than the death-day of empire.   (II.8–14, 24–34)

From Keats's scorn of traditional epic warfare, we can see why he would have had great difficulty continuing *Hyperion* beyond the point where he abandoned it. At some point he was going to have to narrate a battle, either the Titans' attempt to recapture heaven or a flashback to their original defeat.[21] Milton himself had a hard time with this part of his story, and many would say that Books V and VI are poetically the weakest part of *Paradise Lost*.[22] Keats's doubts concerning where his story was taking him surface at the beginning of Book III:

> Thus in alternate uproar and sad peace,
> Amazed were those Titans utterly.
> Oh, leave them, Muse! Oh, leave them to their woes;
> For thou art weak to sing such tumults dire;
> A solitary sorrow best befits
> Thy lips, and antheming a lonely grief.   (III.1–6)

Keats's questioning of his ability "to sing such tumults dire" is not conventional poetic modesty, but a characteristically sane and sober assessment of where his strengths and weaknesses as a poet lay. Keats's genius was indeed for "antheming a lonely grief," but that is a lyric, rather than an epic achievement. Keats shapes his epic material in *Hyperion* so that it becomes a vehicle for examining the nature of the poet, and hence a vehicle for the essentially lyric purpose of self-examination.[23]

Though *Hyperion* may have a Homeric, or rather a pre-Homeric setting, the kind of poetry Keats is writing is far removed from the world of ancient epic. Instead of dealing with the external conflict of god against god, or warrior against warrior, Keats is dealing with the modern theme of internal conflict. His poem avoids narrating actual battles in order to focus on the struggles within its characters as they try to cope with defeat:

> There saw she direst strife – the supreme God
> At war with all the frailty of grief,
> Of rage, of fear, anxiety, revenge,
> Remorse, spleen, hope, but most of all despair.
>
> (II.92–95)

When one first hears what Keats's subject is in *Hyperion*, one might expect him to portray a primitive, even a barbaric world, ruled by brute strength alone. But what strikes us about Keats's Titans is their feebleness.[24] Far from living in a fresh world, at the beginning of time, they live in a world where all possibilities, at least for them, have been played out and time is coming to an end. The mood of their world is not one of dawn, but of the setting sun.[25] The opening lines of the poem are perhaps the most impressive evocation in all poetry of an absolute dead-end:

> Deep in the shady sadness of a vale
> Far sunken from the healthy breath of morn,
> Far from the fiery noon, and eve's one star,
> Sat gray-haired Saturn, quiet as a stone,
> Still as the silence round about his lair;
> Forest on forest hung about his head
> Like cloud on cloud. No stir of air was there,
> Not so much life as on a summer's day
> Robs not one light seed from the feathered grass,
> But where the dead leaf fell, there did it rest.
> A stream went voiceless by, still deadened more
> By reason of his fallen divinity

Spreading a shade; the naiad 'mid her reeds
Pressed her cold finger closer to her lips.

Along the margin-sand large foot-marks went,
No further than to where his feet had strayed,
And slept there since. Upon the sodden ground
His old right hand lay nerveless, listless, dead,
Unsceptred; and his realmless eyes were closed,
While his bowed head seemed listening to the earth,
His ancient mother, for some comfort yet.   (I.1–21)

Confronted with such a fate, Keats's Titans begin to wonder whether anything at all is left for them to do:

　　　　　　　　　　　　But cannot I create?
Cannot I form? Cannot I fashion forth
Another world, another universe,
To overbear and crumble this to naught?
Where is another chaos? Where?   (I.141–45)

Keats's Saturn is a curiously modern Titan, wondering, like a nineteenth-century poet, whether any avenues of creativity remain open to him, whether somewhere something remains as yet unformed on which he might exercise his shaping powers.[26] Keats projected much of himself into the gods he created, portraying them struggling with problems which strike us as modern and sophisticated, rather than ancient and primitive.[27] In the end, even the first version of *Hyperion* is much closer in spirit and substance to *The Prelude* than to the *Iliad*.[28] The modern character of Keats's myth became more fully evident as he reworked it into *The Fall of Hyperion*.

IV

The more we look at *Hyperion*, the more it seems to transform before our eyes, from an ancient epic to a modern, from a Miltonic epic to a Romantic, from a myth of historical progress to a myth of poetic growth, finally, from an epic narrative to a lyric self-examination. We know from Keats's remark about the "egotistical sublime" in Wordsworth[29] that he distrusted the self-absorption of modern poetry, and hoped to be able to get out of himself by turning to the objective poetic forms, the drama and the epic. In *Hyperion*, Keats aspires to be a truly objective narrator, keeping himself out of the poem and letting the story speak for itself. But despite Keats's efforts to avoid speaking in his own voice, his deepest, most personal concerns almost immediately come crowding back into *Hyperion*, until the growth of the poet becomes its central theme. *Hyperion* may be objective in its form, but in celebrating the growth of consciousness, the poem ends up celebrating the very subjectivity of vision it aspires to leave behind. Keats's epic embodies a profound contradiction: Miltonic in form, it is Wordsworthian in content, a basic tension which helps to explain why Keats could not complete the poem as originally conceived.[30]

The idea that Keats's subjectivity gradually wins out over the seeming objectivity of *Hyperion* is borne out by the way in which he recast the poem in *The Fall of Hyperion*.[31] The second version is a great poetic achievement, and most of Keats's changes improve the work artistically.[32] Nevertheless, in an important sense, *The Fall of Hyperion* constitutes an admission of the failure of Keats's epic ambitions in *Hyperion*. Though Keats was planning to incorporate the narrative from *Hyperion* into the second version, he placed it in a frame tale which gives the work more the character of a dream vision than an epic. As many critics have noted, Dante begins to replace Milton as Keats's model in *The Fall of Hyperion*, as shown by the setting in a dark wood or the simple act of changing the name of the poem's divisions from *books* to *cantos*.[33] Keats makes himself a character in the poem, in a very real sense the central character. Any events narrated from the first version must pass through Keats's consciousness to reach us. The idea of a fall is still on Keats's mind; it is in fact now announced in the title of the poem. But, as in the first version, we never see the fall of Hyperion. What we do see is the fall of the poet, out of unthinking and presumably blissful ignorance into a heightened but painful poetic awareness.

The Fall of Hyperion begins in a kind of paradise, a lush garden scene, which, through the mention of "our Mother Eve" (I.31), Keats associates with Eden.[34] But Keats is not satisfied with this earthly paradise, perhaps because it is restricted to purely sensory experience. This is our first indication that the poet is set apart from other men, incapable of being satisfied by their ordinary kind of happiness, and hence incapable of fitting in to the ordinary world. Experiencing an unearthly longing, an "appetite / More yearning than on earth I ever felt" (I.38–39), Keats consumes some kind of forbidden fruit, and, going Milton one better, a forbidden drink as well. The mysterious potion awakens ambivalent feelings in the poet. He obviously desires it, and yet he struggles against its effects (I.53–54). The drink is evidently a narcotic (I.47). Though on one level it overpowers consciousness, on another it leads to a higher form of consciousness, and gives Keats a new power of vision.

Within his dream, Keats awakens to find himself in an ancient, monumental temple, where he meets Moneta, the Latin name for the figure Keats presented as Mnemosyne in *Hyperion*. What follows dramatizes the poet's relation to his Muse. Keats gives the encounter a frightening, nightmarish quality, in sharp contrast to the epic convention of the poet in secure possession of the Muse's favor. When Milton, for example, speaks of his relation to his Muse, it is already well established. Milton accepts the Muse and the Muse accepts Milton. But in *The Fall of Hyperion*, Keats presents himself as struggling with the source of his inspiration, struggling to establish his title to the name of poet.

Far from accepting Keats without question, Moneta challenges his right to be in the temple. In the ensuing action and dialogue, he must prove himself worthy to join the ranks of genuine poets. Though the temple is later identified as Saturn's, on another level of interpretation, it can be regarded as a kind of Chaucerian House of Fame. To be admitted to the temple is to be admitted to the fellowship of poets through the ages, the band of poetic immortals. Moneta offers Keats a form of immortality, presumably the immortality of lasting artistic achievement as opposed to the transiency of ordinary human existence:

> If thou canst not ascend
> These steps, die on that marble where thou art.
> Thy flesh, near cousin to the common dust,
> Will parch for lack of nutriment – thy bones
> Will wither in a few years, and vanish so
> That not the quickest eye could find a grain
> Of what thou now art on that pavement cold.
>
> (I.107–13)

In Keatsian terms, Moneta is challenging the poet to climb into the world of the Grecian Urn.

The agony Keats endures in trying to ascend the steps resembles Apollo's struggle at the end of *Hyperion*, even to the point of both characters shrieking.[35] Keats retains the paradoxical blending of life and death from the earlier version:

> One minute before death, my iced foot touched
> The lowest stair; and as it touched, life seemed
> To pour in at the toes ...
> Then said the veiled shadow: 'Thou hast felt
> What 'tis to die and live again before
> Thy fated hour.'   (I.132–34, 141–43)

Once again Keats sees the poet as having to die into life, losing his
ordinary self in order to gain an artistic identity. Keats develops at
greater length the view of the poet as peculiarly susceptible to
suffering:

> 'None can usurp this height,' returned that shade,
> 'But those to whom the miseries of the world
> Are misery, and will not let them rest.'   (I.147–49)

More specifically, the poet, unable to separate the pains from the
joys of life, experiences both at once:

> Every sole man hath days of joy and pain,
> Whether his labours be sublime or low –
> The pain alone; the joy alone; distinct:
> Only the dreamer venoms all his days,
> Bearing more woe than all his sins deserve.
>   (I.172–76)

The idea that the artist suffers more than other men leads explicitly
in *The Fall of Hyperion* to a notion of compensation:

> Therefore, that happiness be somewhat shared,
> Such things as thou art are admitted oft
> Into like gardens thou didst pass erewhile,
> And suffered in these temples; for that cause
> Thou standest safe beneath this statue's knees.
>   (I.177–81)

The artist's special powers of vision are granted him to make up for
the greater suffering he endures.[36] Presumably the artist's immortal
fame also compensates him for his lack of success in worldly terms.

Keats develops the idea of the artist's peculiar sensitivity to the
point where one begins to sense something almost diseased in the
poet's unfitness for ordinary life.[37] Seemingly uncomfortable with
this extreme position, Keats tries to point out that if he has a
"sickness" it is a "not ignoble" one (I.184). He seems worried
about the sharp division he is creating between art and life, and
wishes that the artist could play a more useful role in society,
becoming a "physician," rather than diseased himself (I.189–90).

His dialogue with Moneta builds up to a nearly frenzied moment of poetic self-recognition, in which Keats tries to assert his true vocation as a poet:

> Apollo! Faded, far-flown Apollo!
> Where is thy misty pestilence to creep
> Into the dwellings, through the door crannies,
> Of all mock lyrists, large self-worshippers
> And careless hectorers in proud bad verse.
> Though I breathe death with them it will be life
> To see them sprawl before me into graves. (I.204–210)

Wordsworth is probably the prototype of the "large self-worshippers" and Byron the prototype of the "careless hectorers."[38] Evidently Keats wants to dissociate himself from his fellow Romantics, largely because he rejects the obsessive concern with self he sensed in Wordsworth.[39]

Keats seems to be struggling against what was happening as he reworked *Hyperion*. Despite his scorn for Wordsworthian or Byronic egotism, Keats increasingly emerges in the new version as a subjective poet himself. Richard Woodhouse claimed that Keats intended to cancel the last part of his dialogue with Moneta (II.187–210), perhaps an indication that he was still uncertain about his role as a poet.[40] Dissatisfied with the kind of poetry he wrote best, Keats always wished that he could be more of a public figure as a poet, like Milton. The direction Keats's dialogue with Moneta finally takes, even if he intended to delete the passage, provides a clue to what was happening throughout the *Hyperion* project: a poet struggling against his own poetic destiny, trying to be something he was not, but in the process extending the limits of what he could do well.

At this point in *The Fall of Hyperion*, Keats modulates back into the original version, and tries to get on with his epic narrative. But this time, Keats has exhausted his thematic material even before he gets to the story he has to tell.[41] The Induction to *The Fall of Hyperion* is more powerful than anything Keats can show in the body of the poem. Once Keats resumes his narrative, he can only repeat themes he has already expressed. As the vision of the Titans unfolds before his eyes, his emphasis falls on the burden of the vision. Moneta herself calls her power of sight "a curse" (I.243), and thus to Keats Moneta becomes another embodiment of the paradoxical yoking of joy and pain, life and death (I.256–63).

Keats repeatedly stresses how he can hardly bear up under the weight of the vision he is experiencing. But he had already shown on the steps of Saturn's Temple what a price the poet pays for the right "to see as a god sees" (I.304).

In *The Fall of Hyperion*, the invocation to the epic overwhelms the epic itself. One can see the potential for this development in *Paradise Lost*. Like the *Hyperion* poems, Milton's epic is fundamentally a story of the growth of understanding through suffering. This overarching theme is reflected in Milton's own story as a poet insofar as it surfaces at all in the poem. Milton's blindness is as paradoxical as the fortunate fall itself, a loss that is in a profounder sense a gain, since it has given him a higher power of vision, a power of inner vision, "to see and tell / Of things invisible to mortal sight" (III.54–55). Milton's blindness is thus a special case of his general understanding of God's providence. At first Milton could not understand why God would visit blindness upon one of His most devoted servants, but he came to see his affliction as part of God's larger plan for his spiritual development. Milton keeps his own story well in the background in *Paradise Lost*. But we can easily imagine how he could have expanded his own role in the epic. The Invocations to Books III and VII are among the most beautiful and moving parts of the poem. Though Samuel Johnson may have been right in claiming that no one ever wished *Paradise Lost* longer than it is, perhaps a little more self-revelation from Milton might have been welcome, more of a glimpse into the poet's struggle to create his masterpiece. That is what Keats gives us in *The Fall of Hyperion* (though he cannot give us the completed masterpiece itself). Keats makes the story of how the poet came to write the poem more important than the story the poem tells. The struggle of the poet to attain poetic vision becomes more interesting than the struggle of Titan against Olympian.

V

The Hyperion myth served as a kind of artistic detour for Keats, a way of getting out of himself at first but of getting back to himself at last. In the process, Keats did not simply abandon myth; rather, he transformed the way it functions in his poetry. As we have suggested, what distinguishes Keats from earlier Romantic myth-makers, particularly Blake and Shelley, is that he uses myth to come to terms with this world, rather than projecting a better world beyond. That explains why we are struck, not by the grandeur of Keats's mythic figures, but by their humanity. There are of course touches of monumentality in Keats's portrayal of the Titans, especially in the first version of his poem. But on the whole, the power in which Keats's gods exceed us is the power to suffer:

> But oh, how unlike marble was that face!
> How beautiful, if sorrow had not made
> Sorrow more beautiful than beauty's self.
>
> (*Hyperion*, I.34–36)

> Some mourning words, which in our feeble tongue
> Would come in these like accents (Oh, how frail
> To that large utterance of the early gods!).
>
> (*Hyperion*, I.49–51)

> Meanwhile in other realms big tears were shed,
> More sorrow like to this, and such-like woe,
> Too huge for mortal tongue or pen of scribe.
>
> (*Hyperion*, I.158–60)

Keats stresses the way that suffering is a humanizing force for the gods.[42] As a result of their fall, the Titans experience emotions they never felt before, emotions which deepen their souls, giving them wider sympathies and a better understanding of each other.

Thea is the first to undergo humanization, as she tries to comfort Saturn:

> One hand she pressed upon that aching spot
> Where beats the human heart, as if just there,
> Though an immortal, she felt cruel pain.   (I.42–44)

Though we feel that for Thea to experience human emotions is a gain, to Coelus, the growing humanity of the Titans is a disgrace:

> For I have seen my sons most unlike Gods.
> Divine ye were created, and divine
> In sad demeanour, solemn, undisturbed,
> Unruffled, like high Gods, ye lived and ruled.
> Now I behold in you fear, hope, and wrath;
> Actions of rage and passion – even as
> I see them, on the mortal world beneath,
> In men who die.   (I.328–35)

Coelus's model of a god seems to be an Aristotelian unmoved mover, with no more passion than a stone. But by our standards, the Titans seem to have become richer, more interesting beings as a result of acquiring emotions. Keats has adapted the figures of ancient poetry to modern purposes by giving them psychological complexity. This explains why he has to show his figures in defeat. Only the frustration of the impulse to act in the external world builds up the richness of the internal world of the mind.

Keats's "Ode to Psyche" suggests that the one realm left for modern poets to explore is the depths of the human psyche, and hence the modern myth-maker must turn inward and "build a fane / In some untrodden region of [the] mind" (ll. 50–51).[43] Keats cannot hope to compete with Homer in describing heroic warfare. But by showing gods who have lost the power to act, who can only suffer inwardly, Keats shifts the focus of attention to the inner world, where the modern poet reigns supreme. Moneta seems to be speaking for Keats when she asserts the value of humanizing myth, denying that the natural world has any meaning except in human terms:

> Mortal, that thou may'st understand aright,
> I humanize my sayings to thine ear,
> Making comparisons of earthly things;
> Or thou might'st better listen to the wind,
> Whose language is to thee a barren noise,
> Though it blows legend-laden through the trees.   (II.1–6)

This scorn for the "legend-laden wind" is a scorn for myth that has not been given human meaning, which in Keats's terms means myth without psychological depth.

Opening up the inner mental world of his divine figures, Keats succeeds in affirming the human condition by showing that even the gods are made better by becoming more human. But for Keats to be human is to be able to suffer, and in the special case of the artist always to feel joy and pain at once. The deepest reason for this conjunction of emotions is that for Keats the joy of creativity is rooted in the pain of suffering. He refuses to separate the creaturely from the creative side of man. In this respect, Keats sees the human condition as fundamentally tragic in *The Fall of Hyperion*.[44]

Even in Blake and Shelley, the Romantic creation myth bordered on tragedy. In *Prometheus Unbound*, for example, the existing world is shot through with tensions and contradictions, conflicting goods and tragic disjunctions:

> The good want power, but to weep barren tears.
> The powerful goodness want: worse need for them.
> The wise want love; and those who love want wisdom;
> And all best things are thus confused to ill.   (I.i.625–28)

The only thing that prevents Shelley's vision from becoming tragic is his hope that this situation is only temporary, a stage in mankind's progression to a higher state, beyond tragedy. But over the years, the tragic vision suppressed by apocalyptic expectations in Romantic myth began to come to the fore. We have already seen this happening in *Frankenstein* and *Cain*, and one might add that Shelley seems to be moving toward a tragic vision of man hopelessly trapped in his current state in his last work, *The Triumph of Life*.[45] What changes the outlook in these works is a loss of confidence in the original Romantic vision of remaking man. As time passes, Romantic authors become less and less confident that paradise can be regained, that any fundamental alteration in the human condition is possible.

From the beginning, what was missing in the *Hyperion* poems was a well-defined end. One of the most important reasons why Keats could not finish either version is that he had no vision of cosmic history culminating in some sort of final moment. At first sight Oceanus's speech seems to embrace the kind of cosmic vistas familiar in Blake and Shelley. But what Oceanus is affirming is a process with no clear resolution:

> as thou wast not the first of powers,
> So art thou not the last; it cannot be.
> Thou art not the beginning nor the end. (II.188–90)

Though Keats sketches out several stages of cosmic history, he leaves shrouded in mystery how the whole process began.[46] Even Coelus, the oldest of all the gods, has a dim view of the day of creation, though he supposedly witnessed it firsthand:

> O brightest of my children dear, earth-born
> And sky-engendered, son of mysteries
> All unrevealed even to the powers
> Which met at thy creating; at whose joys
> And palpitations sweet, and pleasures soft,
> I, Coelus, wonder how they came and whence.
>
> (I.309–14)

The absence of a clear beginning to the story in *Hyperion* is balanced by the absence of a definite end. Though for the moment the Olympians are triumphant, Oceanus suggests that their achievement is no more permanent than Saturn's and they too may someday be displaced: "Yea, by that law, another race may drive /

Our conquerors to mourn as we do now" (II.230–31). This vision
implies that every achievement is in some way limited and destined
to be surpassed. Keats's myth embodies the familiar Romantic
dialectical process, but without any vision of a final synthesis.

When Keats shows the first of the gods wondering of the
primeval divine joys "how they came and whence," he abandons
the original purpose of the Romantic creation myth: to point the
way to recapturing paradise by looking back to man's original
happiness. For Keats, the fall ceases to be a single, definite event, to
be located in a historical past. He no longer uses his vision of the
fall as a clue to remaking man's future, but rather sees fallenness as
the key to understanding man's present.[47] The fall becomes a
perpetual process in the *Hyperion* poems, something everyone must
go through in order to become human. The one defect in the Titans'
understanding of their experience is that they fight against the idea
of fully accepting their fall. The way they continually dwell upon
their loss of paradise, looking wistfully back to their days of calm
and joy, suggests that their greatest hope is to get back to where
they started, to undo the process which has humanized them. As we
saw in *Cain*, nostalgia for paradise can prevent man from making
the most of his world here and now, a lesson Oceanus tries to bring
home to his fellow Titans:

> Now comes the pain of truth, to whom 'tis pain –
> O folly! for to bear all naked truths,
> And to envisage circumstance, all calm,
> That is the top of sovereignty. (II.202–5)

Oceanus wants the Titans to turn their back on their lost paradise,
accept the inevitability of their fall, and become reconciled to their
new world, which, as he tries to show, is not lacking in new beauty.

For Oceanus the highest achievement is to be able to face up to
the suffering in the world. When Apollo has a divine vision later in
the poem, it is a vision of the tragedy in the world, a vision which
above all embraces pain and suffering:

> Knowledge enormous makes a God of me.
> Names, deeds, grey legends, dire events, rebellions,
> Majesties, sovran voices, agonies,
> Creations and destroyings, all at once
> Pour into the wide hollows of my brain,
> And deify me. (III.113–18)

Indeed wherever Apollo looks he sees "creations and destroyings;" everything created in the world of *Hyperion* will someday be destroyed. The reason Keats can affirm the process of destruction is that he knows it clears the way for new creations. The affirmation of historical process in *Hyperion* may ultimately be an affirmation of the destructive power of time, as a liberating force for the new poets of the world.[48] Bearing in mind the theory that the succession of divine dynasties in *Hyperion* may symbolize a succession of poetic generations, one might interpret Keats's portrait of the new displacing the old as expressing his wish that modern poetry might supersede ancient, that the great poets of the past might yield supremacy as gracefully to Keats's generation as Oceanus would have the Titans yield to the Olympians.[49]

In any event, the ability to affirm, and even to embrace, the suffering and transiency of the world is evidently what makes Apollo superior to the gods he displaces.[50] As we meet Apollo in Book III, he is deliberately rejecting the sheltered world of his childhood, and seeking out a wider world, even at the price of suffering. Whatever growth the Titans undergo is thrust upon them. They did not want to leave their paradise, and drag their feet at the prospect of entering the fallen world. Apollo, by contrast, represents the higher ideal in the poem because he is willing to go through with a fall to deepen his insight, even though he is not forced to.[51] As we have seen, in many respects Keats himself assumes Apollo's role in *The Fall of Hyperion*. The poet is best able to accept the fallenness of man's condition, because the poet, needing suffering for growth, understands the profound connection between human creativity and the fall.

VI

The fact that Keats never got beyond the fallen world in his *Hyperion* poems is thus not simply an accident, the result of his failing to complete his work before his death. An apocalyptic climax to the *Hyperion* poems would have been untrue to Keats's distinctive vision of life. Though we have seen that even Blake and Shelley move toward an increasingly open-ended conception of the apocalypse, they both at least began their poetic careers with genuine apocalyptic expectations and kept searching for a way to portray an apocalypse, even if it required rethinking the traditional conception. Although they eventually broke with the orthodox idea of a distinct end to history, they still sought to present poetically the beginning of a radically new age in man's development. But unlike Blake or Shelley, Keats had no faith in any fundamental transformation of the human condition. Speaking of a book about America and lamenting that the evils of society seem to be just as prevalent in what ought to be the state of nature, Keats writes in one of his letters:

... Mankind may be made happy – I can imagine such happiness carried to an extreme – but what must it end in? – Death – and who could in such a case bear with death – the whole troubles of life which are now frittered away in a series of years, would the[n] be accumulated for the last days of a being who instead of hailing its approach, would leave this world as Eve left Paradise – But in truth I do not believe in this sort of perfectibility – the nature of the world will not admit of it – the inhabitants of the world will correspond to itself – Let the fish philosophise the ice away from the Rivers in winter time and they shall be at continual play in the tepid delight of summer. Look at the Poles and at the Sands of Africa, Whirlpools and volcanoes – Let men exterminate them and I will say that they may arrive at earthly Happiness.[52]

Rejecting Romantic apocalyptic expectations, Keats goes on in the same letter to propose a myth of his own, the famous idea of the world as a "vale of Soul-making." Keats dismisses the cosmic salvational scheme of Christianity, and focuses instead on how individual identity emerges out of suffering:

There may be intelligences or sparks of the divinity in millions – but they are not Souls till they acquire identities, till each one is personally itself ... Do you not see how necessary a World of Pains and troubles is to school an Intelligence and make it a soul?[53]

For Keats the meaning of man's suffering cannot be derived from any external source. Man must learn to *make* his suffering meaningful, to create something out of his suffering himself.

Keats's mythic vision in the *Hyperion* poems may well look tentative and even timid by comparison with Blake or Shelley. But what from one viewpoint looks like a failure of nerve on Keats's part – his inability to project an apocalyptic vision – may from an equally valid viewpoint be his greatest strength – his willingness to see life more clearly for what it is because of his refusal to see man's current condition as a passing phase. Perhaps the most powerful

image in *The Fall of Hyperion* is our view of Keats confronting his own
mortality without any illusions, a fallen man staring at a fallen god:

> Without stay or prop
> But my own weak mortality, I bore
> The load of this eternal quietude,
> The unchanging gloom, and the three fixed shapes
> Ponderous upon my senses a whole moon.
> For by my burning brain I measured sure
> Her silver seasons shedded on the night,
> And ever day by day methought I grew
> More gaunt and ghostly. Oftentimes I prayed
> Intense, that death would take me from the vale
> And all its burthens. Gasping with despair
> Of change, hour after hour I cursed myself –
> Until old Saturn raised his faded eyes,
> And looked around and saw his kingdom gone,
> And all the gloom and sorrow of the place.

(I.388–402)

Though Keats would like to throw off the burden of his vision of
man's mortality, he refuses to let his mind abandon the present
moment and run off into pleasing dreams of the past or the future, of
the paradise man lost or the paradise he may regain. Instead Keats
maintains his poetic vigil, staring directly at the world before his eyes,
until a painful but quietly noble vision of man's fallen condition
begins to emerge. When he describes himself as standing "without
stay or prop," what Keats in essence means is without the support of
myth. That may sound like a strange claim to make with regard to a
mythic poem. But the point is that Keats does not derive the kind of
consolation from his mythic vision that most poets do, namely, a
glimpse into a better world. Keats was at times openly contemptuous
of the orthodox view of heaven:

The common cognomen of this world among the misguided and superstitious
is 'a vale of tears' from which we are to be redeemed by a certain arbitrary
interposition of God and taken to Heaven – What a little circumscribe[d]
straightened notion![54]

Keats was evidently also skeptical of the ways in which his fellow
Romantic poets recreated paradise. In his *Hyperion* poems he does
not look to the gods for a vision of a higher destiny for man. For Blake
and Shelley, the gods are a window through which the poet can see
into eternity. What Keats sees in the gods is a mirror of man's own
tragic destiny.

The Return to Rousseau

I

Both Byron and Keats raise doubts about the original Romantic quest for paradise. Could man's yearning for perfect happiness actually be what prevents him from living life to the fullest in the here-and-now? Perhaps if man abandoned his apocalyptic expectations, he could learn to make something out of his seemingly fallen condition. Byron's Cain and Keats's Apollo are distinguished precisely by their ability to live with suffering. The way they face up to painful truths sets them apart from ordinary mortals and thus is the source of their superior vision. In Byron and Keats, a tragic understanding of man's misery as the basis of his creativity begins to emerge out of the ruins of the Romantic dream of paradise.

In this sense, Byron and Keats seem to signify a return to the position of Rousseau, after the long Romantic struggle to overcome the antinomies in human existence the philosopher originally uncovered. In particular, Byron and Keats come back to Rousseau's bifurcation of humanity. Throughout Byron's poetry, he tends to divide humanity into those who live peacefully within society by quietly accepting its beliefs, and those who live on its fringes or beyond its borders, exiled or outlawed for their free-thinking and thus able to see new truths. In Keats, one does not find such a sense of active hostility between two distinct orders of men. But as we have seen in *The Fall of Hyperion*, Keats was inclined toward dividing men into those who accept the world unthinkingly and those who profoundly question its ways. In *Hyperion*, Keats begins with the world divided temporally into two historical stages, a happy but ignorant paradise and a painful but wise fallen world. In *The Fall of Hyperion*, he is working toward the idea that these two states coexist and will always be in tension. Keats contrasts the happy ignorance of the common man, who never probes too deeply into life on earth, with the painful wisdom of the true visionary, who is haunted by his awareness of human transitoriness and

181

tragedy. The dreamer-poet of *The Fall of Hyperion* resembles Rousseau's solitary walker, unable to find a home in conventional society and forced to wander along paths where ordinary men could not sustain themselves.

Besides breaking with the original Romantic hope for a universal redemption which would allow the artist to share his vision with all men, Byron and Keats begin to dismantle the cosmic framework of Romantic creation myths. *Cain* is set in the infinite universe of modern science, which, having no clear beginning and no clear end, will alternate forever between cycles of creation and destruction. Byron pictures human life as an island of meaning in an otherwise meaningless universe. With no recognizable pattern in the history of the cosmos, man cannot take his bearings from anything larger than himself. Keats also could not form a conception of any final state toward which the universe is headed, and he blurs our view of the initial stage as well. Both *Cain* and the *Hyperion* poems portray a universe in perpetual process, with eternal change as its only law.

The two ways in which Byron and Keats depart from the original form of Romantic creation myths are in fact related. The initially clear view of man's beginning and end in Romantics like Blake and Shelley was made possible by their conception of the apocalypse, and that apocalypse was originally supposed to take a political form, the establishment of a universal and democratic community of creative individuals. Basically, it was the idea of the French Revolution as a secular equivalent of the Last Judgment which at first gave shape to Romantic myth. As long as the Romantics viewed the French Revolution as a uniquely privileged moment in history – the beginning of the end of tyranny on earth – they had a fixed point around which to articulate their myths. Once they lost faith in the French Revolution, they lost at one and the same time the natural end-point for their narratives and the means for overcoming the division of mankind into conventional and unconventional men.

The weakening and eventual disintegration of linear narrative form in Romantic myth, evident particularly in the fragmentary character of the *Hyperion* poems, thus mirrors increasing doubts as to whether history is moving toward a universal goal and whether a single solution is possible for the human dilemma. This development is by no means confined to Byron and Keats; they merely begin at a point which other Romantics reached only late in their poetic careers. We have already seen how Blake moved from closed to open forms in his creation myths, as he began to conceive of the apocalypse in psychological rather than political terms. Although Blake refused to allow his thought to develop in a tragic direction, one senses him moving in his later works away from his original notion of the artist at the center of a liberated society and toward a less optimistic picture of the artist isolated by his visionary powers from the ordinary run of men.

We have also already discussed the tension between a linear and a cyclical conception of history in *Prometheus Unbound*. On the surface, Shelley's poem seems to promise a permanent liberation for mankind, but he throws out disquieting hints that man's fight for freedom may be unending. Throughout Shelley's work, one senses this conflict between different views of man's destiny. His idealistic vision of what man can become has to struggle with his skeptical awareness of how difficult it is to overcome the limitations of material existence. In Shelley's final work, *The Triumph of Life*, his doubts seem to win out over his hopes, resulting in perhaps the most deeply tragic vision any English Romantic produced. Significantly, Rousseau himself appears in Shelley's poetry just when he is beginning to wonder whether there may be unresolvable contradictions in human existence. Looking at the spectacle of Napoleon's rise and fall, the focus of the Romantics' disillusionment with politics, Shelley asks "why God made irreconcilable / Good and the means of good" (ll. 230–31).

In *The Triumph of Life*, Shelley begins to think of salvation as the exclusive privilege of only a few, and not, as in *Prometheus Unbound*, the destiny of mankind as a whole. Life has triumphed over the spirits of almost all men, including many of the great names of history, with a mere handful of exceptions:

> All but the sacred few who could not tame
> Their spirits to the Conqueror, but as soon
> As they had touched the world with living flame
>
> Fled back like eagles to their native noon,
> Or those who put aside the diadem
> Of earthly thrones or gems, till the last one
>
> Were there; for they of Athens and Jerusalem
> Were neither mid the mighty captives seen
> Nor mid the ribald crowd that followed them.
>
> (ll. 128–36)

When one has to be a Socrates or a Jesus to achieve redemption, clearly we have travelled a long way from the Romantics' original democratic faith. *The Triumph of Life* comes very close to the spirit of Rousseau's *Reveries* in its idea that the majority of men are doomed to go through life in chains, while only a special few can escape by turning their backs completely on society.[1]

Admittedly, the fact that *The Triumph of Life* remained unfinished when Shelley died makes it difficult to pin down its meaning. Some critics have argued that if Shelley had lived to complete the poem, he would have given it an optimistic turn.[2] If, for example, Shelley had died after writing only the first act of *Prometheus Unbound*, the surviving fragment would make a very depressing impression.[3] Given the references to *The Divine Comedy* in *The Triumph of Life*, in a completed version Rousseau might have proved to be the Virgil to Shelley's Dante, capable of showing the poet the infernal and purgatorial aspects of the world, but not of taking him into paradise.[4] What is missing from *The Triumph of Life* is precisely the apocalyptic vision that in Shelley's earlier works transforms a tragic view of human life into a hopeful one. A completed version of the poem might have supplied this vision and thus have had a wholly different emotional impact.

But in a way it is presumptuous of us to assume that we know how to complete a poem which Shelley himself could not see his way to finishing. Perhaps *The Triumph of Life* is no more fragmentary than *The Fall of Hyperion*. It is in fact remarkable that Shelley and Keats should have concluded their poetic careers with works which resemble each other so closely.[5] Both are dream visions modelled on Dante, both involve visions within the vision, both focus on mysterious female figures, both include a magic potion which effaces consciousness. And both works seem to have remained incomplete, not because the poets were denied a chance to finish them, but because they could not find a way to round out their visions, to answer the questions they raised.

We cannot know whether Shelley foresaw how to end his poem, but, from what we have, we can see that he was uncertain about how to begin his narrative. Like *The Four Zoas*, *The Triumph of Life* is a poem in search of its own beginning. From the very first moment of his vision, Shelley is questing for origins. But the crowd of men he sees is oblivious of either pole of Romantic myth: "none seemed to know / Whither he went, or whence he came" (ll. 47–48).[6] Shelley's vision plunges him *in medias res*, confronting him with a stark image of the fallen world. He wants to know the source of this suffering, presumably so that he can find a way to overcome it. The poem thus becomes a series of unanswered questions:

> Struck to the heart by this sad pageantry,
> Half to myself I said, "And what is this?
> Whose shape is that within the car? & why" –
>
> I would have added – "is all here amiss?" (ll. 176–79)

Rousseau appears in response to Shelley's enquiries, but only becomes the occasion for further questions about origins: "'Whence comest thou and whither goest thou? / How did thy course begin,' I said, 'and why?'" (ll. 296–97).

The Triumph of Life reveals its connection with Romantic creation myths in the way it persistently pairs the questions "whence?" and "whither?", linking knowledge of man's destiny to knowledge of his origins. But Rousseau proves to be a questionable guide:

> Whence I came, partly I seem to know,
>
> And how and by what paths I have been brought
> To this dread pass, methinks even thou mayst guess;
> Why this should be my mind can compass not;
>
> Whither the conqueror hurries me still less.
>
> (ll. 300–304).

In order to help Shelley understand his vision, Rousseau has to recount an enigmatic vision of his own. Yet Rousseau frustrates Shelley's curiosity from the start, claiming that the precondition of his vision was forgetfulness of his past:

> Whether my life had been before that sleep
> The Heaven which I imagine, or a Hell
>
> Like this harsh world in which I wake to weep,
> I know not. (ll. 332–35)

Shelley appropriately has Rousseau raise doubts concerning the very Romantic enterprise he inspired, the search for a prior paradise in human life.[7] Rousseau recognizes the possibility that paradise may be only a human fiction, and even seems to undermine the basic purpose of Romantic creation myths: "Thou wouldst forget thus vainly to deplore / Ills, which if ills, can find no cure from thee" (ll. 327–28).

Rousseau nevertheless goes on to narrate his own visionary experience. Confronted by a spirit who ought to be able to initiate him into the deepest mysteries, all Rousseau can do is to pose the same task Shelley assigned to him: "Shew me whence I came, and where I am, and why –" (l. 398). The Spirit does grant Rousseau a vision, but it is a vision of the chariot and triumphant procession of life. In other words, the poem has circled in upon itself and we are right back where we started from. Shelley has a vision of the Triumph of Life, wonders about its origin, seeks an answer to his questions from Rousseau, and Rousseau finally replies by narrating Shelley's original vision back to him. If Shelley had continued, *The Triumph of Life* might have become a set of Chinese boxes, an unending cycle of questions within questions. As Paul de Man describes the poem:

Questions of origin, of direction and of identity punctuate the text without ever receiving a clear answer. They always lead back to a new scene of questioning which merely repeats the quest and recedes in infinite regress ... We have to imagine the same sequence of events repeating themselves for Shelley, for Rousseau and for whomever Rousseau chose to question in his turn as Shelley questioned him. The structure of the text is not one of question and answer, but of a question whose meaning, as question, is effaced from the moment it is asked. The answer to the question is another question, asking what and why one asked, and thus receding ever further from the original query.[8]

The Triumph of Life remained unfinished for the same reason *The Four Zoas* did. Like Blake, Shelley discovered that the quest for origins is never-ending. No matter what one chooses as one's starting point, one can always push the enquiry into origins further back into the past.

II

The Triumph of Life epitomizes the structural difficulties Romantic myth-makers encountered. Once Shelley loses faith in political action as a means of achieving universal salvation for mankind, the shape of his myth begins to dissolve. With his apocalyptic vision slipping away, he has no clear end-point for his narrative, and finds it difficult to reach a fixed starting point as well. But we must not dwell exclusively on the negative aspects of this development. The dissolution of form in later Romantic myths does not simply reflect a process of disillusionment, the fading of an earlier Romantic dream. As we saw in analyzing *The Four Zoas*, the break with the neatness of a linear paradise–fall–paradise pattern gives Blake's new myth an open-ended quality, and thereby serves the positive purpose of embodying the Romantic ideal of freedom and unceasing creativity for man. In breaking out of the rigidity of the traditional pattern of creation myths, Romantic myth-makers gradually work their way back to a fundamental insight of Rousseau's *Second Discourse*: the ideal of human perfection is ultimately incompatible with the ideal of human freedom. If one sets up a finished model of human nature in the past, one implies an eventual end to human history in the future, and hence to human striving and development.

Observing the struggle to remain within the bounds of the traditional creation myth in works like *The Four Zoas* and *The Fall of Hyperion*, one begins to suspect that in the deepest sense the genre was never truly appropriate to the Romantics' distinctive vision. Indeed what we are observing in the development of Romantic creation myths is a group of artists gradually breaking down the limits of a traditional genre they imposed upon themselves in the first place. Wanting to be able to address men in familiar forms to reach as wide an audience as possible, Romantic myth-makers were naturally attracted to the well-established Biblical pattern of creation, fall, and apocalypse. The gnostic approach to myth at first seemed to offer the Romantics a perfect vehicle for their vision. They originally hoped to infuse the old and familiar forms with new and unfamiliar content, preserving the outlines of traditional creation myths while gnostically inverting their meaning. But the Romantics eventually came to see that in myth form very often *is* content, and to work within traditional mythic structures is often to remain bound by traditional religious assumptions. In the end, Romantic myth-makers could not work comfortably within the clearly defined structure of Biblical myth because they did not share the Bible's clearly defined idea of man's destiny.

Whether one looks at the Bible or its recreation in *Paradise Lost*, both works provide a clearly linear view of cosmic history, with a definite moment of creation, a definite moment of the fall, and a definite path toward eventual salvation determined by divine providence. This certainty of narrative shape reflects the ethical certainty of the Biblical tradition. The Bible has a very definite idea of what the good life for man is, and it does not hesitate to spell out this ideal, sometimes in overwhelming detail. One might sum up the Biblical idea of the good life as humble obedience to God. In the Garden of Eden man began in a state of perfect obedience to divine commandments, and if he is to achieve salvation, he must return to that subservience to God in the end.

As we have repeatedly seen, the Romantics, like Rousseau, had a vaguer conception of human nature than we find in the Biblical tradition, or for that matter, in the classical or even the early modern rationalist traditions. This indeterminateness in the idea of man is necessary to preserve the possibility of human freedom and individuality. The Romantics do not presume to tell a given man what to become; they only enjoin him to become whatever best expresses his inner being. This ideal of individual development is incompatible with laying down a single pattern of cosmic development in a creation myth. In effect, Romantic myth-makers gradually worked toward the idea that there are as many different creations, falls, and apocalypses as there are distinct individuals in the world. As Blake puts it: "the last Judgment begins & its Vision is seen by the [*Imaginative Eye*] of Every one according to the situation he holds ... to different People it appears differently as every thing else does ... whenever any Individual Rejects Error & Embraces Truth a last Judgment passes upon that Individual."[9]

Thus the development of the Romantic creation myth can be viewed as an attempt to find open-ended narrative patterns suited to the new open-ended vision of human possibilities presented in Rousseau. Conceiving of life as a continual process of change and growth, Romantic authors hesitated in the end to confine themselves to the strait-jacket of linear myth. One can see this tendency even in Romantic works which are by no means creation myths, but which still reflect the Romantic interest in the story of paradise and the fall. For example, though obviously not a mythic poem, Byron's *Don Juan* shows many signs of following Biblical patterns. Byron compares the experience of love to paradise,[10] and throughout the early cantos draws parallels between his characters and both Adam and Eve.[11] Hence the archetype of the fall is always hovering in the background of Byron's poem.[12] Byron begins with the story of an exile from "paradise," and then goes on to tell what amounts to a tale of a flood in Book II, with explicit references to Noah.[13] But *Don Juan* does not continue to follow the linear narrative of the Bible. Instead, Byron shapes his poem into a potentially unending cycle of innocence and experience, with its hero never reaching any kind of higher or final state. Juan's chief distinction as a hero is his unflagging resilience, his ability to go through experiences that would shatter most men, pick up the pieces in his life, and resume his quest for happiness. Byron never allows him to settle in to any fixed situation, no matter how enjoyable or comfortable it may seem. Whenever Juan is on the verge of finding a form of paradise, he must be expelled again in order to continue his growth and development.

Accordingly, the virtue Byron comes to focus on in the later cantos is something he calls "mobility," the refusal to become frozen in any given role in society and the insistence instead on treating one's identity as something to be constantly shaped and reshaped like a work of art.[14] One can get a feel for the distance Byron has travelled from traditional epic by contrasting the chameleon character of Juan[15] with the steadfastness, moral constancy, and singlemindedness of purpose typical of the conventional epic hero. What gives a clear narrative structure to the traditional epic is the hero's well-defined mission. Byron's narrative, by contrast, must remain open-ended because he wants to leave his hero free to wander all the world and experience life in its infinite variety.

On the whole, *Don Juan* remains within the horizons of everyday human life. But at one point, Byron gives us a glimpse of the cosmic framework in which his poem is set. Byron begins by consigning his own thought to oblivion, and then develops a universal image of chaos:

> But let it go: — it will one day be found
>   With other relics of "a former World,"
> When this World shall be *former*, underground,
>   Thrown topsy-turvy, twisted, crisped, and curled,
> Baked, fried, or burnt, turned inside-out, or drowned,
>   Like all the worlds before, which have been hurled
> First out of, and then back again to chaos —
> The superstratum which will overlay us.
>
> So Cuvier says: — and then shall come again
>   Unto the new creation, rising out
> From our old crash, some mystic, ancient strain

Of things destroyed and left in airy doubt;
Like to the notions we now entertain
Of Titans, giants, fellows of about
Some hundred feet in height, *not* to say *miles*,
And mammoths, and your winged crocodiles.
(IX.xxxvii–viii)

Referring to contemporary geological theories, Byron develops the understanding of the cosmos we have already seen in *Cain*. But he adds a twist: he uses his new myth to explain the form all the old ones took. He comes up with a view of the history of the cosmos which explains why men are persistently haunted by the dream of paradise. The way the world repeatedly returns to chaos leaves men with vague memories of an earlier state which was better, and which they image as Eden.

Byron's myth thus does not present the ascending spiral so common in Romantic poetry, but just the reverse. Fantasizing about what a disinterred George IV would look like to future ages, Byron presents cosmic history as a descending spiral:

Think if then George the Fourth should be dug up!
    How the new worldlings of the then new East
Will wonder where such animals could sup!
    (For they themselves will be but of the least:
Even worlds miscarry, when too oft they pup,
    And every new creation hath decreased
In size, from overworking the material –
Men are but maggots of some huge Earth's burial.)

How will – to these young people, just thrust out
    From some fresh Paradise, and set to plough,
And dig, and sweat, and turn themselves about,
    And plant, and reap, and spin, and grind, and sow,
Till all the arts at length are brought about,
    Especially of War and taxing, – *how*
I say, will these great relics, when they see 'em,
Look like the monsters of a new Museum!   (IX.xxxix–xl)

Despite its obvious playfulness, this passage has many of the elements we have seen in serious Romantic creation myths. It provides a naturalistic reinterpretation of the Biblical story of creation, and even follows Rousseau in suggesting that man develops all his civilized arts in response to his loss of paradise.[16] But in *Don Juan* the complex account of what went wrong in man's development in *The Book of Urizen* is reduced to the comic one-liner: "Even worlds miscarry, when too oft they pup." Byron suggests that man's inability to hold on to paradise is somehow rooted in the nature of things. Paradise is something which is perpetually being lost; indeed when man wakes up into history, it always seems to be just at the moment of leaving Eden. But Byron is willing to renounce any apocalyptic expectations in order to prevent man from settling in to any one rigid form. Like Don Juan, man must keep moving in order to keep from stagnating. Only in a chaotic universe can man go on creating forever.

III

With Byron's idea that paradise is only something to be lost, and not to be regained, we seem to have come full circle. Romantic myth-makers were originally inspired in their search for paradise by the speculations of Rousseau concerning the state of nature. But as we saw from the beginning, Rousseau himself doubted the possibility of man ever overcoming the basic tensions in his existence. Many Romantics tried to prove Rousseau wrong, but some came back in the end to the idea that paradise may be only a vain dream, and one which may unfit man for ordinary life. In this respect, the development of the creation myth in Romanticism points ahead to important developments in nineteenth- and twentieth-century thought, and helps to suggest the links between Romantic and modern literature. For example, the movement we have seen from linear to cyclical patterns in the myths of Blake, Shelley, Byron, and Keats looks forward to Nietzsche's myth of the eternal recurrence. As Nietzsche shows in *Thus Spoke Zarathustra*, a cyclical myth eliminates the notion of privileged moments in history, and thus allows man to go on creating and recreating himself forever. This helps to explain why a twentieth-century poet like Yeats was attracted to a cyclical notion of history, and even tried to set up his own myth of history in *A Vision*. As a poem like "The Double Vision of Michael Robartes" suggests, Yeats is in many respects the modern heir of the Romantic creation myth. He certainly shares the insight that the only way for man to keep his creative horizons open is to renounce the eternity of any of his achievements:

> Everything that man esteems
> Endures a moment or a day.
> Love's pleasure drives his love away,

The painter's brush consumes his dreams;
The herald's cry, the soldier's tread
Exhaust his glory and his might:
Whatever flames upon the night
Man's own resinous heart has fed.[17]

By looking back at Romantic creation myths from the perspective of the twentieth century, we can see that just when poets like Shelley and Keats abandoned their efforts at shaping a cosmic myth, they were on the verge of articulating a truly modern understanding of the horizons of human life, one which grounds an ideal of human freedom and autonomy in a vision of an infinite and open-ended universe. Consider the paradoxical character of the idea of the fall presented in *The Fall of Hyperion* or *The Triumph of Life*. Keats and Shelley sever their understanding of the fallen world from any traditional framework of paradise and apocalypse. That is, they tell the story of a fall, but give no clear view of the state from which man fell or the state to which he might aspire to undo the fall. It sounds strange to conceive of man's existence as fallen, without speaking of what lies beyond the borders of the fallen world. But this is exactly the understanding of human existence developed in what is perhaps the most characteristic work of twentieth-century philosophy, Heidegger's *Being and Time*. Heidegger continually speaks of man as fallen into the world, but he manages to do so without resorting to the underpinning of traditional myth. He thus finds a way to speak of human existence within a human horizon, refusing to refer to any transcendent grounding of man's life and thereby making man himself responsible for his being. The two poles between which Romantic myth originally moved – the creation and the apocalypse – drop out of view in *Being and Time*:

So neither must we take the fallenness of Dasein as a 'fall' from a purer and higher 'primal status' ... We would also misunderstand the ontological–existential structure of falling if we were to ascribe to it the sense of a bad and deplorable ontical property of which, perhaps, more advanced stages of human culture might be able to rid themselves.[18]

Heidegger's dense prose is obviously worlds removed from Romantic poetry. And yet like *The Fall of Hyperion* and *The Triumph of Life*, *Being and Time* presents fallenness, not as a passing phase, but as *the* human condition.[19] The way the impulse of the Romantic creation myth seems to drift off and subside in the final fragmentary works of Keats and Shelley may at first suggest the failure of the genre, as if the disaster of the French Revolution simply destroyed the hopes for the recreation of man that originally inspired Romantic myth-makers. But what from one point of view may look like a failed vision, from another point of view looks remarkably prophetic. The later Romantic attempts at myth-making dispense with the certainty of traditional mythic form and take a step toward imaginatively embodying the open horizons of modern man's understanding of his place in the world. Though Romantic creation myths originally strike us as merely recreations of traditional forms, they are in fact more genuinely creative than may at first appear. In studying Romantic creation myths, we are witnessing the genesis of the imaginative framework of modern literature.

Notes

Preface

1 The best general discussion of gnosticism is still Hans Jonas's classic work, *The Gnostic Religion* (Boston: Beacon Press, 1963). For an anthology of primary Gnostic sources, see Werner Foerster, ed., *Gnosis: A Selection of Gnostic Texts* (Oxford: Clarendon Press, 1972). For a survey of contemporary research and theories concerning gnosticism, see Ugo Bianchi, ed., *The Origins of Gnosticism* (Leiden: E. J. Brill, 1970). This volume contains a useful summary by Jonas of his understanding of gnosticism, "Delimitations of the Gnostic Phenomenon – Typological and Historical," pp. 90–108. Throughout my discussion I use *gnosticism* as a generic term referring to the form of heresy available throughout the history of religion; when referring specifically to the original practitioners of this heresy, who flourished around the time of Christ, I use *Gnosticism* as a proper name.

2 See Jonas, *Gnostic Religion*, pp. 92–94.

3 Henry Crabb Robinson reports that when arguing theology with Blake, he heard "the doctrine of the Gnostics repeated with sufficient consistency to silence one so unlearned as myself." See G. E. Bentley, Jr., Ed., *Blake Records* (Oxford: Clarendon Press, 1969), p. 545. On Blake's knowledge of Gnosticism, see Morton D. Paley, *Energy and the Imagination* (Oxford: Clarendon Press, 1970), pp. 66–67; Stuart Curran, "Blake and the Gnostic Hyle: A Double Negative," *Blake Studies*, 4 (1972), 130–33; and Leopold Damrosch, Jr., *Symbol and Truth in Blake's Myth* (Princeton: Princeton University Press, 1980), pp. 256–57. As these studies point out, Blake did not necessarily share the doctrinal beliefs or moral attitudes of the original Gnostics; in fact, he was probably opposed to them. But while rejecting the specific content of Gnostic myth, Blake obviously learned something from its form, and found a way of adapting its typical pattern of inverting gods and devils to embody his distinctive vision in his own myths.

4 For a detailed study of Shelley's knowledge and use of Gnosticism, see James Rieger, *The Mutiny Within: The Heresies of Percy Bysshe Shelley* (New York: George Braziller, 1967).

5 For a general survey of creation myths, see Philip Freund, *Myths of Creation* (Levittown: Transatlantic Arts, 1975) and David Maclagan, *Creation Myths: Man's Introduction to the World* (London: Thames and Hudson, 1977).

6 See especially Harold Bloom, *Poetry and Repression* (New Haven: Yale University Press, 1976), pp. 1–27, and for his fullest discussion of gnosticism and literature to date *Agon: Toward a Theory of Revisionism* (New York: Oxford University Press, 1982), pp. 3–90.

7 On the problem of canon formation, see Harold Bloom, *Poetry and Repression*, pp. 28–34.

8 An excellent example of this point occurs in the so-called "Tripartite Tractate," one of the texts from *The Nag Hammadi Library in English*, ed. James M. Robinson (San Francisco: Harper & Row, 1977). This account of the creation occupies forty-two pages in Robinson's edition; it does not get to the making of Adam until the twenty-seventh page.

9 See Douglas Bush, *Mythology and the Romantic Tradition in English Poetry* (1937; rpt. New York: Norton, 1969), pp. 3–50 and Alex Zwerdling, "The Mythographers and the Romantic Revival of Greek Myth," *PMLA*, 79 (1964), 447–56. Samuel Johnson's censure of "Lycidas" in his *Life of Milton* may be taken as representative of late eighteenth-century attitudes toward the use of myth in poetry.

10 See Leslie Brisman, *Romantic Origins* (Ithaca: Cornell University Press, 1978), pp. 11–20.

11 See especially Jonas, *Gnostic Religion*, pp. 241–65.

12 Consider the implications of Bloom's statement in *Agon*: "The origins and aims of poetry together constitute its powers, and the powers of poetry, however they relate to or affect the world, rise out of a loving conflict with previous poetry, rather than out of conflict with the world" (p. viii).

13 See *Agon*, p. 50.

14 For the political significance of creation myths, see Judith N. Shklar, "Subversive Genealogies," *Daedalus*, 101 (1972), 129–59.

15 For a recent example of this tendency, see Samuel S. B. Taylor, "Rousseau's Romanticism," in Simon Harvey, ed., *Reappraisals of Rousseau* (Manchester: Manchester University Press, 1980), pp. 2–23.

16 Babbitt himself was aware of the one-sidedness of his approach to Rousseau; see Irving Babbitt, *Rousseau and Romanticism* (1919; rpt. Cleveland: Meridian Books, 1955), pp. 10–11.

17 Jean-Jacques Rousseau, *The Confessions*, trans. J. M. Cohen (Harmondsworth: Penguin Books, 1954), p. 361.

18 M. H. Abrams, *Natural Supernaturalism* (New York: Norton, 1971), p. 13.

19 I am of course aware that *Frankenstein* was written three years before *Prometheus Unbound*, but I still think that it is profitable to read Mary Shelley's work as an "answer" to her husband's. By the summer of 1816, Mary was undoubtedly already aware of the tendencies in her husband's thought which we have access to largely in the written form of *Prometheus Unbound*. Since the ideals put to the test in *Frankenstein* are expounded most eloquently in *Prometheus Unbound*, I feel justified in violating the principle of chronology and will discuss the later work first for the sake of clarifying the relationship between the two. The idea of reading *Frankenstein* and *Prometheus Unbound* as companion pieces is pursued brilliantly in Christopher Small, *Mary Shelley's Frankenstein: Tracing the Myth* (Pittsburgh: University of Pittsburgh Press, 1973); see especially p. 240. For the contrary approach of reading *Prometheus Unbound* as "a reply to *Frankenstein*," see Paul Sherwin, "*Frankenstein*: Creation as Catastrophe," *PMLA*, 96 (1981), 900.

Introduction: A Discourse on Eden

1 *The Geneva Manuscript*, Book I, chapter ii, in Jean-Jacques Rousseau, *On the*

Social Contract, trans. Judith R. Masters (New York: St. Martin's, 1978), pp. 158–59.

2 See Northrop Frye, *A Study of English Romanticism* (New York: Random House, 1968), pp. 17–18 and Abrams, *Natural Supernaturalism*, especially pp. 179–83. On Milton's myth, see Isabel Gamble MacCaffrey, *Paradise Lost as "Myth"* (Cambridge: Harvard University Press, 1959), pp. 23–43. For the mythological background of Milton's epic, see J. M. Evans, *Paradise Lost and the Genesis Tradition* (Oxford: Clarendon Press, 1968).

3 See Abrams, *Natural Supernaturalism*, p. 51 and Northrop Frye, *The Return of Eden* (Toronto: Toronto University Press, 1965), p. 110.

4 To draw a rough analogy, the *Second Discourse* is to nineteenth-century literature what a work like Freud's *The Interpretation of Dreams* is to twentieth-century literature. One would not have to prove that a given twentieth-century author had actually read *The Interpretation of Dreams* in order to argue that he was influenced by Freud's idea of the unconscious.

5 For a convenient summary of Blake's references to Rousseau, see S. Foster Damon, *A Blake Dictionary* (1965; rpt. New York: E. P. Dutton, 1971), pp. 351–52.

6 See David V. Erdman, *Blake: Prophet Against Empire* (1954; rpt. Garden City: Doubleday, 1969), pp. 416–22 and Edward Duffy, *Rousseau in England* (Berkeley: University of California Press, 1979), pp. 56–57.

7 *Remarks on the Writing and Conduct of J. J. Rousseau* (London: T. Cadell, 1767). Excerpts from this edition have been reprinted by the Augustan Reprint Society, ed. Karl Guthke (Los Angeles: William Andrews Clark Memorial Library, 1960). The full text is available in a Swiss edition listed under the name Johann Heinrich Füssli, ed. Eudo C. Mason (Zurich: Fretz & Wagmuth, 1962). For the influence of this book on Blake, see Erdman, *Blake*, pp. 42–43, 129 (n. 35), 130 (n. 36), 178 (n. 7), and 428–29 (n. 10). For a general account of the relationship between Blake and Fuseli, see Leonard M. Trawick, "William Blake's German Connection," *Colby Library Quarterly*, 13 (1977), 229–45.

8 For general studies of the relationship of Shelley and Rousseau, see Duffy, *Rousseau*, pp. 86–105 and Hans Meyer, *Rousseau und Shelley: Ein typologischer Vergleich* (Würzburg: Konrad Triltsch, 1934). For studies of Rousseau's influence in specific works of Shelley, see Donald L. Maddox, "Shelley's *Alastor* and the Legacy of Rousseau," *Studies in Romanticism*, 9 (1970), 82–98; G. M. Matthews, "On Shelley's 'The Triumph of Life,'" *Studia Neophilologica*, 34 (1962), 104–34; and Donald H. Reiman, *Shelley's "The Triumph of Life": A Critical Study* (Urbana: University of Illinois Press, 1965).

9 Frederick Jones, ed., *Mary Shelley's Journal* (Norman: University of Oklahoma Press, 1947), p. 225.

10 Duffy, *Rousseau*, pp. 90–91. For the reference to Rousseau, see Shelley's note to "And Statesmen Boast of Wealth" in David Lee Clark, ed., *Shelley's Prose* (Albuquerque: University of New Mexico Press, 1954), p. 113.

11 For the influence of Rousseau on Godwin, see the Preface to William Godwin, *Enquiry Concerning Political Justice* (Harmondsworth: Penguin Books, 1976), p. 69.

12 For Shelley's knowledge of Monboddo, see *Mary Shelley's Journal*, pp. 138–39. For an account of Monboddo's thought, see E. L. Cloyd, *James Burnett, Lord Monboddo* (Oxford: Clarendon Press, 1972).

13 See Arthur Lovejoy, "Monboddo and Rousseau," in *Essays in the History of Ideas* (Baltimore: Johns Hopkins University Press, 1948), pp. 38–61.

14 Earlier thinkers occasionally questioned the definition of man as the rational animal, but never as radically as Rousseau did. Swift, for example, in a famous letter to Alexander Pope (Sept. 29, 1725), wrote that he had assembled "materials toward a treatise, proving the falsity of that definition *animal rationale*, and to show it would be only *rationis capax*." See. W. D. Taylor, ed., *Select Letters of Jonathan Swift* (London: G. Bell, 1926), p. 201. A consideration of the context of this statement, especially in light of the entire body of Swift's writings, will show that Swift's model of human nature is still based on reason as man's distinctive characteristic; it is just that Swift is recognizing the sad fact that the majority of men do not live up to that model. In Swift's view, because they are not governed by reason, most men are not fully human. Swift's formulation thus only sounds revolutionary; in fact he is making a rather traditional point. Rousseau, by contrast, genuinely breaks with the classical understanding of man. He does not provide a critique of mankind for not using its reason, but rather a critique of reason itself, as he questions whether reason is basic to man as man.

15 See Paul de Man, *Allegories of Reading* (New Haven: Yale University Press, 1979), pp. 139–40. Cf. Godwin, *Political Justice*, p. 140.

16 Allan Bloom, "Jean-Jacques Rousseau," in Leo Strauss and Joseph Cropsey, eds., *History of Political Philosophy*, 2nd ed. (Chicago: Rand McNally, 1972), pp. 536–37.

17 Leo Strauss, *Natural Right and History* (Chicago: University of Chicago Press, 1953), p. 271.

18 See Ernst Cassirer, *The Question of Jean-Jacques Rousseau*, trans. Peter Gay (Bloomington: Indiana University Press, 1963), p. 65.

19 De Man, *Allegories of Reading*, p. 140. Cf. Godwin, *Political Justice*, pp. 144–45.

20 Cassirer, *Rousseau*, p. 78; Frye, *English Romanticism*, p. 28; and Babbitt, *Rousseau and Romanticism*, p. 49.

21 See Ronald Grimsley, *Rousseau and the Religious Quest* (Oxford: Clarendon Press, 1968), p. 96.

22 See Roger D. Masters, *The Political Philosophy of Rousseau* (Princeton: Princeton University Press, 1968), p. 116. On the general importance of the footnotes in the *Second Discourse*, see Masters, pp. 108–9.

23 Letter to William Wordsworth, May 30, 1815. See Earl Leslie Griggs, ed., *Collected Letters of Samuel Taylor Coleridge* (Oxford: Clarendon Press, 1955), IV, 574. For further literary reflection of the orangoutan issue, see stanza four of Schiller's poem, "Rousseau," and Thomas Love Peacock's novel, *Melincourt* (1817). In the almost Kafka-like sixth chapter of this work, Peacock tests the Rousseau–Monboddo hypothesis by introducing a primate from Angola, named Sir Oran Haut-Ton, who is eventually put up for Parliament. Filled with footnotes to the *Second Discourse*, as well as to Monboddo's two principal works, *The Origin and Progress of Language* and *Antient Metaphysics*, this chapter in *Melincourt* is excellent evidence for the currency of the ideas of Rousseau and Monboddo in the early nineteenth century.

24 Strauss, *Natural Right*, p. 252.

25 See John Andrew Bernstein, *Shaftesbury, Rousseau, and Kant* (Rutherford, New Jersey: Fairleigh Dickinson University Press, 1980), p. 108 and Leo Strauss, "The Three Waves of Modernity," in Hilail Gildin, ed., *Political Philosophy: Six Essays by Leo Strauss* (Indianapolis: Bobbs-Merrill, 1975), p. 94.

26 Babbitt, *Rousseau and Romanticism*, p. 110.

27 Frye, *English Romanticism*, pp. 9–10.

28 See Shklar, "Subversive Genealogies," pp. 139–40.

29 Leo Strauss, *The City and Man* (Chicago: Rand McNally, 1964), pp. 43–44.

30 Cassirer, *Rousseau*, pp. 72–76. Cassirer quotes Kant to show that he understood Rousseau's enterprise on the model of theodicy: "Newton was the first to see order and regularity combined with great simplicity, where disorder and ill-matched variety had reigned before. Since then comets have been moving in geometric orbits. Rousseau was the first to discover in the variety of shapes that men assume the deeply concealed nature of man and to observe the hidden law that justifies Providence. Before then, the objections of Alfonso and Manes still had validity. After Newton and Rousseau, God is justified, and from now on Pope's maxim is true" (p. 72).

31 Edward Davies, *Celtic Researches* (London: J. Booth, 1804), p. 5.

32 See Jacques Barzun, *Classic, Romantic, and Modern* (Chicago: University of Chicago Press, 1961), pp. 21–22 and Arthur Lovejoy, "The Supposed Primitivism of Rousseau's *Discourse on Inequality*," in *Essays in the History of Ideas*, pp. 14–37. Shelley understood this point, as his "Essay on Christianity" makes clear: "Rousseau certainly did not mean to persuade the immense population of his country to abandon all the arts of life, destroy their habitations and their temples and become the inhabitants of the woods." See *Shelley's Prose*, p. 210.

33 Strauss, *Natural Right*, p. 282.

34 Strauss, *Natural Right*, pp. 254–55. For a statement of this position, see Cassirer, *Rousseau* and Lester Crocker, "Order and Disorder in Rousseau's Social Thought," *PMLA*, 94 (1979), 247–60.

35 See Leo Strauss, *What is Political Philosophy?* (New York: Free Press, 1959), p. 53 and Allan Bloom, "Rousseau," pp. 550–52.

36 See Strauss, *Natural Right*, pp. 281, 285; Cassirer, *Rousseau*, pp. 55–56; and Barzun, *Classic, Romantic*, pp. 23–25.

37 The *Letter to d'Alembert* is available in English, translated by Allan Bloom, under the title *Politics and the Arts* (Glencoe, Illinois: Free Press, 1960). In Babbitt's one reference to this work, in order to maintain his view of Rousseau as a proto-Romantic, he must completely misread Rousseau's intention: "Rousseau assailed Molière in the name of instinct ... and fought sense with sensibility. The hostility of Rousseau to Molière ... is that of a romantic Bohemian to a philistine of genius" (p. 37).

38 *Social Contract*, p. 56.

39 *Ibid.*

40 See Leo Strauss, "On the Intention of Rousseau," in *Hobbes and Rousseau*, ed. Maurice Cranston and Richard S. Peters (Garden City: Doubleday, 1972), pp. 254–90.

41 For a particularly memorable statement of this tendency in Rousseau's character, see *Confessions*, pp. 183–84: "In all matters constraint and compulsion are unbearable to me: they would make me dislike even pleasure. It is said that

among the Mohammedans a man goes through the streets at dawn to command all husbands to do their duty by their wives. At that hour I should be a bad Turk."
42 See Earl Wasserman, "The English Romantics: The Grounds of Knowledge," *Studies in Romanticism*, 4 (1964–65), 17–34.
43 Babbitt, *Rousseau and Romanticism*, p. 186. The best confirmation of this point is Hölderlin's lyric, "Der Rhein," which at one point becomes a kind of free translation of Rousseau's experience at Lake Bienne in his fifth reverie. For a discussion of Hölderlin's relationship to Rousseau's *Reveries*, see Jean Starobinski, "Rousseau's Happy Days," *New Literary History*, 11 (1979), 157–58.
44 Cf. Shelley's similar conception of the state of reverie in his fragmentary essay, "On Life": "Those who are subject to this state called reverie feel as if their nature were dissolved into the surrounding universe, or as if the surrounding universe were absorbed into their being. They are conscious of no distinction" (R & P, p. 477). On this parallel between Shelley and Rousseau, see Duffy, *Rousseau*, pp. 109–10.
45 Strauss, *Natural Right*, p. 292 and Grimsley, *Rousseau*, pp. 66, 99–101.
46 Strauss, *Natural Right*, p. 293.
47 Samuel Taylor, "Rousseau's Romanticism," p. 19.
48 Strauss, "On the Intention of Rousseau," pp. 284–85.
49 "A Vindication of Natural Diet," *Shelley's Prose*, p. 83. Sometimes this Romantic ideal even inspired practical efforts at reforming the world, as in the young Coleridge's plans to establish a utopian community in America: "What I dared not expect from constitutions of government and whole nations, I hoped from Religion and a small company of closer individuals, and formed a plan, as harmless as it was extravagant, of trying the experiment of human perfectibility on the banks of the *Susquehannah*; where our little society, in its second generation was to have combined the innocence of the patriarchal ages with the knowledge and genuine refinements of European culture." See Section the First, Essay VI, in *The Friend*, ed. Barbara E. Rooke (Princeton: Princeton University Press, 1969), I, 224.
50 See D. F. Rauber, "The Fragment as Romantic Form," *Modern Language Quarterly*, 30 (1969), 212–21. One study of Romanticism which focuses specifically on unfinished poems is Edward Bostetter, *The Romantic Ventriloquists* (Seattle: University of Washington Press, 1975). See especially the Introduction, pp. 3–11. See also Thomas McFarland, *Romanticism and the Forms of Ruin* (Princeton: Princeton University Press, 1981), especially pp. 3–55.
51 Frye, *English Romanticism*, p. 107.

1 The Demonic Creator

1 See Hazard Adams, "Blake, *Jerusalem*, and Symbolic Form," *Blake Studies*, 7 (1975), 143–66.
2 Despite his subsequent attempts at creation myths, Blake never fully repudiated *The Book of Urizen*, as shown by the fact that he "reissued" the poem rather late in his career – in 1818, according to Erdman (E, p. 804), in 1815, according to

Kay and Roger Easson, eds., *William Blake: The Book of Urizen* (New York: Random House, 1978), p. 41. Though this last version of the poem, the so-called Copy G, involves several efforts at rearrangement and revision, it is still substantially the same work Blake originally wrote.

3 Mark Schorer, *William Blake: The Politics of Vision* (1947; rpt. New York: Vintage Books, 1959), p. 115.

4 Harold Bloom, *The Visionary Company* (1961; rpt. Ithaca: Cornell University Press, 1971), p. 71; Warren Stevenson, *Divine Analogy: A Study of the Creation Motif in Blake and Coleridge* (Salzburg: Institut für Englische Sprache und Literatur, 1972), p. 88; and Mollyanne Marks, "Structure and Irony in Blake's 'The Book of Urizen,'" *Studies in English Literature*, 15 (1975), 579–90.

5 For an analysis of the view of God in the opening chapters of Genesis, see Umberto Cassuto, *A Commentary on the Book of Genesis*, trans. Israel Abrahams (Jerusalem: Magnes Press, 1961), I, 7–70.

6 Harold Bloom, *Blake's Apocalypse* (Garden City: Doubleday, 1963), p. 178. See *Paradise Lost*, VII.168–73. On the doctrine of creation by contraction in Lurianic Kabbalah see Gerschom Scholem, *Kabbalah* (New York: Quadrangle, 1974), pp. 128–35.

7 See S. Foster Damon, *William Blake: His Philosophy and Symbols* (New York: Peter Smith, 1947), p. 116 and Clark Emery, ed., *William Blake: The Book of Urizen* (Coral Gables: University of Miami Press, 1966), pp. 34–40. The identification of Urizen with the power of reason in man is accepted by all Blake critics. One possible explanation for Urizen's name is that it is a pun on "Your Reason." See Damon, *Blake Dictionary*, p. 419. For a survey of Urizen's role in Blake's poetry, see Milton O. Percival, *William Blake's Circle of Destiny* (New York: Columbia University Press, 1938), pp. 20–29.

8 E. D. Hirsch, Jr., *Innocence and Experience* (Chicago: University of Chicago Press, 1964), pp. 73–74.

9 For Blake's view of eighteenth-century theories of knowledge, see Northrop Frye, *Fearful Symmetry* (1947; rpt. Princeton: Princeton University Press, 1969), pp. 14–29.

10 Schorer, *Politics of Vision*, p. 238; Damon, *Blake Dictionary*, p. 51; Stevenson, *Divine Analogy*, p. 107; and Damrosch, *Symbol and Truth*, p. 253.

11 See Erdman, *Prophet Against Empire*, pp. 242–63, especially n. 28 and n. 34.

12 Damon, *Blake Dictionary*, p. 419. Urizen's name may be derived from the Greek verb *ourizein* ("to mark out boundaries"), the source of our word *horizon*.

13 Talking about Urizen's motives raises an interesting theoretical difficulty in Blake's mythic mode. Strictly speaking, Urizen, as pure reason, should have no motives at all, since he should have no desires, fears, or any other emotions. Blake has in fact made his task much easier for himself by making Urizen at times an embodiment of the abstract principle of reason, at times a rounded character, with a full set of human faculties and hence the will to act. In a sense, Blake begs the question in his myth by making Reason energetic enough in itself to begin its war with Energy. Blake's remaking of his myth in *The Four Zoas* seems to recognize the fact that both Reason and Energy (Urizen and Luvah–Orc) had to be implicated in the fall from the beginning. In any case, in discussing Blake's myth, one must always bear in mind that his characters function both as parts of a larger whole and as wholes themselves. As a result, one

often finds oneself in the logically awkward position of speaking of Reason's passions. On this problem, see Damrosch, *Symbol and Truth*, p. 158.

14 Cf. *The Four Zoas*, 121:3–5, 19–22.

15 This famous passage from Rousseau actually appears transformed into poetry in one of the minor examples of Romantic creation myths, Peacock's *Ahrimanes* (1813–15):

> But years passed on, and strange perversion ran
> Among the dwellers of the peaceful isle:
> And one, more daring than the rest, began
> To fell the grove, and point the massy pile;
> And raised the circling fence, with evil wile,
> And to his brethren said: These bounds are mine.   (I.x)

See *The Halliford Edition of the Works of Thomas Love Peacock*, ed. H. F. B. Brettsmith and C. E. Jones (1924–34; rpt. New York: AMS Press, 1967), VII. Rousseau's name even appears in the margin of the manuscript of *Ahrimanes* (*Works*, VII, p. 514), in Peacock's notes to himself for further reading.

16 On primitive man's lack of foresight and planning, see Rousseau, *Second Discourse*, pp. 117, 153.

17 Leslie Tannenbaum, "Blake's Art of Crypsis: *The Book of Urizen* and *Genesis*," *Blake Studies*, 5 (1972), 158–60.

18 For an eighteenth-century account of the role of language in separating man from his animal nature, see Johann Gottfried Herder, *Essay on the Origin of Language*, trans. Alexander Gode (New York: Frederick Ungar, 1966), especially pp. 107–19.

19 See Arthur Lovejoy, "Supposed Primitivism," pp. 29–30.

20 See Masters, *Rousseau*, pp. 171–75.

21 On the complexity of Blake's view of man's original state, see Schorer, *Politics of Vision*, pp. 112–16.

22 Harold Bloom, *Blake's Apocalypse*, pp. 58–59 and Stevenson, *Divine Analogy*, pp. 70–71.

23 Rousseau's strategy was clearly understood and analyzed by Fichte, whose *Von der Pflichten der Gelehrten* ("On the Duties of Scholars," a set of lectures from 1794–95) contains one of the most revealing near-contemporary reactions to Rousseau. See the fifth lecture, in *Pflichten* (Hamburg: Felix Meiner, 1971), pp. 44–54. Fichte states Rousseau's principle simply: "Ihm ist Rückkehr Fortgang" (p. 45; "For him, return is progress"). Fichte continues: "Ahead of us lies what Rousseau under the name of the state of nature, and the poets under the name of the Golden Age, place behind us ... That which we should become is pictured as something we have already been, and that which we have yet to reach is presented as something we have lost" (my translation). At about the same time, Schiller used very similar language in describing a form of poetry he called the *idyll*. He criticizes pastoral poems, which try to portray a life of primitive innocence: "Set *before the beginnings of civilization*, they exclude together with its disadvantages its advantages ... *Theoretically*, then, they lead us backwards, while *practically* they lead us forwards and ennoble us. Unhappily they place that purpose *behind* us, *toward* which they should, however, lead us, and hence they imbue us with a sad feeling of loss, not with joyous feelings of hope"

(Schiller's italics). See *Naive and Sentimental Poetry*, trans. Julias Elias (New York: Frederick Ungar, 1966), p. 149. Blake's attempt in *The Book of Urizen* to gloss over the primitive elements in man's beginnings might be regarded as an effort to avoid what Schiller sees as a possible defect of poetic portrayals of paradise. The whole of Schiller's discussion of the form he calls the idyll is very helpful for understanding the problem Romantic myth-makers faced in portraying man's original state. It particularly helps to explain Blake's fascination with the idea of an archetypal civilization deep in the British past: "The Britons (say historians) were naked civilized men, learned, studious, abstruse in thought and contemplation; naked, simple, plain in their acts and manners; wiser than after-ages" (*Descriptive Catalogue*, pp. 39–40; E, p. 542). Here Blake tries to overcome Rousseau's antinomy between nature and civilization by positing that his ancestors once combined the advantages of both. See also *Jerusalem*, Pl. 3: "The Primeval State of Man, was Wisdom, Art, and Science."

24 See Adams, "Blake, *Jerusalem*, and Symbolic Form," p. 144. For Eliot's use of the term, see "The Metaphysical Poets" in *Selected Essays* (New York: Harcourt, Brace, 1950), pp. 241–50.

25 Harold Bloom, *Blake's Apocalypse*, p. 181.

26 Emery, *Urizen*, pp. 27–28.

27 For a survey of Los's role in Blake's poetry, see Percival, *Circle of Destiny*, pp. 36–40 and Damon, *Blake Dictionary*, pp. 246–50.

28 See Hirsch, *Innocence and Experience*, pp. 74–75 and Anne K. Mellor, *Blake's Human Form Divine* (Berkeley: University of California Press, 1974), p. 96.

29 Harold Bloom, *Blake's Apocalypse*, p. 182 and Hirsch, *Innocence and Experience*, pp. 77–78.

30 Cf. Schiller's similar characterization of the self-division of modern culture: "While in one place a luxuriant imagination ravages the hard-earned fruits of the intellect, in another the spirit of abstraction stifles the fire at which the heart might have warmed itself and the fancy been enkindled." See *On the Aesthetic Education of Man*, trans. Reginald Snell (New York: Frederick Ungar, 1965), p. 39. In many ways, the *Aesthetic Education* states philosophically what Blake presents poetically and mythically in *The Book of Urizen*, especially the notion of the aesthetic imagination as the mediator between reason and passion.

31 For an excellent discussion of Blake in relation to eighteenth-century poetry, see Frye, *Fearful Symmetry*, pp. 147–77.

32 Harold Bloom, *Blake's Apocalypse*, pp. 182–83.

33 *Twilight of the Idols*, Maxims and Arrows, no. 7, trans. Walter Kaufmann, in *The Portable Nietzsche* (New York: Viking Press, 1954), p. 467.

34 See Jonas, *Gnostic Religion*, pp. 62–68.

35 Cassuto, *Commentary*, I, 57. For Gnostic interpretations of this passage, see Elaine Pagels, *The Gnostic Gospels* (New York: Random House, 1979), pp. 49–50, 56. Blake may have derived the idea of the originally hermaphroditic nature of man from Jacob Böhme. See Stevenson, *Divine Analogy*, p. 112 and Abrams, *Natural Supernaturalism*, pp. 154–63.

36 *Symposium*, 189D–190C.

37 Blake's treatment of the masculine and feminine elements in the human mind seems to anticipate Jungian psychology. Blake's notion of the feminine emanation seems particularly close to Jung's concept of the anima. See Carl Jung, *Two*

Essays in Analytical Psychology, trans. R. F. C. Hull (Cleveland: Meridian Books, 1956), pp. 198–233 and *Aion: Researches into the Phenomenology of the Self*, trans. R. F. C. Hull (New York: Pantheon Books, 1959), pp. 11–22.

38 The prophet's alternation between wrath and pity is reflected in the disagreement between *The Book of Urizen* and *The Book of Los* as to Los's motives in the fall. In the first version of Blake's creation account, Los becomes implicated in the fall because he seems to pity Urizen and builds him a body to heal his wounds. When Blake takes a second look at the same creation story in *The Book of Los*, he pictures a sterner Los ("stiffend, hardned," 4:14), experiencing the occupational hazard of all prophets, "impatience" (4:15). In the second version, Los gets disgusted with Urizen's state and tries to smash it out of existence, "stamping [it] furious to dust" (4:20). In *The Book of Los*, it is not pity but "the Prophetic wrath, strug'ling for vent" (4:19) which draws Los into the fall. The opposition of wrath and pity is represented in Blake's major prophecies by the divisions of Rintrah and Palamabron. See Damon, *Blake Dictionary*, pp. 321, 349–50. The idea that for Blake the two basic oppositions in the fallen world are: reason vs. passion (desire) and wrath vs. pity is suggested by the diagram on Pl. 54 of *Jerusalem* (reproduced in E, p. 203).

39 Stevenson, *Divine Analogy*, pp. 97–98. In Plato's *Symposium*, Zeus is said to divide up the originally bisexual human beings in order to divert them from their plans for storming heaven by getting them absorbed in a search to reunite with their lost halves (190D–192E).

40 Harold Bloom, *Blake's Apocalypse*, p. 185.

41 This is the main thrust of Freud's thought on the subject, but see *The Interpretation of Dreams*, trans. James Strachey (New York: Avon Books, 1965), p. 599, where Freud speaks of "the envy which is felt for the young by those who have grown old," as he analyzes a dream which expressed his hidden wish to see his son have an accident. For a general comparison of Blake and Freud, see Diana Hume George, *Blake and Freud* (Ithaca: Cornell University Press, 1980). For a specific contrast of their views on the Oedipus complex, see especially pp. 113–21.

42 Harold Bloom, *Blake's Apocalypse*, p. 185 and Stevenson, *Divine Analogy*, p. 100.

43 When Blake retold this part of his creation myth in *The Four Zoas*, he seems to have reversed his position as to who begins the battle between youth and age, portraying the Oedipus complex as prior. In the later version, Orc has time to reach puberty before any conflict begins ("fourteen summers & winters had revolved over"), and gives Los good reason to be jealous: "Los beheld the ruddy boy / Embracing his bright mother & beheld malignant fires / In his young eyes discerning plain that Orc plotted his death" (60:6–9). If this account is taken at face value, it would be one more indication that *The Four Zoas* reflects Blake's growing disillusionment with Orc as a revolutionary force. Once again, Blake seems to be suggesting that passion is as fully implicated in the fall as reason. On the other hand, in order to justify the hostility he already feels for Orc, Los may be misreading Orc's affection for his mother, and projecting his own jealousy onto his son, seeing hostile intentions where none actually exist. Blake's phrase "discerning plain" may be ironic. Blake offers no independent or objective

confirmation of Orc's intentions. See Damrosch, *Symbol and Truth*, p. 269 and George, *Blake and Freud*, p. 118.

44 Tannenbaum, "Art of Crypsis," pp. 151, 160, 163.

2 The Myth Unbound

1 Harold Bloom, *Blake's Apocalypse*, pp. 190–91.

2 *Ibid.*, p. 192.

3 Erdman argues that Fuzon may be specifically identified with Robespierre. See *Prophet Against Empire*, pp. 314–15.

4 Frye, *Fearful Symmetry*, pp. 308–9.

5 For Erdman's justification of this arrangement, as well as a summary of the textual problems surrounding Night VII, see E, p. 836. See also Brian Wilkie and Mary Lynn Johnson, *Blake's Four Zoas: The Design of a Dream* (Cambridge: Harvard University Press, 1978), pp. 271–73.

6 For a contrary view, that VIIb is the later version, see Paley, *Energy and the Imagination*, p. 263.

7 Compare, for example, *The Four Zoas*, 91:17 with *America*, 2:2 (see Harold Bloom, *Blake's Apocalypse*, p. 267) and the building of the Temple in *The Four Zoas* (95:31–96:18) with the scene of the Temple and the Stone of Night in *Europe*, 10:1–31.

8 Harold Bloom, *Blake's Apocalypse*, p. 271.

9 *Ibid.*, p. 275 and Wilkie and Johnson, *Four Zoas*, pp. 143–48.

10 On the role of the spectre in Blake, see Percival, *Circle of Destiny*, pp. 90–106; Frye, *Fearful Symmetry*, pp. 292–99; Damon, *Blake Dictionary*, pp. 380–83; and Harold Bloom, *Blake's Apocalypse*, pp. 275–80.

11 See Wilkie and Johnson, *Four Zoas*, p. 165.

12 See Christine Gallant, *Blake and the Assimilation of Chaos* (Princeton: Princeton University Press, 1978), pp. 79–80.

13 Abrams, *Natural Supernaturalism*, pp. 333–34, 339–42.

14 Harold Bloom, *Blake's Apocalypse*, pp. 310–11.

15 See Gallant, *Assimilation of Chaos*, pp. 101, 114; Wilkie and Johnson, *Four Zoas*, pp. 228–29; and especially the excellent discussion in Damrosch, *Symbol and Truth*, pp. 336–48.

16 Wilkie and Johnson, *Four Zoas*, pp. 213–14.

17 *Ibid.*, pp. 216–17.

18 For a general discussion of Beulah, see Harold Bloom, *Visionary Company*, pp. 20–31 and Damrosch, *Symbol and Truth*, pp. 220–33.

19 Harold Bloom, *Blake's Apocalypse*, pp. 299–300 and Gallant, *Assimilation of Chaos*, pp. 99–100, 103–4.

20 See E, p. 966 and Wilkie and Johnson, *Four Zoas*, p. 225.

21 Wilkie and Johnson, *Four Zoas*, pp. 7–8. This pattern is suggested by what appears to be a motto for *The Four Zoas* on p. 2 of the manuscript: "Rest before Labour."

22 See Harold Bloom, *Blake's Apocalypse*, pp. 377–78. The Eden–Beulah dialectic is reflected even in the versification of the major prophecies. See the Preface to *Jerusalem* (Pl. 3): "The terrific numbers are reserved for the terrific parts – the mild & gentle, for the mild & gentle parts."

23 Percival, *Circle of Destiny*, pp. 49–59.
24 *Marriage*, Pl. 3. See Percival, *Circle of Destiny*, pp. 9, 48–49 and Gallant, *Assimilation of Chaos*, p. 115.
25 Douglas B. Smith, "Blake's Conception of Imagination in *Jerusalem*: The Harmonizing Apocalypse," Undergraduate Thesis, Harvard 1972, p. 5 (unpublished).
26 Consider in this context Blake's characterization of the city Los builds in *Jerusalem*: "continually building & continually decaying desolate! / In eternal labours" (53:19–20). See Percival, *Circle of Destiny*, pp. 287–89 and Damrosch, *Symbol and Truth*, pp. 234–35, 242–43. For similar doubts in Shelley about the value of a static paradise, see Jean Hall, *The Transforming Image: A Study of Shelley's Major Poetry* (Urbana: University of Illinois Press, 1980), p. 91.
27 Leslie Brisman, *Romantic Origins*, pp. 226–28, 249.
28 See John Beer, *Blake's Visionary Universe* (Manchester: Manchester University Press, 1969), p. 148. See above, Chapter 1, n. 13 and n. 43.
29 For a useful summary of the various accounts, see Appendix B in Wilkie and Johnson, *Four Zoas*, pp. 255–60 (they identify fourteen separate accounts). See also Beer, *Visionary Universe*, pp. 148–58.
30 See Leslie Brisman, *Romantic Origins*, pp. 224, 238, 259.
31 Leslie Brisman characterizes *The Four Zoas* this way: "a story about origins becomes a story about originating stories about origins – a story about originality" (p. 272).
32 *Ibid.*, pp. 235, 252–53, 262.
33 Wilkie and Johnson, *Four Zoas*, p. 87.
34 See Leslie Brisman, *Romantic Origins*, pp. 226–27, who points out that in *The Four Zoas* "we are directed to questions of regeneration rather than generation." See also p. 254. For a parallel point in Blake's illustrations to the Book of Job, see Northrop Frye, *Creation and Recreation* (Toronto: University of Toronto Press, 1980), p. 58.
35 Wilkie and Johnson, *Four Zoas*, p. 139.
36 Strauss, *Natural Right*, pp. 293–94 and Frye, *Creation*, p. 49.
37 For a parallel discussion of the movement from closed to open forms in Blake, see Mellor, *Human Form Divine*, especially pp. 40–101.

3 The Prelude to Apocalypse

1 See Jonas, *Gnostic Religion*, pp. 96–97.
2 For a general discussion of the Prometheus myth, see Károly Kerényi, *Prometheus: Archetypal Image of Human Existence*, trans. Ralph Manheim (New York: Pantheon Books, 1963). See also Edward B. Hungerford, *Shores of Darkness* (1941; rpt. Cleveland: Meridian Books, 1963), p. 166 and Lawrence John Zillman, *Shelley's Prometheus Unbound: A Variorum Edition* (Seattle: University of Washington Press, 1959), pp. 723–29.
3 Preface to *Prometheus Unbound*, R & P, 133.
4 R & P, 498. Cf. Blake, *Marriage*, Pl. 5–6 and Godwin, *Political Justice*, p. 309.
5 See I.i.546–63, 584–85, 594–604, 631. See Earl Wasserman, *Shelley: A Critical Reading* (Baltimore: Johns Hopkins University Press, 1971), pp. 291–303; Ross

G. Woodman, *The Apocalyptic Vision in the Poetry of Shelley* (Toronto: University of Toronto Press, 1964), pp. 42–45; Stuart Curran, *Shelley's Annus Mirabilis* (San Marino, California: Huntington Library, 1975), pp. 54–55; and Carlos Baker, *Shelley's Major Poetry* (Princeton: Princeton University Press, 1948), pp. 98–100.

6 See Baker, *Shelley's Major Poetry*, p. 98; Curran, *Annus Mirabilis*, p. 57; and Susan Hawk Brisman, "'Unsaying His High Language': The Problem of Voice in *Prometheus Unbound*," *Studies in Romanticism*, 16 (1977), 62.

7 Wasserman, *Shelley*, p. 106 and Harold Bloom, *Shelley's Mythmaking* (1959; rpt. Ithaca: Cornell University Press, 1969), pp. 92–93.

8 Woodman, *Apocalyptic Vision*, p. 117. On the dating of *Prometheus Unbound* and *The Cenci*, see R & P, 130.

9 Paul A. Cantor, "'A Distorting Mirror': Shelley's *The Cenci* and Shakespearean Tragedy," in G. Blakemore Evans, ed., *Shakespeare: Aspects of Influence* (Cambridge: Harvard University Press, 1976), p. 97.

10 Curran, *Annus Mirabilis*, pp. 122–23.

11 See Frye, *English Romanticism*, p. 96.

12 See Carl Grabo, *Prometheus Unbound: An Interpretation* (Chapel Hill: University of North Carolina Press, 1935), p. 31; Frye, *English Romanticism*, p. 108; David Perkins, *The Quest for Permanence* (Cambridge: Harvard University Press, 1959), pp. 159–60; and Gerald McNiece, *Shelley and the Revolutionary Idea* (Cambridge: Harvard University Press, 1969), p. 227.

13 For Shelley's reaction to the French Revolution, see particularly the preface to his *The Revolt of Islam*. See also Grabo, *Prometheus*, pp. 38–39; Wasserman, *Shelley*, pp. 303–5; McNiece, *Revolutionary Idea*, pp. 222–23; and Kenneth Neill Cameron, "The Political Symbolism of *Prometheus Unbound*," in R. B. Woodings, ed., *Shelley: Modern Judgments* (Nashville: Aurora Publishers, 1970), pp. 103–4.

14 R & P, 240. See Frye, *English Romanticism*, pp. 118–19.

15 Frye, *English Romanticism*, p. 88.

16 In her note to *Prometheus Unbound* (1839), Mary Shelley states this principle: "The prominent feature of Shelley's theory of the destiny of the human species was, that evil is not inherent in the system of creation, but an accident that might be expelled." Unfortunately, the way Mary Shelley goes on to formulate her husband's philosophy makes it sound simplistic, as if overcoming the evil in the universe were an easy matter: "Shelley believed that mankind had only to will that there should be no evil, and there would be none" (Zillman, *Prometheus*, p. 684). It is important to realize that for Shelley this act of will is not a simple achievement.

17 On this general point, see section 1019 of Nietzsche's *The Will to Power*.

18 See Frederick Pottle, "The Role of Asia in the Dramatic Action of Shelley's *Prometheus Unbound*," in George M. Ridenour, ed., *Shelley: A Collection of Critical Essays* (Englewood Cliffs, New Jersey: Prentice-Hall, 1965), pp. 133–43. See also Abrams, *Natural Supernaturalism*, p. 304; Hungerford, *Shores of Darkness*, p. 183; and G. Wilson Knight, *The Starlit Dome* (1941; rpt. London: Methuen, 1959), p. 211.

19 See Pottle, "Role of Asia," p. 141; Frye, *English Romanticism*, p. 113; Harold Bloom, *Visionary Company*, p. 309; and Curran, *Annus Mirabilis*, pp. 46–47.

20 See Pottle, "Role of Asia," p. 142; Rieger, *Mutiny Within*, p. 139; and Curran, *Annus Mirabilis*, pp. 99–100.

21 See Daniel Hughes, "Prometheus Made Capable Poet in Act One of *Prometheus Unbound*," *Studies in Romanticism*, 17 (1978), 3–11.

22 For a survey of critical opinion concerning Demogorgon, see Zillman, *Prometheus*, pp. 313–20. See also Rieger, *Mutiny Within*, p. 143.

23 Harold Bloom, *Visionary Company*, p. 310.

24 Curran, *Annus Mirabilis*, pp. 100–101 and Susan Brisman, "Problem of Voice," p. 81.

25 In this one respect, Shelley appears to differ from Rousseau, since, as we have seen, for Rousseau autonomy is one of the chief characteristics of natural man.

26 Here Shelley has reshaped the traditional myth to make Prometheus look better and Jupiter worse. He exaggerates Prometheus's power, by making it seem as if he could simply hand cosmic rule over to Jupiter, and thereby makes Jupiter seem all the more guilty of ingratitude in his treatment of Prometheus. See Hungerford, *Shores of Darkness*, pp. 167–68.

27 Jupiter's reign also resembles what might be called the "second creation" in *Paradise Lost*. After man's disobedience in the Garden of Eden, God, much as Shelley's Jupiter does, readjusts the heavens to produce the alternation of the seasons and hence extremes of climate to make man suffer. See *Paradise Lost*, X.651–706.

28 See Susan Brisman, "Problem of Voice," pp. 57–58.

29 For a suggestive attempt at a paraphrase of this dialogue, see Pottle, "Role of Asia," pp. 140–41.

30 *Ibid.*, p. 140 and Susan Brisman, "Problem of Voice," p. 83. Man's misguided tendency to anthropomorphize his experience is the theme of a number of Shelley's lyrics, most notably "Mont Blanc" and "Hymn to Intellectual Beauty" (see especially stanza 3).

31 See Frye, *English Romanticism*, p. 90.

32 Small, *Frankenstein*, p. 321.

33 Pottle, "Role of Asia," p. 141; Susan Brisman, "Problem of Voice," p. 85; and Hall, *Transforming Image*, p. 89.

34 Harold Bloom, *Shelley's Mythmaking*, p. 123.

35 See Zillman, *Prometheus*, p. 444 and Grabo, *Prometheus*, p. 69. From this perspective, the fact that Demogorgon refers to the spiritual principle as "Almighty God" at one point (II.iv.ll) introduces a regrettable inconsistency into Shelley's presentation. Perhaps "Almighty God" must be regarded in this context as a purely conventional expression. We must bear in mind that throughout II.iv, Shelley is operating at the boundary of human expression, and is constantly frustrated by his inability to find words to embody his thoughts (see II.i.108–22).

36 Frye, *English Romanticism*, pp. 96–97.

37 See Grabo, *Prometheus*, pp. 35–36; Woodman, *Apocalyptic Vision*, p. 62; and John W. Wright, *Shelley's Myth of Metaphor* (Athens: University of Georgia Press, 1970), p. 31.

38 See Woodman, *Apocalyptic Vision*, p. 62 and Hall, *Transforming Image*, p. 18. For a general discussion of this "tragedy of culture," see Ernst Cassirer, *The*

Logic of the Humanities, trans. Clarence Smith Howe (New Haven: Yale University Press, 1961), pp. 182–217.

39 *Defence* (R & P, 482); Rousseau develops a similar view of the development of language in the *Second Discourse* (see especially pp. 123–26).

40 On this point, see Martin Heidegger, *Being and Time*, trans. John Macquarrie and Edward Robinson (New York: Harper and Row, 1962), p. 282.

41 On this process of "semantic entropy," see Wright, *Myth of Metaphor*, pp. 29–31 and Susan Brisman, "Problem of Voice," p. 70.

42 See D. G. James, *The Romantic Comedy* (London: Oxford University Press, 1948), p. 129.

43 See Richard H. Fogle, "The Abstractness of Shelley," in Ridenour, *Shelley*, p. 15.

44 "On Life" (R & P, 478). On Shelley's linguistic skepticism, see Wasserman, *Shelley*, pp. 266–69; Perkins, *Quest for Permanence*, pp. 109–10; and Gerald Bruns, *Modern Poetry and the Idea of Language* (New Haven: Yale University Press, 1974), pp. 58–63.

45 Perkins, *Quest for Permanence*, pp. 106–7 and Fogle, "Abstractness of Shelley," p. 17.

46 See Small, *Frankenstein*, p. 229 and Bush, *Mythology*, p. 144.

47 See Fogle, "Abstractness of Shelley," p. 19. Zillman, *Prometheus*, p. 39, quotes a reviewer in the *Literary Gazette* of 1820 who cleverly refers to Shelley's *"dramatis impersonae."*

48 *English Romanticism*, p. 115. See also Woodman, *Apocalyptic Vision*, p. xiii.

49 See Hungerford, *Shores of Darkness*, p. 193 and Frye, *English Romanticism*, pp. 111, 114.

50 On the apocalypse as a recovery of an original innocence, see III.iii.33, 90–107.

51 Knight, *Starlit Dome*, p. 217 and Small, *Frankenstein*, p. 238.

52 "The Mental Traveller," l. 62. See Perkins, *Quest for Permanence*, p. 161 and Curran, *Annus Mirabilis*, pp. 96, 104, 109–110.

53 Grabo, *Prometheus*, p. 171 and Frye, *English Romanticism*, pp. 115–16.

54 Cf. Rousseau's distinction between "natural or physical" inequality and "moral or political inequality" (SD, 101; see also 180–81). Cf. Godwin, *Political Justice*, pp. 181–84.

55 See Melvin M. Rader, "Shelley's Theory of Evil," in Ridenour, *Shelley*, pp. 103–10. In his view of evil, Shelley was probably influenced by Godwin. See especially *Political Justice*, p. 83: "though the evils that arise to us from the structure of the material universe are neither trivial nor few, yet the history of political society sufficiently shows that man is of all other beings the most formidable enemy of man."

56 See, for example, *Emile, or On Education*, trans. Allan Bloom (New York: Basic Books, 1979), p. 222: "Men are not naturally kings, or lords, or courtiers, or rich men. All are born naked and poor: all are subject to the miseries of life, to sorrows, ills, needs, and pains of every kind. Finally, all are condemned to death. This is what truly belongs to man. This is what no mortal is exempt from. Begin, therefore, by studying in human nature what is most inseparable from it, what best characterizes humanity."

57 On the difficulty with this passage, see James, *Romantic Comedy*, pp. 65–66.

58 Small, *Frankenstein*, p. 239 and Harold Bloom, *Visionary Company*, p. 317.

59 Rieger, *Mutiny Within*, pp. 152–55.

60 Frye, *English Romanticism*, pp. 114–15.
61 See Grabo, *Prometheus*, pp. 196–98; Hall, *Transforming Image*, pp. 97–98; and Michael G. Cooke, *Acts of Inclusion* (New Haven: Yale University Press, 1979), pp. 188–89, 223.
62 Perkins, *Quest for Permanence*, pp. 110–15, 167–69.
63 Letter to John Gisborne, Oct. 22, 1821. See Roger Ingpen, ed., *The Letters of Percy Bysshe Shelley* (London: G. Bell, 1914), II, 920.

4 The Nightmare of Romantic Idealism

1 Of recent versions of the Frankenstein story I have read, the most inventive and symbolically rich is *Frankenstein: The True Story* (New York: Avon Books, 1973), a screenplay written by Christopher Isherwood and Don Bachardy for a 1973 television movie. In the same year, an interesting science fiction treatment of the theme appeared, Brian Aldiss's *Frankenstein Unbound* (New York: Random House, 1973). Both works develop the connections between the Frankenstein story and the events in the Byron–Shelley circle at the time Mary conceived the novel.
2 See, for example, Harold Bloom's Afterword to his edition of *Frankenstein*, pp. 213–14. On the Prometheus archetype in *Frankenstein*, see also Small, *Frankenstein*, pp. 48–55 and Martin Tropp, *Mary Shelley's Monster* (Boston: Houghton Mifflin, 1976), pp. 56–57.
3 See Small, *Frankenstein*, pp. 57–70, 64–65; Tropp, *Mary Shelley's Monster*, pp. 69–80; James Rieger, "Introduction" to *Frankenstein* (Indianapolis: Bobbs-Merrill, 1974), p. xxxii; and Burton R. Pollin, "Philosophical and Literary Sources of *Frankenstein*," *Comparative Literature*, 17 (1965), 103–4.
4 See, for example, William Walling, *Mary Shelley* (New York: Twayne Publishers, 1972), pp. 42–47 and Milton A. Mays, "*Frankenstein*: Mary Shelley's Black Theodicy," *Southern Humanities Review*, 3 (1969), 146–53.
5 See Small, *Frankenstein*, pp. 59, 66, 186 and George Levine, "*Frankenstein* and the Tradition of Realism," *Novel*, 7 (1973), 23.
6 See, for example, Harold Bloom, "Afterword," p. 213; Levine, "Tradition of Realism," p. 18; Small, *Frankenstein*, p. 122; and Tropp, *Mary Shelley's Monster*, pp. 8, 81.
7 See especially Tropp, *Mary Shelley's Monster*, pp. 17, 59 and Rieger, *Mutiny Within*, pp. 237–47. The most elaborate and convincing attempt to link Frankenstein and Shelley can be found in Small, *Frankenstein*, pp. 100–121. Small establishes the parallels between Frankenstein's intellectual development and Shelley's, above all their common interest in alchemy, chemistry, and technological progress, and their fascination with death as the key to life. "Victor" was Shelley's childhood name for himself (p. 101). Small concludes of Frankenstein: "If he is not Shelley he is a dream of Shelley" (p. 102).
8 See Robert Kiely, *The Romantic Novel in England* (Cambridge: Harvard University Press, 1972), p. 161; Wilfred Cude, "Mary Shelley's Modern Prometheus: A Study in the Ethics of Scientific Creativity," *Dalhousie Review*, 52 (1972), 218; and D. J. Palmer and R. E. Douse, "*Frankenstein*: A Moral Fable," *The Listener*, 68 (1962), 281. Frankenstein himself, in thinking of his

enthusiasm as a creator, mentions "an artist occupied by his favorite employment" (55).

9 See M. K. Joseph, "Introduction" to *Frankenstein* (London: Oxford University Press, 1969), p. xiv and Mary Poovey, "My Hideous Progeny: Mary Shelley and the Feminization of Romanticism," *PMLA*, 95 (1980), 332–33. For the connection between *Frankenstein* and Mary Shelley's doubts about her husband's idealism, see P. D. Fleck, "Mary Shelley's Notes to Shelley's Poems and *Frankenstein*," *Studies in Romanticism*, 8 (1967), 226–54.

10 See Tropp, *Mary Shelley's Monster*, pp. 21–22.

11 See Small, *Frankenstein*, p. 73.

12 In the original version of *Frankenstein* (1818), Victor and Elizabeth are in fact cousins. As Small points out, "Elizabeth" was the name of Percy Shelley's mother and of his "favourite sister" (*Frankenstein*, p. 103).

13 See Levine, "Tradition of Realism," p. 21. Consider in this context the argument Frankenstein uses to repulse Walton's offer of friendship: "the companions of our childhood always possess a certain power over our minds which hardly any later friend can obtain. They know our infantine dispositions, which, however they may be afterwards modified, are never eradicated" (201).

14 Kiely, *Romantic Novel*, p. 164.

15 See Tropp, *Mary Shelley's Monster*, p. 64. Hawthorne's short story, "The Birthmark," which resembles *Frankenstein*, also presents science as the product of sublimated sexuality. See Frederick Crews, *The Sins of the Fathers: Hawthorne's Psychological Themes* (New York: Oxford University Press, 1966), pp. 111–12, 125–26, 156–57.

16 Kiely, *Romantic Novel*, pp. 165–66.

17 Rieger, *Frankenstein* (*The 1818 Text*), p. 29.

18 See Sherwin, "Creation as Catastrophe," p. 899. That Frankenstein himself is thinking of the poetic imagination at this moment is evident from the fact that he says of the animated monster: "it became a thing such as even Dante could not have conceived" (57). Mary Shelley's choice of words in her recollection of the animation scene in her original dream is also revealing: "His success would terrify the artist; he would rush away from his handi-work, horror-stricken" (xi). Frankenstein is even more repelled by his second attempt at creating life (see pp. 156–57). Like a Romantic artist, he loses his enthusiasm for the task of creation once he is forced to repeat it. The second time around, Frankenstein's work is, as it were, commissioned by the monster, and hence not the free projection of Frankenstein's mind.

19 See Tropp, *Mary Shelley's Monster*, pp. 24, 37–40, 43, 48, 50 and Small, *Frankenstein*, pp. 186, 214.

20 See Kiely, *Romantic Novel*, p. 165; Small, *Frankenstein*, p. 191; Tropp, *Mary Shelley's Monster*, pp. 22–23; and Sherwin, "Creation as Catastrophe," p. 887. Mary Shelley's own mother, Mary Wollstonecraft, died as a result of bearing her, and perhaps she was familiar with the results of this kind of association in her father's neglect of her as a child.

21 See Tropp, *Mary Shelley's Monster*, p. 42. Frankenstein's suicidal longings are revealed long before the conclusion of his tale. See, for example, p. 82: "I was tempted to plunge into the silent lake, that the waters might close over me and my calamities forever."

22 For the influence of Rousseau on Mary Shelley, see Small, *Frankenstein*, p. 62; Tropp, *Mary Shelley's Monster*, pp. 71, 162–63 (n. 12); and Pollin, "Sources of *Frankenstein*," p. 106. Mary Shelley's journal records that she read the *Emile* and the *Nouvelle Héloïse* in 1815. She was reading the *Reveries* from Thursday, August 1 to Sunday, August 4, 1816, that is, exactly when she was at work writing *Frankenstein*. See *Mary Shelley's Journal*, pp. 48, 55–56. I have been unable to find any evidence that Mary Shelley read the *Second Discourse*, but she certainly was exposed to the work's ideas through the writings and conversations of both her father and her husband.

23 This was Percy Shelley's interpretation of *Frankenstein*: in his review of the book (unpublished in his lifetime), he stated its moral this way: "Treat a person ill and he will become wicked." See *Shelley's Prose*, p. 307.

24 See Note (e) of the *Second Discourse*, pp. 187–88. It might be argued that in making the monster a vegetarian, Mary Shelley was influenced not by Rousseau but by her husband's early essay, *A Vindication of Natural Diet* (1813). But since Shelley's essay is itself heavily influenced by Rousseau – he advances the same evidence as Rousseau from comparative anatomy to prove that man is by nature a frugivorous animal – this example shows how the influence of Rousseau might have reached Mary Shelley indirectly, if not directly.

25 See Harold Bloom, "Afterword," p. 222. A late example of this Romantic fire motif is Nietzsche's brief poem, "Ecce Homo," in the prelude to *The Gay Science*.

26 See Carl Jung, *Two Essays*, p. 318 (n. 1).

27 See Levine, "Tradition of Realism," p. 21. The solipsism of Frankenstein's imagination becomes evident once all his relations are dead and he believes that he can possess them within his mind: "During the day I was sustained and inspirited by the hope of night, for in sleep I saw my friends, my wife, and my beloved country ... Often ... I persuaded myself that I was dreaming until night should come and that I should then enjoy reality in the arms of my dearest friends" (195). Walton views Frankenstein's confusion of dream and reality as "the offspring of solitude and delirium": "he believes that when in dreams he holds converse with his friends ... they are not the creations of his fancy, but the beings themselves who visit him from the regions of a remote world" (200). This passage should be compared with Mary Shelley's description of her own childhood day-dreaming: "I was not confined to my own identity, and I could people the hours with creations far more interesting to me at that age than my own sensations" (viii).

28 These are precisely the ways in which Rousseau thinks natural man excels civilized man. For the monster's advantages, see for example p. 115: "I was more agile than they and could subsist upon coarser diet: I bore the extremes of heat and cold with less injury to my frame; my stature far exceeded theirs."

29 See Frye, *English Romanticism*, p. 44 and Elizabeth Nitchie, *Mary Shelley: Author of "Frankenstein"* (New Brunswick, New Jersey: Rutgers University Press, 1953), p. 187.

30 Consider the monster's comment: "Once I falsely hoped to meet with beings who, pardoning my outward form, would love me for the excellent qualities which I was capable of unfolding" (209).

31 See, for example, Byron's Cain, who echoes Milton's Adam:

What had *I* Done in this? I was unborn;
I sought not to be born; nor love the state
To which that birth has brought me.   (I.i.67–69)

Later Cain seeks to excuse his crime because of the bad timing of his conception:

After the fall too soon was I begotten,
Ere yet my mother's mind subsided from
The serpent, and my sire still mourned for Eden.
That which I am, I am. I did not seek
For life nor did I make myself.   (III.i.506–10)

32 Frankenstein predicts a similar attitude in the mate he is creating for the monster; he suspects that she "might refuse to comply with a compact made before her creation" (158).

33 See Joseph, "Introduction," p. xiv: "If Prometheus, in the romantic tradition, is identified with human revolt, is the monster what the revolt looks like from the other side – a pitiful botched-up creature?" A similar, though even more grotesque, image for the creator's disgust at the creatureliness of man is developed in John Barth's "Petition" in *Lost in the Funhouse* (New York: Grosset & Dunlop, 1969). Barth pictures the artist-half of man as the weaker of a pair of Siamese twins, perpetually repulsed by the grossness of his more physical half, who takes active pleasure in life, while his frail brother remains "an observer of life, a mediator, a taker of notes, a dreamer if you will ... being out of reach except to surrogate gratifications" (pp. 62, 65).

34 Sherwin, "Creation as Catastrophe," pp. 892, 895.

35 Something similar happens in the other great nineteenth-century myth of scientific creativity gone awry, Robert Louis Stevenson's *Dr. Jekyll and Mr. Hyde*. Dr. Jekyll's attempt to distill out the good part of man only results in turning his evil impulses loose in the monstrous form of Mr. Hyde. See Palmer and Douse, "Moral Fable," p. 284.

36 For insight into this aspect of *Frankenstein*, see the chapter, "The Ugliest Man," in Part IV of Nietzsche's *Thus Spoke Zarathustra*, which becomes in effect a dialogue between the creature and the creator in man, and explores the connection between creaturely *ressentiment* and the murder of the creator-god. In Nietzsche's terms, the problem with the monster is that he is so thoroughly a creature that he cannot create his own values and hence is forced to accept them ready-made from his creator and his creator's race. That is why the monster can become creative only in destruction. The most he can do is to attempt what Nietzsche calls the slave revolt in morals, merely reversing the values of his "natural lord and king" (95). It is in this context that we can best understand the monster's echo of Milton's Satan: "Evil thenceforth became my good" (209).

37 On the issue of moral responsibility in *Frankenstein*, and its relation to Percy Shelley's own capacity for psychological projection, see Small, *Frankenstein*, pp. 171–95.

5 The Metaphysical Rebel

1 For an account of the initial reception of *Cain*, including its legal history and a sampling of contemporary reviews, see Steffan, *Lord Byron's Cain*, pp. 9–18, 330–426.

2 See Northrop Frye, *Fables of Identity* (New York: Harcourt, Brace, 1963), p. 181.
3 For the original Gnostic view of the Cain story, see Jonas, *Gnostic Religion*, p. 95. There was even a Gnostic sect called the Cainites.
4 See also I.i.197–99, 352–54, 394–95, II.ii.167.
5 *Paradise Lost*, XII.587. See Peter Thorslev, Jr., *The Byronic Hero* (Minneapolis: University of Minnesota Press, 1962), p. 179 and Paul Siegel, "'A Paradise Within Thee' in Milton, Byron, and Shelley," *Modern Language Notes*, 56 (1941), 615–17.
6 In a sentence in the preface to *Cain* (suppressed in the first edition), Byron wrote: "I am prepared to be accused of Manicheism, or some other hard name ending in *ism*" (Steffan, p. 156). On Manicheanism, see Jonas, *Gnostic Religion*, pp. 206–37.
7 See Bostetter, *Romantic Ventriloquists*, p. 288; Steffan, p. 48; and Leonard Michaels, "Byron's *Cain*," *PMLA*, 84 (1969), 76–77.
8 (Italics in the original.) Letter to John Murray, Nov. 3, 1821. See Byron, *Letters and Journals*, ed. Rowland E. Prothero (1898–1901; rpt. New York: Octagon Books, 1966), V, 470.
9 See Frye, *Fables of Identity*, p. 181.
10 See M. K. Joseph, *Byron the Poet* (London: Victor Gollancz, 1964), p. 121.
11 Preface to *Cain* (Steffan, p. 157).
12 Byron of course does not use this precise analogy, but very well might have, if he had known of dinosaurs. Consider Lucifer's comparison of prehistoric and modern elephants (II.ii.132–47). For Byron's notion of prehistoric "behemoths," see his letter to Thomas Moore, Sept. 19, 1821 (*Letters*, V, 368).
13 See Steffan, pp. 45, 290 and Paul Elledge, "Imagery and Theme in Byron's *Cain*," *Keats–Shelley Journal*, 15 (1960), 51.
14 Herman Melville, *Moby Dick* (Indianapolis: Bobbs–Merrill, 1964), Chapter XXXVI, pp. 220–21.
15 See Albert Camus, *The Rebel: An Essay on Man in Revolt*, trans. Anthony Bower (New York: Vintage Books, 1956), pp. 23–104. Camus calls the generation of Romantic revolutionaries the "Sons of Cain" (pp. 26–35). The relevance of Camus to Byron is noted in Thorslev, *Byronic Hero*, p. 197.
16 See Camus, *The Rebel*, p. 10.
17 See Camus, *The Rebel*, p. 48: the metaphysical rebel "creates a human injustice parallel to divine injustice. Since violence is at the root of all creation, deliberate violence shall be its answer."
18 See, for example, *Lara*, I.xviii.337–48. For the significance of crime in Romantic drama, see Robert Langbaum, *The Poetry of Experience* (New York: Norton, 1963), pp. 58–59 and Terry Otten, *The Deserted Stage* (Athens: Ohio University Press, 1972), p. 52.
19 Cf. Michaels, "*Cain*," p. 77.
20 See Thorslev, *Byronic Hero*, pp. 65–83.
21 *Portable Nietzsche*, pp. 150–51.
22 Lucifer does make several references to the coming of Christ (I.i.163–66, 541–42, II.i.16–20), but they all occur in contexts that suggest the arbitrariness of God, not his interest in man's salvation.

23 See Robert Gleckner, *Byron and the Ruins of Paradise* (Baltimore: Johns Hopkins University Press, 1967), p. 327.

24 See Small, *Frankenstein*, p. 221.

25 Since "Darkness" was written in the summer of 1816, at just the time Mary Shelley was beginning *Frankenstein*, the poem cannot actually be referring to Shelley's drama, which was not written until 1819. Nevertheless, Byron "anticipates" Shelley's poetic vision of the end of this world, even down to the detail of kingless thrones (ll. 10–11). Of course both poems have a common source in the apocalyptic traditions of the Bible.

26 See Small, *Frankenstein*, pp. 56–57.

27 See particularly II.i.178–90. Byron's attraction to scenes of universal cataclysm is also evident in the fragmentary drama *Heaven and Earth*, which deals with the coming of Noah's Flood. Because Byron failed to finish the play, it ends with a vivid impression of the human race being annihilated. The anti-apocalyptic character of the play can be seen in one particularly striking reversal of traditional imagery:

> even the brutes in their despair,
> Shall cease to prey on man and on each other,
> And the striped tiger shall lie down to die
> Beside the lamb, as though he were his brother;
> Till all things shall be as they were,
> Silent and uncreated, save the sky.   (I.iii.177–82)

The traditional apocalyptic reconciliation of the beasts is here given a negative character because it is brought about only in death, indeed in universal destruction.

28 For this notion, Poe's *Eureka* provides the closest analogue to *Cain*. See Daniel Hoffman, *Poe Poe Poe Poe Poe Poe Poe* (Garden City: Doubleday, 1972), especially pp. 286–87.

29 See Frye, *English Romanticism*, p. 34. For the relation between death and the primal unity in *Eureka*, see Hoffman, *Poe*, p. 291.

30 On Beddoes, see Frye, *English Romanticism*, pp. 51–85.

31 On this subject, see the brilliant epilogue to Jonas's *Gnostic Religion*, "Gnosticism, Existentialism, and Nihilism," pp. 320–40.

32 Usually, the Romantic rebel believes that he has evidence of substantial injustice in the world order. But the fact that, deep down, he will settle for no less than perfection is evident in the slight grounds that are in some cases able to touch off metaphysical rebellion. Kleist's Michael Kohlhaas, for example, is willing to bring chaos to all Germany over an incident involving two horses. In *The Brothers Karamazov*, Dostoevsky provides the ultimate test-case for metaphysical rebellion. Ivan Karamazov refuses to accept a world order perfect in all respects except that its eternal harmony requires the suffering of a single child. See Part II, Book V, Chapter IV ("Rebellion"). On Dostoevsky and metaphysical rebellion, see Camus, *The Rebel*, pp. 55–61.

33 See Camus, *The Rebel*, pp. 26–35.

34 On this point in Aristotle, see Strauss, *The City and Man*, pp. 41–43.

35 Cf. Jerome McGann, *Fiery Dust: Byron's Poetic Development* (Chicago: University of Chicago Press, 1968), p. 273.

36 See Langbaum, *Poetry of Experience*, p. 61 and Otten, *Deserted Stage*, p. 50.

37 On the limits of Lucifer's knowledge, see McGann, *Fiery Dust*, pp. 255–58. For how "death and mortality define, paradoxically, a moral advance in existence," see McGann, pp. 269–70.
38 The idea that immortal spirits might risk their status to descend to earth in order to experience the superior pleasures of human love is the thematic germ of Byron's *Heaven and Earth*.
39 See Otten, *Deserted Stage*, pp. 50–51.

6 Romantic Myth and Tragic Vision

1 Ronald A. Sharp, *Keats, Skepticism, and the Religion of Beauty* (Athens: University of Georgia Press, 1979), p. 135 and Geoffrey H. Hartman, "Spectral Symbolism and Authorial Self in Keats's *Hyperion*," in *The Fate of Reading* (Chicago: University of Chicago Press, 1975), p. 61.
2 Douglas Bush, *English Poetry* (1952; rpt. New York: Oxford University Press, 1963), p. 144.
3 Helen E. Haworth, "The Titans, Apollo, and the Fortunate Fall in Keats's Poetry," *Studies in English Literature 1500–1900*, 10 (1970), p. 587.
4 Walter Jackson Bate, *John Keats* (Cambridge: Harvard University Press, 1963), p. 587.
5 Hungerford, *Shores of Darkness*, p. 153.
6 On Milton's use of this strategy, see Harold Bloom, *A Map of Misreading* (New York: Oxford University Press, 1975), pp. 125–43.
7 In this context, see especially *Hyperion*, I.277–83 and II.132–35, and *The Fall of Hyperion*, I.65–71. In the history of philosophy, one finds a similar tactic in combatting the prestige of the classical philosophers Plato and Aristotle by suggesting that their wisdom derived from more ancient sources. This strategy was used as early as Francis Bacon's ironically titled *The Wisdom of the Ancients* (1609), and survives well into the twentieth century, particularly if one considers Heidegger's interest in and use of the Pre-Socratics.
8 See Bate, *Keats*, p. 409 and Douglas Bush, *John Keats* (New York: Macmillan, 1966), pp. 105–8.
9 James, *Romantic Comedy*, p. 135 and Pierre Vitoux, "Keats's Epic Design in *Hyperion*," *Studies in Romanticism*, 14 (1975), 169.
10 Bate, *Keats*, p. 399; Harold Bloom, *Visionary Company*, p. 395; and Paul Sherwin, "Dying into Life: Keats's Struggle with Milton in *Hyperion*," *PMLA*, 93 (1978), 385.
11 Sharp, *Skepticism*, p. 137 and Frye, *English Romanticism*, p. 148.
12 See Knight, *Starlit Dome*, p. 286 and Vitoux, "Epic Design," p. 170.
13 See Sharp, *Skepticism*, pp. 133, 145 and Haworth, "Fortunate Fall," pp. 637–49.
14 For a contrary view, in fact a political interpretation of *Hyperion*, see Kenneth Muir, "The Meaning of *Hyperion*," in *John Keats: A Reassessment* (Liverpool: Liverpool University Press, 1969), pp. 105–6. For evidence of Keats's thorough-going disillusionment with politics, see his letter to George and Georgiana Keats, Oct. 14, 1818. Specifically, Keats had clearly undergone the typical Romantic disillusionment with Napoleon: "Notwithstand[ing] the part which the Liberals take in the Cause of Napoleon I cannot but think that he has done more harm to

the life of Liberty than any one else could have done." See Hyder Edward Rollins, ed., *The Letters of John Keats* (Cambridge: Harvard University Press, 1958), I, 396–97. The infrequency with which Keats comments on political matters in his letters is one index of his comparative lack of interest in the subject. A typical observation appears in a letter to George and Georgiana Keats, Sept. 24, 1819: "The first political duty a Man ought to have a Mind to is the happiness of his friends" (Rollins, II, 213). In short, Keats claims that one's first political duty is something apolitical.

15 For a discussion of this genre, with particular reference to Blake, see Geoffrey H. Hartman, "Blake and the Progress of Poesy," in *Beyond Formalism* (New Haven: Yale University Press, 1970), pp. 193–205. For the relevance of this genre to Keats, see Sharp, *Skepticism*, pp. 131–32 and Sherwin, "Dying into Life," p. 385.

16 Edward Hungerford develops this theory in great detail; see *Shores of Darkness*, pp. 137–62. The most convincing piece of evidence for Hungerford's hypothesis is the Invocation to Book IV of Keats's *Endymion* (ll. 1–29), a passage which charts the progress of the poetic muse from Asia to Greece to Rome and finally to England.

17 See Hungerford, *Shores of Darkness*, pp. 142–43 and D. G. James, *Romantic Comedy*, p. 140. On Keats's life-long interest in the figure of Apollo, see Walter Evert, *Aesthetic and Myth in the Poetry of Keats* (Princeton: Princeton University Press, 1965).

18 Allott notes this parallel in her edition (p. 403). See also Vitoux, "Epic Design," p. 172.

19 Letter to Richard Woodhouse, Oct. 27, 1818 (Rollins, I, 387).

20 Harold Bloom, *Poetry and Repression*, p. 121.

21 Hungerford, *Shores of Darkness*, pp. 150–51 and Vitoux, "Epic Design," p. 176.

22 See Hungerford, *Shores of Darkness*, p. 150 and Hartman, *Fate of Reading*, p. 60.

23 For a general discussion of the relation of lyric and narrative forms in Romantic poetry, see A. C. Bradley, "The Long Poem in the Age of Wordsworth," in *Oxford Lectures on Poetry* (London: Macmillan, 1909), pp. 177–205. See also Hartman, *Fate of Reading*, p. 60: "If Wordsworth wrote 'lyrical ballads,' ... Keats can write 'lyrical epics.'"

24 See Hartman, *Fate of Reading*, who describes Saturn's condition this way: "As if a god, or a whole generation of gods, had suffered a stroke" (p. 60).

25 See I.2–3, 203, 288, 298, II.5–6, 374–75. In this context, recall Hyperion's inability to bring on the dawn when he desires it. See also *Fall*, I.85–86. On this point, see Harold Bloom, *Poetry and Repression*, pp. 122–23.

26 Sherwin, "Dying into Life," p. 391.

27 See Bate, *Keats*, p. 392 and Sherwin, "Dying into Life," p. 391. On the general principle of projecting a "belatedness" as an "earliness," see Harold Bloom, *Map of Misreading*, p. 138.

28 Abrams, *Natural Supernaturalism*, pp. 128–29.

29 Letter to Richard Woodhouse, Oct. 27, 1818 (Rollins, I, 387).

30 James, *Romantic Comedy*, p. 141; Bush, *Mythology*, p. 119; and Bate, *Keats*, p. 407.

31 James, *Romantic Comedy*, pp. 146–47; Abrams, *Natural Supernaturalism*, p. 127; and Anne K. Mellor, *English Romantic Irony* (Cambridge: Harvard University Press, 1980), p. 101.

32 Muir, *Keats*, pp. 115–21.

33 See Harold Bloom, *Visionary Company*, p. 391 and Abrams, *Natural Supernaturalism*, p. 127. For a different view, see Stuart M. Sperry, Jr., "Keats, Milton, and *The Fall of Hyperion*," *PMLA*, 77 (1962), 77–84. Sperry argues that the departures from Milton in the second version are merely stylistic, not thematic.

34 Keats's paradise is a peculiar one: it lacks the freshness of Eden. Though the garden offers food in abundance, the "feast of summer fruits" consists of leftovers (they "seemed refuse of a meal / By angel tasted," I.30–31). As Bate writes: "the dreamer is very much a latecomer; this is a place where others have already been" (*Keats*, p. 590). Perhaps Keats is imaging his own relationship to poetic tradition. As a poet, he is forced to sustain himself on what is left over from Milton's paradise. Leslie Brisman speaks of "Keats ingesting Miltonic scraps" (*Romantic Origins*, p. 93). See also Sperry, "Keats, Milton," pp. 78–79.

35 Compare *Fall*, I.126 with *Hyperion*, III.135. Compare also *Fall*, I.302–4 with *Hyperion*, III.113–20. In both versions, suffering intense pain is the necessary prelude to achieving the immortality of divine vision. The fact that Apollo speaks of drinking a "bright elixir" (III.119) in the earlier version shows how closely these two scenes were linked in Keats's mind. For the original meeting of Apollo and Mnemosyne, Keats substitutes a scene in which he himself encounters the muse in *The Fall of Hyperion*. For the identity of Keats and Apollo, see Sharp, *Skepticism*, p. 147. See also James, *Romantic Comedy*, p. 144 and Mellor, *Romantic Irony*, p. 105.

36 Cf. Rousseau's assessment of the dreamy life of the solitary walker: "an unfortunate person who has been cut off from human society and who can no longer do anything here-below useful and good for another or for himself can find compensation for all the human felicities in this state, compensations which fortune and men could not take away from him" (R, 69).

37 See Frank Kermode, *Romantic Image* (New York: Random House, 1957), pp. 7–10. Kermode goes on to link Keats with the aestheticism and decadence of later nineteenth-century writers.

38 Harold Bloom, *Visionary Company*, p. 429 and Bostetter, *Romantic Ventriloquists*, pp. 168–69.

39 See in particular Keats's letter to John Hamilton Reynolds, Feb. 3, 1818 (Rollins, I, 223–25).

40 Allott, pp. 669–70.

41 Abrams, *Natural Supernaturalism*, pp. 128–29; Bush, *Keats*, p. 172; and Muir, *Keats*, p. 122.

42 Abrams, *Natural Supernaturalism*, p. 126; Bate, *Keats*, p. 401; and Harold Bloom, *Visionary Company*, p. 395.

43 See Bate, *Keats*, p. 488 and Sharp, *Skepticism*, pp. 35–36. On the exploration of the psyche as the distinctive task of the modern poet, see Keats's praise of Wordsworth in his letters, especially the letter to John Hamilton Reynolds, May 3, 1818, in which Keats explains why "Wordsworth is deeper than Milton,"

largely because Milton "did not think into the human heart, as Wordsworth has done" (Rollins, I, 281–82).

44 See I.277, 444. See also James, *Romantic Comedy*, p. 148 and Harold Bloom, *Poetry and Repression*, p. 113.

45 For a discussion of *The Triumph of Life*, see the first section of my Conclusion. As I will show, in many ways *The Fall of Hyperion* and *The Triumph of Life* are very similar.

46 Leslie Brisman speaks of Keats's aim as the "restoration of the mystique of origins" (*Romantic Origins*, p. 101).

47 See Harold Bloom, *Poetry and Repression*, p. 123 and Eric Smith, *Some Versions of The Fall* (London: Croom Helm, 1973), pp. 160–61.

48 Abrams, *Natural Supernaturalism*, p. 126 and Sherwin, "Dying into Life," p. 389.

49 See Stuart A. Ende, *Keats and the Sublime* (New Haven: Yale University Press, 1976), p. 111 and Sherwin, "Dying into Life," p. 385. In his notion of the "progress of poetry," Keats renounces the Romantic dream of the "definitive poet." Like Shelley in his *Defence*, Keats came to realize that no one poet can be the first or the last of his tribe. This lesson is perhaps reflected in Oceanus's advice to Saturn in *Hyperion*, II.188–90.

50 Sharp, *Skepticism*, pp. 138–39.

51 See Abrams, *Natural Supernaturalism*, pp. 126–27; Bush, *Keats*, p. 103; Muir, *Keats*, p. 109; and Vitoux, "Epic Design," p. 178.

52 Letter to George and Georgiana Keats, April 21, 1819 (Rollins, II, 101).

53 Rollins, II, 102.

54 Letter to George and Georgiana Keats, Feb. 14–May 3, 1819 (Rollins, II, 101–2). On the general subject of Keats's skepticism, see Sharp, *Skepticism*, especially pp. 9–26.

Conclusion: The Return to Rousseau

1 Duffy, *Rousseau*, p. 113.

2 See Reiman, Shelley's *"Triumph"*, pp. 34–36, 46–48, 84–86; Duffy, *Rousseau*, pp. 148–49; and Hall, *Transforming Image*, pp. 151–64.

3 Baker, *Shelley's Major Poetry*, p. 268.

4 Reiman, Shelley's *"Triumph"*, pp. 39–40.

5 Harold Bloom, *Visionary Company*, p. 352.

6 Cf. *Hyperion*, I.314: "I, Coelus, wonder how they came and whence."

7 Leslie Brisman, *Romantic Origins*, p. 176.

8 "Shelley Disfigured," in Harold Bloom, ed., *Deconstruction and Criticism* (New York: Seabury Press, 1979), pp. 43–44.

9 "A Vision of the Last Judgment," pp. 70, 68–69, 84 (E, 554–5, 562). See Damon, *William Blake*, p. 152 and Damrosch, *Symbol and Truth*, pp. 28–29.

10 See, for example, I.cxxvii, II.clxxxix, cxciii, cciv, IV.x.

11 See, for example, I.xviii, clxxx, II.ccxiii. See Cooke, *Acts of Inclusion*, p. 231.

12 On the pattern of the fall in *Don Juan*, see George Ridenour, *The Style of Don Juan* (New Haven: Yale University Press, 1960), especially chapters 2 and 3.

13 See II.viii, lxvi, xcv.

14 See XV.xcvi–xcviii. See also Ridenour, *Don Juan*, pp. 162–66 and Mellor, *Romantic Irony*, pp. 55–56.

15 See XIV.xxxi, XV.xi, xvi.

16 Ridenour, *Don Juan*, p. 29.

17 "Two Songs from a Play," in *Collected Poems* (New York: Macmillan, 1956), p. 211.

18 Heidegger, *Being and Time*, p. 220.

19 Heidegger's link to Romanticism is suggested by his abiding interest in Hölderlin. See especially his collection of essays, *Erläuterungen zu Hölderlins Dichtung* (Frankfurt: Vittorio Klostermann, 1971).

Index

Abrams, M. H., xvi, 196–97, 203, 207, 217–19
Adams, Hazard, 200, 203
Aldiss, Brian, 210
Allott, Miriam, xx, 217–18
Aristotle, 174, 215–16

Babbitt, Irving, xiv–xv, 16–17, 196, 198–200
Bachardy, Don, 210
Bacon, Francis, 216
Baker, Carlos, 207, 219
Barth, John, 213
Barzun, Jacques, 199
Bate, Walter Jackson, 216–18
Beddoes, Thomas Lovell, 147, 215
Beer, John, 206
Bernstein, John Andrew, 199
Blake, William, ix–xi, xiii, xviii, xx, 5, 11–12, 22–24, 29–74, 77–78, 82–85, 88, 97, 130, 145–46, 155–56, 162–63, 173, 175–76, 178–80, 182–83, 186–88, 191, 195, 197, 200–6, 219
Bloom, Allan, 198–99, 209
Bloom, Harold, xi–xiii, xx, 157, 195–96, 200–5, 207–10, 212, 216–19
Böhme, Jacob, 203
Bolingbroke, Henry St. John, 45
Bostetter, Edward, 200, 214, 218
Bradley, A. C., 217
Brisman, Leslie, 196, 206, 218–19
Brisman, Susan Hawk, 207–9
Bruns, Gerald, 209
Bush, Douglas, 196, 209, 216–19
Byron, Lord, ix, xvi, xviii–xx, 23–24, 108, 132, 135–55, 163, 172, 181–82, 188–91, 210, 212–16

Cameron, Kenneth Neill, 207

Camus, Albert, 143, 148, 214–15
Cantor, Paul A., 207
Cassirer, Ernst, 198–99, 208–9
Cassuto, Umberto, 201, 203
Cloyd, E. L., 197
Coleridge, Samuel Taylor, xvii, 9, 97, 198, 200
Cooke, Michael G., 210, 219
Cowper, William, 44
Crews, Frederick, 211
Crocker, Lester, 199
Cude, Wilfred, 210
Curran, Stuart, 195, 207–8

Damon, S. Foster, 197, 201, 203–5, 219
Damrosch, Leo, 195, 201–2, 205–6, 219
Dante, 93, 169, 184, 211
Darwin, Charles, 8, 142
Davies, Edward, 14, 199
De Man, Paul, 186, 198
Dostoevsky, Fyodor, 145, 215
Douse, R. E., 210, 213
Dryden, John, 44
Duffy, Edward, 197, 200, 219

Easson, Kay, 201
Easson, Roger, 201
Eliot, T. S., 42, 203
Elledge, Paul, 214
Emery, Clark, 201, 203
Ende, Stuart A., 219
Erdman, David V., xx, 58, 197, 200–1, 205
Evans, J. M., 197
Evert, Walter, 217

Fichte, Johann Gottlieb, xvi, 202
Fleck, P. D., 211
Fogle, Richard H., 209

221

Index

Index